Reading Time in the Long Poem

Reading Time in the Long Poem

Milton, Thomson and Wordsworth

Tess Somervell

Edinburgh University Press is one of the leading university presses in the UK. We publish academic books and journals in our selected subject areas across the humanities and social sciences, combining cutting-edge scholarship with high editorial and production values to produce academic works of lasting importance. For more information visit our website: edinburghuniversitypress.com

© Tess Somervell 2023, 2024

Edinburgh University Press Ltd
The Tun – Holyrood Road
12(2f) Jackson's Entry
Edinburgh EH8 8PJ

First published in hardback by Edinburgh University Press 2023

Typeset in 11/13 Adobe Sabon by
IDSUK (DataConnection) Ltd

A CIP record for this book is available from the British Library

ISBN 978 1 4744 8613 2 (hardback)
ISBN 978 1 4744 8614 9 (paperback)
ISBN 978 1 4744 8615 6 (webready PDF)
ISBN 978 1 4744 8616 3 (epub)

The right of Tess Somervell to be identified as the author of this work has been asserted in accordance with the Copyright, Designs and Patents Act 1988, and the Copyright and Related Rights Regulations 2003 (SI No. 2498).

Contents

List of Figures	vi
Acknowledgements	vii
Abbreviations	viii
Introduction	1

PART I MILTON

1. His Prospect High: The Nunc Stans in *Paradise Lost*	17
2. More than Delphic: Miltonic History and Hermeneutics	48
3. A Full-grown Beauty: Reading *Paradise Lost*	68

PART II THOMSON

4. Shade Softening into Shade: Georgic Causation in *The Seasons*	89
5. The Broken Scene: Thomson's Tales	116
6. Unforced Method: Reading *The Seasons*	141

PART III WORDSWORTH

7. Years Flowed In Between: Chronos and Kairos in *The Prelude*	161
8. Hung O'er the Deep: Wordsworth's Allusions and Revisions	181
9. A Feeling of the Whole: Reading *The Prelude*	202
Conclusion	222
Bibliography	225
Index	240

Figures

Figure 5.1 William Kent, 'Summer' in James Thomson, *The Seasons* (London: A. Millar, 1730).   127

Figure 5.2 Richard Westall, 'Summer', engraved by John Romney, in James Thomson, *The Seasons* (London: John Sharpe, 1825).   129

Figure 5.3 John Calcott Horsley, 'Musidora', engraved by J. Thompson, in James Thomson, *The Seasons* (London: Longman, Brown, Green, and Longmans, 1847).   130

Acknowledgements

Some material in Chapter 5, on the Damon and Musidora tale in 'Summer', appeared in an earlier form as 'Versions of Damon and Musidora: The Realization of Thomson's Story in Revisions and Illustrations', *Studies in the Literary Imagination* 46.1 (2013): 47–70. Some material on Wordsworth's allusions to Thomson and Milton appeared in an earlier form as 'Mediating Vision: Wordsworth's Allusions to Thomson's *Seasons* in *The Prelude*', *Romanticism* 22.1 (2016): 48–60. Thanks to the editors of *Studies in the Literary Imagination* and *Romanticism* for permission to reproduce this work here.

The research that has gone into this book was funded by an Arts and Humanities Research Council doctoral award and a British Academy Postdoctoral Fellowship. I am grateful for the support and advice of many teachers, colleagues, friends and readers: Laura Ashe, Mishtooni Bose, Peter Conrad, Jeff Cowton, Jeremy Davies, Richard De Ritter, Peggy Elliott, Katherine Fender, Mina Gorji, Freya Johnston, Robert Jones, Louise Joy, Sandro Jung, Pippa Marland, Peter McDonald, Anna Mercer, Seamus Perry, Sophie Read, Corinna Russell, Katarina Stenke, Christopher Tilmouth, Stefan Uhlig and Kwinten Van De Walle. Thanks also to my students at Cambridge, Leeds and Oxford. At Edinburgh University Press, Michelle Houston and Susannah Butler have been fantastic editors, and the Press's readers provided valuable feedback; and Belinda Cunnison has been an excellent copy editor. Special thanks go to David Higgins for his guidance through my postdoctoral research; my doctoral examiners David Fairer and Ruth Abbott for their counsel on the direction of the project and for their encouragement since; Fred Parker for his support as my doctoral advisor; and Phil Connell for his intellectual generosity, kindness and generally being the ideal doctoral supervisor. Finally, thank you to Scott, my parents and the rest of my family.

Abbreviations

References for the following works are given after quotations in the text.

PL	Milton, John, *Paradise Lost*, ed. Barbara Lewalski (Oxford: Blackwell, 2007).
TS	Thomson, James, *The Seasons*, ed. James Sambrook (Oxford: Clarendon Press, 1981). Unless otherwise stated, references are to the 1744–6 edition.
TP	Wordsworth, William, *The Fourteen-Book Prelude*, ed. W. J. B. Owen (Ithaca: Cornell University Press, 1985), in *The Cornell Wordsworth*, ed. Stephen Parrish, 21 vols (Ithaca: Cornell University Press, 1975–2007), xiv.

Unless otherwise stated, references are to the fourteen-book 1850 *Prelude*. References to the 1805 thirteen-book *Prelude* are to the AB-Stage Reading Text in the Cornell edition, i: *The Thirteen-Book Prelude*, ed. Mark L. Reed (1991).

Introduction

In an 1817 letter to Benjamin Bailey, John Keats recalls Leigh Hunt asking why poets should 'endeavour after a long Poem'. Keats offers two answers to this question. The second, that a long poem is the ultimate test of a poet's 'Invention, which I take to be the Polar Star of Poetry', is often quoted. Less remarked upon is the first answer Keats gives to Hunt's question, about the value of a long poem not for the poet but for the reader:

> Do not the Lovers of Poetry like to have a little Region to wander in, where they may pick and choose, and in which the images are so numerous that many are forgotten and found new in a second Reading: which may be food for a Week's stroll in the Summer? Do not they like this better than what they can read through before Mrs. Williams comes down stairs? a Morning work at most.[1]

For Keats, a long poem is not something to 'read through', from beginning to end, in one sitting. It is a space in which to wander, and within which any direction can be taken. Parts may be extracted at the reader's whim, read out of order, and read and reread again. (Elsewhere Keats writes that 'I long after a stanza or two of Thomson's Castle of Indolence'.[2]) On the other hand, Keats – on whose insights into the long poem I will draw a number of times in this book – is keenly aware of the poet's 'management' of a long poem, their arrangement of parts into a structure that rewards reading in chronological order. In his annotations to *Paradise Lost*, he notes the effects of coming to the opening of Book 3 *after* the first two books:

> The management of this Poem is Apollonian – Satan first 'throws round his baleful eyes' the[n] awakes his legions, he consu[l]ts, he sets forward on his voyage – and just as he is getting to the end of

it we see the Great God and our first parent, and that same satan all brough[t] in one's vision – we have the invocation to light before we mount to heaven – we breathe more freely – we feel the – – great Author's consolations coming thick upon him at a time when he complains most – we are getting ripe for diversity . . .[3]

Keats's readings of individual 'images' within this long poem depend on his understanding of their place in relation to other images, what comes 'first' or 'before', and how the reader is made 'ripe' through their linear reading.

Does it matter whether we read a long poem – by which I mean a book-length poem, with lines running to the thousands, rather than the hundreds – from beginning to end, as a whole that unfolds in one direction, or whether we read it as a series of parts that can be taken in any order? And did this matter in the long eighteenth century, the heyday of the long poem in English? In this book I argue that this distinction matters, and has mattered to readers and poets. The distinction is between taking a poem as a temporal form (a voyage, a 'getting' or a 'coming', to echo Keats) and taking it as a spatial form (a region in which to wander). All readers, of course, do both, but it is important to recognise the implicit temporality and spatiality in each reading method and what this means when we combine them in our reading practice. To 'pick and choose' between parts is to map time onto space, and to rearrange elements of that theoretical linear temporal experience. The long poem, then, is a medium in which to shape and reshape time, to question relationships between moments and events, and therefore to question causation itself, at the level of form as well as content. Over the course of the long eighteenth century, when ethical and epistemological debates about causation were fraught, the long poem emerged and developed as the form that could posit and balance different shapes of time alongside and against one another.

Reading time in the long poem, of course, involves both analysis of the theme of time within particular long poems, and consideration of the way reading a long poem is itself a reading of time. Whether we conceive of a long poem as a diachronic or synchronic form has implications for that poem's portrayal of time and thus its portrayal of freedom, power and perception. When we appreciate (1) the ethical imports of time in these poems, and (2) the way reading these poems involves particular approaches to time, then our readings of these poems take on new ethical significance. The way we read the poems, and navigate between their parts and wholes, becomes a way of thinking through causation, and the various ethical issues that these poems relate to causation (free will, physico-theology and self-formation). Keats's accounts of reading long poems above hint at some of the ethical questions involved: his wording implies that to read out of order is to 'pick and choose', an assumption of freedom on the part of the reader; to read in order is to submit to the 'great Author's' sublime 'management'.

The recent 'temporal turn' in eighteenth-century studies emphasises the period's rejection of 'cyclical or repetitious forms' in favour of 'newer expressions of directional time'.[4] Studies have connected developments in philosophy, historiography, technology and socio-economics, from the increasing influence of Newton's theory of absolute time to improvements in clockmaking and the growth of capitalistic labour relations, with trends in literature and art, like the rise of the novel and the retheorisation of musical tempo.[5] Critics identify exceptions, of course, but these exceptions prove the rule, and are framed as forms of resistance to a dominant masculine, imperial, linear temporality.[6] The recent temporal turn in criticism, then, reasserts an older critical history of a temporal turn within the long eighteenth century itself, a shift from spatial to temporal modes of thinking. In 1979 Lewis White Beck wrote that in the eighteenth century 'Human time replaces divine eternity as the proper object and concern of man', noting that 'At the beginning of the century, the grand chain [of being] was vertical; at the end, horizontal or perhaps gently sloping upward . . . a temporal process', which enabled the development of theories of evolution.[7] In 1982, John Sitter argued that 'the significant shift [of the mid-eighteenth century] is from spatial to temporal theodicy, from proportion to process . . . the transformation of Providence into Process'.[8] It is difficult to locate any specific turning point from space to time as the dominant epistemological dimension. Martin Priestman, for example, locates the 'broad epistemic shift' a little later in the century than Sitter,[9] from 'the Enlightenment belief that all knowledge could be laid out in a "*tabula*"', 'that fixed formal spaces . . . are the best way to make sense of otherwise inchoate matter',[10] to the Romantic belief that the world must be understood in terms of 'the individual object's development through time'.[11]

What makes this transition particularly difficult to parse is that, even if temporal structures of sequence, succession and process became the preferred frameworks for thinking about the universe and humankind, space was still the default framework for thinking about time. European languages depended then as they do now upon spatial metaphors in order to think, let alone talk, about time. Even if the circle is replaced by the arrow or the straight line, these spatial images retain a hint of an idea of time as something that can be grasped and held still, and as something made up of extended parts that exist simultaneously. This book is about poets' figurative uses of space to imagine and represent time, at both the level of content and the level of form. Specifically, it is about how John Milton, James Thomson and William Wordsworth employ the prospect – the spatially extended landscape – to think about time. I am aiming to articulate, in a way, a 'chronotope' for the long poem from the Restoration to the Romantic period. Mikhail Bakhtin's term, however, is generally used to describe the way literal time and literal space interrelate in given genres and discourses, whereas the prospect view is used in these poems both as a literal space in which time exists (as when, in the essential strategic move of the prospect poem, real prospect views give rise to reflections on historical progress) and as a figure for time (as when Wordsworth imagines seeing 'beneath me stretched / Vast prospect of the world which I had been' [XIV.380–1]). Characters and speakers in these poems read time by mapping them onto real or imagined extended landscapes. This is to imagine moments as contiguous rather than continuous with one another, and therefore might seem to remove all sense of time's movement and flow. In fact, it opens new and multiple ways in which different moments can be understood to relate to one another, including but not limited to the linear. It allows these poets to combine the virtues of the 'tabula' with the virtues of 'process', and to compensate for the shortcomings of each, in order to deal with epistemological and ethical problems that arise in contemporary debates, and personal anxieties, about time. It allows them to imagine and represent a perspective of time that can comprehend both time as a flowing movement, in which causation is linear and sequential, and time as stasis, in which every moment is spontaneously derived from within or above, and independent of times around it. It is through such representations of time that these poets stage their interventions into debates about free will, science and nature, and the role of the poet.

I have taken as my three case studies *Paradise Lost*, *The Seasons* and *The Prelude*, for several reasons. The most important are their common thematic interest in time and causation, and their particularly prominent uses of spatial landscape figures for thinking about time. Two other reasons, related to one another, are that they represent a direct line of influence in the development of the long poem (specifically that of the long poem in blank verse), and that they have been widely read and discussed. In this book I offer readings of the poems themselves, but also of their reception by readers who have reflected on the experience of reading the long poem. I hope that through these three case studies a broader story will emerge about the (very) long poem across the (very) long eighteenth century, about how it was written and how it was read. The long poem as a category, which encompasses but is not limited to epic and romance, has not received much critical attention or theorisation, with occasional important exceptions such as Adam Roberts's *Romantic and Victorian Long Poems: A Guide* (1999) and Katarina Stenke's thesis 'Parts and Wholes in Long Non-Narrative Poems of the Eighteenth Century' (2013).[12] But this category is essential to understanding and discussing the generic modulations and combinations that have occurred in the writing, publishing and reading of English-language poetry. The eighteenth-century long poem bucks the trend of a shift from spatial to temporal thinking in the period; although it thinks constantly about time, structurally it leans into non-narrative forms, with the related genres of georgic (following Virgil and Hesiod), the philosophical poem (following Lucretius), and the prospect poem (following, principally, John Denham) overtaking epic and romance as the most popular and successful types of long poem. The story of the long poem in the long eighteenth century, then, is one of tension between the luxurious appeal of spatial elaboration and the exciting tug of narrative momentum.

These genres may seem no more interested in questions of time, fate and the relationship between cause and effect – indeed, in their relative lack of narrative they may seem far less interested – than genres like tragic drama and the novel. Perhaps this is one reason for the long poem's comparative neglect in recent studies of time and literature, within and outside eighteenth-century studies. The excellent recent books *Time and Literature* and *Literature and Contingency* contain no chapters on the long poem, and only occasionally refer in passing to epic; they focus overwhelmingly on prose forms, especially the novel, and their few chapters on poetics discuss mainly lyric.[13] In *Reading the Times: Temporality and History in Twentieth-Century Fiction*, Randall Stevenson writes of the novel's unique 'profound *inner* potentials for reshaping time':

> Of all inventions, then or since, the novel may be the best equipped to resist or reorient the relentless, measured passage of time. In its bound, printed form, it may be the only artefact ever devised whose physical shape allows its users to keep the dimension of time so

firmly under their thumb, or thumbs. The past of the story safely remains mostly under the reader's left thumb, in the section of the novel already read, while the future waits placidly under the right.[14]

Although the novel's scale is containable, it is long enough to separate past from future. In this we can contrast the novel with the short lyric poem which conventionally represents the intensity of a single moment, whole and perfect in itself. It cannot be read instantaneously, of course, and even a short poem consists of parts – this is why Hegel could declare that 'the outpouring of lyric' was the true temporal form, portraying 'the momentary emergence of feelings and ideas in . . . temporal succession', as opposed to the way epic narrative 'juxtaposes [phenomena] or interweaves them in rather a spatial extension'.[15] But the fact that our eyes can take in the whole of a short poem on the page at one glance means that it is easier to conceive of the poem as one whole, which may have distinct parts like individual lines but whose parts appear to exist in simultaneity. Rebecca Bushnell has argued that short poems have a unique capacity to reshape time, because '[l]ike a film, a written poetic text permits cuts and editing, "rewinding" or rereading, and repetition of words and images. In particular, in the case of a short text, the poem appears as an object of analysis in which the parts exist synchronically as well as diachronically.'[16] Wordsworth wrote of sonnets that 'Instead of looking at this composition as a piece of architecture, making a whole out of three parts, I have been much in the habit of preferring the image of an orbicular body, a sphere or a dew-drop'.[17]

A novel, in Stevenson's account, is more like a building, even if it fits into a book: we can view the whole from a distance, as it were, just as we can hold a whole book in our hands, but to get into and through it takes time. Stevenson points out that longer literary forms have 'profound *inner* potentials for reshaping time' because they can disjoin fabula and syuzhet (story and plot), using our expectation that the chronology of reading will follow the chronology of story to rearrange and suggest new, non-linear relationships between moments and events. Of course, a long poem is just as well-equipped to do all this. The novel is not the only 'artefact devised' to keep the past 'already read' under one thumb and the future under another. The fact that Stevenson makes this claim may be partly due to the recession of the long poem from popular and even from widespread critical view. But it may also testify to the fact that we do not expect poems, even narrative ones like *Paradise Lost*, to relay 'the past of the story' in such neat order as we expect from novels.

Nor do we expect necessarily to have to read the whole of a long poem from beginning to end – at least not after we have done so once – as we expect novels to demand. The readers of long poems have, far more than the readers of novels, sought to cope with the demands of length by focusing on local parts. Sometimes they argue for a hierarchy of certain parts over others; sometimes they extract parts altogether. While focus on particular sections is a feature of almost all literary criticism, it seems to me that readers have been more willing to either lose sight of or restructure the whole of a long poem than the whole of a novel. It is as though a novel is greater than the sum of its parts, whereas a long poem's parts are greater than its whole. Two likely reasons for this are the common assumption that poetry offers greater local intensity than prose and the long poem's evolution in the eighteenth century into a non-narrative form. Long poems have been rearranging chronologies and questioning the need for chronology at all for far longer than novels. But we must remember that a linear reading experience, if not a linear plot or any plot at all, remains the default assumption for a long poem as well as a novel, and that linear conception of time is then 'reshaped' when readers like Keats treat a poem like a 'Region to wander in', a selection of parts that they can move between at will.

Keats's conception of the long poem as a 'little Region to wander in' anticipates Joseph Frank's theory of 'spatial forms' in the twentieth century, a theory that Frank applied to long poems as well as novels. He coined the term in 1945 to describe a modernist conception of literature as spatially extended. In his essay on 'Spatial Form and Modern Literature' Frank posited that when encountering certain modernists 'the reader is intended to apprehend their work spatially, in a moment of time, rather than as a sequence'.[18] Even in their long poems, Frank argued, Eliot and Pound attempted to make 'the poem itself one vast image'. They 'undermine[d] the inherent consecutiveness of language, frustrating the reader's normal expectation of a sequence and forcing him to perceive the elements of the poem juxtaposed in space rather than unrolling in time'.[19] The reader was 'forced' to think of the poem this way through a structural method Frank called 'reflexive reference': techniques such as internal allusion, transitions between passages, foreshadowing, repetition and contradiction, that oblige the reader to consider parts side by side instead of in sequence, and so perceive them as simultaneous in time, even when those parts are separated by many lines or pages. Comparing different points in the poem in this way requires the reader to think of the text as a whole composed of many parts that are laid out in space, like a painting: the mind conceives of the whole at once, and then can move between the constituent parts in any order. The text might direct the movement of the mind through its methods of reflexive reference, in the same way that a painting can direct the movement of the eye, but that movement need not correspond with the chronological ordering of the parts. Of course, recognising the operations of spatial form requires as a kind of default the initial conception of the text in what Frank calls temporal form, with its different parts representing different moments in a linear reading experience. It is only by apprehending the text in this way that we can then perceive how reflexive reference reshapes it into spatial form. Frank does not explicitly pursue the implication that, having done so, we then perceive the parts not just as places located in space, but as moments located in time, albeit in time that no longer possesses its familiar linear shape.

It is notable that Frank contrasted the modernist spatial form with eighteenth-century theories of literature, particularly Gotthold Ephraim Lessing's argument in *Laokoon* (1766) that because language unfolds over time literature is necessarily a temporal medium, compared to the spatial medium of visual art. But in 1979, Paul K. Alkon argued that a 'partial grammar of spatial forms ... evolved in the eighteenth century', that in *Tristram Shandy* 'readers are constantly invited to make some effort at apprehending many parts of the book at once' and that these memories 'called into play during a reading are part of a work's temporal structure'.[20] Alkon's use of the idea of spatial forms to study Defoe's novels, and the value of this approach for studying eighteenth-century literature more generally, has gone underappreciated. The conception of texts as spaces whose parts exist in simultaneity was available to writers and readers in the seventeenth, eighteenth and early nineteenth centuries as well as in the early twentieth. Readers described long poems as buildings, trees, tapestries and landscapes: regions to wander in. This book is part of the current 'temporal turn' in eighteenth-century studies, then, but argues that the eighteenth-century temporal turn didn't necessarily reject spatial forms of thinking; rather, it used spatial forms to think about the various shapes that time might take.

The non-narrative generic traditions for the long poem that rose to prominence from the late seventeenth century, before receding from view again in the early nineteenth, particularly the cousin-genres of georgic and prospect poem, offered very particular models for thinking about time that distinguished the long poem from other long literary forms, including other genres of long poem. Tragedy and comedy (the primary generic structures for both drama and prose fiction in the period) involve an inexorable pull towards a determined conclusion, whether death or marriage (and any divergences from this conclusion still take their energy from resistance to it). Epic cycles and romances, while their structures are more repetitive, similarly proceed through fulfilments and conclusions of quests, journeys and conflicts. But a georgic poem or a prospect poem is less interested in articulating a beginning or an end than in what lies between. Georgic is the genre that seeks to know the causes of things, but also knows the limitations of how far we can understand the relation between action and outcome, cause and effect. The prospect poem offers a vision of history, but by locating historical events upon an extended spatial scene renders them simultaneous with one another and therefore causally disconnected. Drawing on these emerging generic frameworks for the long poem, even Milton, whose most obvious generic source is epic, can unsettle both his portrayal of cause and effect and his poem's own dependence on narrative chronology.

This book is divided into three sections, one on each of *Paradise Lost*, *The Seasons* and *The Prelude*. Each section is divided into three chapters. The first chapter of each section explains the particular contemporary debates about causation, and contexts for thinking about time, that the poem engages with. It explores how each poem constructs in its content a binary temporality that can accommodate an apprehension of time as both moving and static, flowing and disjointed, in order to hold both possibilities in suspension. The second chapter of each section turns to the time of writing and reading as these processes are depicted in the poems themselves, whether in portraits of the poet, narratives of creative expression and receptive interpretation, or the acts of revision and adaptation that are registered within these texts. In the third chapter of each section, I survey the critical and popular reception of each poem, and argue that the question of how to read these poems in and through time – whether they should be conceived as chronologically unfolding from beginning to end, or as wholes whose parts exist in simultaneity and can be encountered in any order – has not only divided readers, but has had implications for their understanding of the relationship and power dynamic between author and reader. This combination of chapters in each section demonstrates, I hope, a useful methodological approach that brings together thematic, narratological and structural analysis with reception history in order to understand the ethical and aesthetic implications of reading time in the long poem.

Chapter 1 argues that *Paradise Lost* is an early experiment in the prospect poem, as it both establishes that all the events it narrates take place within the view of God 'beholding from his prospect high / Wherein past, present, future he beholds' (III.77–8), and uses shorter prospect poems to frame its characters' reflections on free will and causation. Milton adapts the use of the prospect view to grapple with questions about freedom and time from Boethius's theory of God's nunc stans, and his image of God viewing all times from a high peak. This image, of all times laid out spatially as though on a landscape, allows Milton and his characters to understand each moment as isolated, deriving its significance directly from above, and/or as part of a connected timeline, deriving significance from its causes and consequences. Shifting between these conceptions of time allows Milton and his characters to obscure God's role in characters' choices and actions, and to ascribe continuity of character and therefore responsibility to creatures, but to draw up the causal drawbridge before it leads to their creator.

Chapter 2 looks more closely at depictions of authorial composition and readerly interpretation across several of Milton's works. The similes in *Paradise Lost* are examples of the poet-narrator's own reading of time, and demonstrate a kind of 'commonplacing' of history. Although his drawing together of different points in history suggests a radical restructuring of time, chronology irrupts into the similes to distance the poet from his subject. In Milton's prose works of scriptural exegesis, and in his depictions of a kind of 'live' scriptural exegesis in *Paradise Regain'd*, a similar principle applies: readers must extract pieces of Scripture to compare different parts of the text, but remain alert to the contexts that those pieces had in their original placements.

Chapter 3 turns to the reception of *Paradise Lost*, arguing that the question of whether the poem should be approached as a spatial or temporal form, and whether it should be understood synchronically or diachronically, distinguishes two important schools of interpretation. The Romantic or post-Romantic reading approaches the poem as a spatial form, a region in which to wander, and empowers readers to extract and privilege particular parts of the poem, especially the early 'satanic' books. The 'Fishian' reading that came to prominence in the 1960s, on the other hand, stresses the importance of a linear reading that privileges the end of the poem over the beginning. The former approach frames the reading experience in terms of the reader's autonomy as well as their ease and enjoyment, with the reader portrayed as a gentleman flicking through the book at his leisure and whim; whereas the latter portrays the reader as a long-distance runner, whose strenuous effort to read the poem culminates in submission to the poet's intentions.

Chapter 4 turns to Thomson's *The Seasons*, arguing that Thomson, like Milton, develops a binary conception of time in order to engage, albeit in a non-committal way, in a contemporary debate about causation. By obscuring whether the movement of his poem is across time or space – whether his natural description narrates change over time or variation across space – Thomson is able to suggest both the independence and interconnectedness of each moment in time and each occasion or event in the natural world. As in *Paradise Lost*, the crucial question is whether God is an immediate cause, intervening at each moment to shape the world, or a first or original cause, deferred from the present by time and a long chain of intermediate or secondary causes. For Milton this was a question primarily of human freedom; for Thomson it is a question of physico-theology, and God's specific role in the nonhuman world. By positing both possible shapes of time, Thomson is able to articulate a georgic cyclical temporality in which processes of growth and decay can continue flowing, but the concepts of 'before' and 'after' have little currency.

Chapter 5 addresses a potential counter-argument to the theory of Thomson's portrayal of time that I developed in Chapter 4. There are episodes of *The Seasons* that seem to depend more clearly on narrative time: the interpolated tales, and the depictions of the poet-narrator's own creative process. I argue here that even these seemingly narrative passages undermine the supposed chronological order of their parts. I look more closely at a specific tale, the story of Damon and Musidora in 'Summer', and show that in its content as well as its reception – by Thomson in his revisions, and by artists in their illustrations – this tale both endorses and questions the ongoing flow of time.

Chapter 6, like Chapter 3, focuses on readers' reception. Readers of *The Seasons* have disagreed over whether the poem is about spatial variety, and therefore its parts may be read in any order, or whether it is a poem about continuous change, and therefore must be read from beginning to end and in the proper order. *The Seasons* has been excerpted and anthologised extensively, despite the difficulty of defining where a 'part' begins or ends. Without advocating for one or the other hermeneutic method, I show in this chapter how these different reading approaches and conceptions of the poem's structure have implications for how the reader receives *The Seasons*' ethical and epistemological claims.

Chapter 7 identifies Wordsworth's *The Prelude* as a landmark in the history of the long poem when the non-narrative forms favoured in the eighteenth century started to be felt insufficient. Wordsworth still wishes to privilege certain times, seeming even to extract them from the extended timeline of his autobiographical narrative – these are the so-called 'spots of time', whose very name suggests their conception of both a life and a poem as spatial forms. But Wordsworth's desire to trace his own progress as a poet requires a linear temporality and a continuity that the spots of time model does not provide. In this chapter I look more closely at a few examples of the spots of time and show how they function not as spots but as prospects – the initial focus on a specific moment in a specific place opens out into a wider view of space and a longer process of time. This chapter, then, argues for the importance for Wordsworth of chronos over kairos, although critical emphasis has almost always been on the latter. The return to a world of moving time that is dramatised in the spots of time is a return to intersubjective, communal forms of time and therefore a movement from isolation to society.

Chapter 8 approaches both Wordsworth's allusions and his revisions as depictions and dramatisations of the poet's engagement with the literary past. Wordsworth's allusions to Milton and Thomson, I argue, reveal the mediation of the time that has flowed in between in the form of the long literary history of the eighteenth century. His extensive revisions to *The Prelude* similarly hint that versions of the poem represent moments in time that are part of a continuous, additive process, because the revisions often retain traces of and subtly allude to, rather than fully displace, their origins in past versions of the poem.

Chapter 9 maps the kairos/chronos distinction onto critical readings of *The Prelude*. Victorian reviewers of *The Prelude* as well as earlier reviewers of *The Excursion* repeatedly describe Wordsworth's long poems as uneven landscapes, with particular parts that rise above, or should be extracted from, the less impressive ground. Even some early readers, however, suggested that both the order of the parts and the more prosaic sections that connect the more attractive spots of time are necessary to understanding the progress that Wordsworth narrates. In this chapter I argue that, despite the temptation to privilege the spots of time and treat them as self-contained lyrics, the long journey of reading *The Prelude* makes visible the losses, gains and recuperations that Wordsworth undergoes both in his life and in the fictional writing process.

The three sections of this book can be read out of order, or extracted entirely. But together they tell a story about the development of the long poem in the long eighteenth century: its transition, as early as in *Paradise Lost*, towards the non-narrative forms of georgic, prospect poem, and philosophical poem; the apotheosis of the non-narrative long poem in *The Seasons*, its capacity to represent non-linear shapes of time, and the natural-philosophical arguments that this conception of time could articulate; and its lingering decline in the Romantic period, as Wordsworth feels the tug of ongoing narrative history yet still finds the prospect poem a useful framework, and landscape a useful figure, for thinking about the multiple ways in which moments in time can speak to one another.

Notes

1. John Keats, *The Letters of John Keats*, ed. Maurice Buxton Forman, 4th edn (Oxford: Oxford UP, 1952), 52.
2. Ibid., 302.
3. John Keats and John Milton, *Keats's Paradise Lost: A Digital Edition*, ed. Daniel Johnson, Beth Lau and Greg Kucich (*The Keats Library*, 2020) <http://keatslibrary.org/paradise-lost/> (accessed 5 July 2021), 62.
4. Jesse Molesworth, 'Introduction: The Temporal Turn in Eighteenth-Century Studies', *The Eighteenth Century* 60.2 (2019): 129–38 (130).
5. See for example Christina Lupton, *Reading and the Making of Time in the Eighteenth Century* (Baltimore: Johns Hopkins UP, 2018), and Roger Mathew Grant, *Beating Time & Measuring Music in the Early Modern Era* (Oxford: Oxford UP, 2014).
6. See for example Jonathan Sachs, 'Eighteenth-century Slow Time', *The Eighteenth Century* 60.2 (2019): 185–205.
7. Lewis White Beck, 'World Enough, and Time', in *Probability, Time, and Space in Eighteenth-Century Literature*, ed. Paula R. Backscheider (New York: AMS Press, 1979): 113–39 (114).
8. John Sitter, *Literary Loneliness in Mid-Eighteenth-Century England* (Ithaca: Cornell UP, 1982), 158.
9. Martin Priestman, *The Poetry of Erasmus Darwin: Enlightened Spaces, Romantic Times* (Aldershot: Ashgate, 2013), 31.
10. Ibid., 29.
11. Ibid., 31.
12. Adam Roberts, *Romantic and Victorian Long Poems: A Guide* (London: Routledge, 1999). Katarina Stenke, 'Parts and Wholes in Long Non-narrative Poems of the Eighteenth Century' (unpublished doctoral thesis, University of Cambridge, 2013).

13. Thomas M. Allen, ed. *Time and Literature* (Cambridge: Cambridge UP, 2018); Christina Lupton and Carston Meiner, ed. *Literature and Contingency* (London and New York: Routledge, 2020). The essays in *Literature and Contingency* first appeared in a special issue of *Textual Practice*, 32.3 (2018).
14. Randall Stevenson, *Reading the Times: Temporality and History in Twentieth-Century Fiction* (Edinburgh: Edinburgh UP, 2018), 19.
15. G. W. F. Hegel, *Aesthetics: Lectures on Fine Art*, II, trans. T. M. Knox (Oxford: Clarendon Press, 1975). Quoted in Ryan Netzley, *Lyric Apocalypse: Milton, Marvell, and the Nature of Events* (New York: Fordham UP, 2015), 17.
16. Rebecca Bushnell, 'Time and Genre', in Allen, ed. *Time and Literature*: 44–56 (49).
17. William Wordsworth, letter to Alexander Dyce (Spring 1833), in *The Romantics on Milton*, ed. Joseph Wittreich (Cleveland: Case Western Reserve UP, 1970), 137.
18. Joseph Frank, 'Spatial Form in Modern Literature, Part 1', *The Sewanee Review* 53 (1945): 221–40 (225).
19. Ibid., 227.
20. Paul K. Alkon, *Defoe and Fictional Time* (Athens, GA: University of Georgia Press, 1979), 12, 106.

Part I

Milton

Chapter 1

His Prospect High: The Nunc Stans in *Paradise Lost*

Paradise Lost is a prospect poem. This is not only true of Book 11, in which Adam enjoys a panorama of biblical history from the highest hill in Paradise. Book 11 is Milton's most obvious adaptation of the prospect poem, a nascent and mainly Royalist genre that had been inaugurated by John Denham's *Coopers Hill* (1642). But the whole of *Paradise Lost* can, and should, be understood as an experiment in the prospect poem, because we are told that everything relayed in the poem occurs within the sight of God the Father, watching from his elevated position in Heaven, as well as within the sight of Milton's muse, from whose high 'view' 'Heav'n hides nothing' (I.27). The first three books of *Paradise Lost* all open with a high eminence from which characters survey. In Book 1, the muse is located on the 'secret top' (6) of various mountains, and Milton's own poem is projected to soar 'Above th' *Aonian* Mount' (15). This opening, establishing the prospect poem's common method of analogy between literal and figurative heights, echoes that of *Coopers Hill*, in which Denham imagines his poetic 'flight' from the hill's 'auspicious height', 'Through untrac'd wayes'.[1] At the start of Book 2, Satan is placed 'High on a Throne' in Hell (1), raised to a 'bad eminence' (6). And in Book 3, we are introduced to God as the definitive surveyor and surveillor, whose prospect view informs and enables that of Milton's muse because it encompasses all the places and times described in *Paradise Lost*, from the Creation to the composition of the poem and beyond:

> Now had the Almighty Father from above,
> From the pure Empyrean where he sits
> High Thron'd above all highth, bent down his eye,
> His own works and their works at once to view:

> About him all the Sanctities of Heaven
> Stood thick as Starrs, and from his sight receiv'd
> Beatitude past utterance; on his right
> The radiant image of his Glory sat,
> His onely Son; on Earth he first beheld
> Our two first Parents, yet the onely two
> Of mankind, in the happie Garden plac't,
> Reaping immortal fruits of joy and love,
> Uninterrupted joy, unrivald love
> In blissful solitude; he then survey'd
> Hell and the Gulf between, and *Satan* there
> . . .
> Him God beholding from his prospect high,
> Wherein past, present, future he beholds,
> Thus to his onely Son foreseing spake.
> (III.56–79)

As in Book 11, these lines dramatise the pun on 'prospect', as a temporal as well as a spatial term, that was inherent in the genre. God is first shown moving his eyes across space, from Heaven 'about him' down to Earth, then across a space 'between' to Hell. Like Denham's prospector in *Coopers Hill*, his 'eye . . . swift as thought' (which is not instantaneous) 'contracts the space / That lyes between' particular spatial reference points.[2] This establishes the 'powerful feeling' of the 'spatial sublime' that Gordon Teskey has described in the poem: an awareness of the 'giant vistas' and 'vast distances' that make every location 'continuous in space with . . . worlds beyond'.[3] But again as in Denham's poem, here the spatial topography is actually quite limited, focusing on a small number of spatial reference points in the panorama and remaining extraordinarily vague about where they stand in relation to one another, because Milton's real interest is not in describing a landscape but in the temporal 'prospects' that these points open up: the visions of past and future time that a spatial point represents and stimulates. Marvell dramatises this conventional transition, from space to time, overtly in his country-house-poem-meets-prospect-poem, 'Upon Appleton House': 'While with slow eyes we these [features of the landscape] survey . . . We opportunely may relate / The progress of this house's fate.'[4] God's divine panorama in *Paradise Lost* literalises this conventional association between spatial prospect and historical 'progress'. Here in Book 3, the spatial topography shifts into a literal temporal equivalent, a 'prospect high / Wherein past, present, future he beholds'. Here is the temporal peculiarity of the prospect poem, which explicitly frames its past and future prospects as parts of a linear historical 'progress', but whose spatial rendering of time collapses the sequence into simultaneity. As well as the simultaneity of all space described by Teskey, in this scene Milton establishes the simultaneity of all times as they appear in God's view. Every moment in time appears, in God's perspective, like a coordinate on a map, coexistent with every other moment. Everything that *Paradise Lost* contains, therefore, everything it has to say about God's 'works and their works', is an elaboration of this prospect: an imperfect rendering, in the form of poetry, of an image that God sees all 'at once'.

The prospect poem, then, is not only a modish mode in *Paradise Lost*, introduced in particular passages, but one of the poem's shaping genres, informing its overall form as well as content. On one hand, it is partly in retrospect – in the light of Milton's reception and influence in the eighteenth century – that *Paradise Lost*'s status as prospect poem, and the importance of recognising this generic status, become visible. On the other, critics such as David Quint and Ann Boynes Coiro have argued that, contrary to common assumption, Milton did directly respond to the poetry of his contemporaries in *Paradise Lost*, including early prospect poems like *Coopers Hill* and Edmund Waller's 'On St. James's Park', which suggests that he understood the (potentially dangerous) capacity of the prospect poem for fashioning narratives of national and biblical history.[5] It is important to recognise the prospect poem as a shaping genre for Milton's project, not only in order to understand Milton's later influence and his engagement with his contemporaries, but because genre is Milton's primary resource for thinking through his key philosophical, theological, and ethical question: that of free will. By combining genres such as epic, tragedy and scriptural history, and the particular temporalities associated with those genres, Milton combines different conceptions of time and causation, blended together in a recipe for divine justification. And I contend that it was the prospect poem, inflected with modes of its cousin-genre georgic, that Milton found to be one of the most fruitful poetics for exploring and balancing the competing temporal demands of freedom and responsibility.

What are these temporal demands? Free will is a fraught issue in Christian theology, to put it mildly, and has occupied readers of *Paradise Lost* since its publication. Often it is upon this question that the seeming self-contradictions in the poem hinge. In Book 10 the Father declares that 'Conviction to the Serpent none belongs' (84). Later in the same book Milton describes how 'To Judgement he proceeded on th' accus'd / Serpent though brute, unable to transferre /

The Guilt on him who made him instrument / Of mischief' (164–7). Can the snake, a passive instrument of Satan, be held responsible for his part in bringing about the Fall? Many of the famous disagreements in critical interpretation of the poem also centre upon the question of free will: how far does the poem convince us that Satan, Adam and Eve are responsible for their own falls and therefore justly punished? Or can they, unlike the snake, 'transferre / The Guilt' of their sins elsewhere, and especially up, or back, to God? These are questions of causation – Milton's opening address beseeches the inspiring spirit to 'say first what cause / Mov'd our Grand Parents ... to fall off' (I.28–30) – and therefore of time. James P. Driscoll sums up the problem in terms that make clear its temporal dimension:

> the doctrine [of free will] gives Satan and men stable, continuous identities so that God may hold them responsible for their sins. At the same time it leaps beyond process and borrows from flux to grant those identities spontaneous mutation in order to free God from responsibility for the evil choices of the beings he creates. ... The doctrine offers no viable way to unify the conflicting definitions of identity it posits; it only provides a blurred question mark to shroud the contradiction.[6]

A temporality that will 'justifie the ways of God to men' must not only accommodate both continuity and spontaneity, but must use each to 'shroud' the shortfalls of the other. While it is not possible to resolve the tensions in the doctrine of free will that *Paradise Lost* articulates, it is possible to draw out some of the techniques by which Milton holds these tensions in suspension and 'blurs' their fault-lines. His central method, I argue, is the development of a fundamentally binary apprehension of time based on the medieval theory of eternity as a *nunc stans*: an 'abiding now' or 'now that remains', an atemporal existence that encompasses all times within it. In its original articulation by Boethius, the nunc stans was imagined as a prospect view from a peak. Milton picks up on this use of the prospect to visualise time and thereby understand free will, and recognises the potential of a newly fashionable seventeenth-century genre to develop the image.

In this chapter I begin by outlining Milton's engagement, in Book 3, with Boethius's theory of the nunc stans, contextualising this engagement within mid-seventeenth-century debates about the term and its visualisation. The second half of this chapter examines other moments when characters use their own prospect views to contemplate the multiple possible causal or acausal relationships that pertain between events, demonstrating the consistency with which Milton associated questions of free will with the prospect poem genre. In its ability to balance progress with simultaneity, process with spontaneity, the prospect poem allowed Milton and his characters to identify causal responsibility in actors when good turns to evil, but then to draw up the causal chain before the source of that evil is apprehended in God, leaving the buck to stop with one of his creatures, such as Adam in Book 10: 'first and last / On mee, mee onely, as the sourse and spring / Of all corruption' (X.831–3).

The Nunc Stans

The need to distinguish between different conceptions, or apprehensions, of time in *Paradise Lost* has long been recognised. Judith Scherer Herz, Amy Boesky and Anthony Welch have all recently written about the multiple temporal structures at play in the poem, and have shown (in the tradition of the New Milton Criticism) how the conflicts between these structures open up inconsistencies and contradictions that work to destabilise the idea of time itself, and time's capacity to narrate events that touch or take place in eternity.[7] The basic distinction most commonly identified is between providence and possibility: the temporality of God, who foreknows all events from the beginning, and the temporality experienced by those characters who feel that the future genuinely lies open. Gary Saul Morson has argued that this temporal binary characterises all narrative literature by virtue of assumed authorial foreknowledge: 'Readers of literary narrative have a double experience: they both identify with characters and contemplate structure . . . identification and foreshadowing may both be present, which means that the reader's experience of the work involves an overlap of distinct temporalities.'[8] But he acknowledges, in his analysis of the 'double experience' of time in *Oedipus*, that narratives including prophecies or foreknowing characters, like Tiresias or Milton's God, dramatise and draw attention to this doubleness. The most prominent recent scholar of Milton's philosophy of time, Ayelet C. Langer, has focused not on the distinction between divine and human temporalities, but on the distinction between what she takes to be the fallen experience of time, which occupies an isolated present and can apprehend succession but not causation, and the unfallen experience of time as a fluid medium in which one moment leads causally into the next in continuous movement.[9] But as in most analyses of time in the poem,

Langer holds the temporal experience of God in eternity apart from these in turn.

While my reading retains Langer's fundamental distinction between two apprehensions of time that perceive either continuous causation or moments that are disjointed from one another, I propose that this distinction does not lie between fallen and unfallen perspectives, or even between the human and the eternal as in most formulations of the poem's different temporalities. Such a distinction is contained within the apprehension of God. God's nunc stans perspective allows him to apprehend both the causal relationships that connect events to one another, and each event in isolation. Such a perspective can accommodate both providence and possibility, and can incorporate both the continuity and the spontaneity that are essential to a structure of free will that does not implicate God. Furthermore, both fallen and unfallen characters, Milton shows, are able to approach this dual apprehension of time, although their capacity to reconcile the two perspectives is limited. In *Paradise Lost*, it is not only the reader, as in Morson's account, but numerous characters who experience an 'overlap' of temporalities. Even those characters who cannot 'contemplate' the entire 'structure' as God can are aware of its existence in eternity. I aim to understand these temporal ambiguities and paradoxes as a deliberate function of the poem's Christian argument, with roots in a canonical theological tradition that was very honest about its own foundation in anxiety. Aporias, logical gaps and leaps, and contradictions in the portrayal of time are not invitations to an against-the-grain reading, then, but an orthodox assertion that our most accurate understanding of free will is one that embraces and combines seemingly incompatible temporalities.

It is no good asking 'what is time in *Paradise Lost*?' without asking 'what is eternity in *Paradise Lost*?' Eternity, according to early medieval church fathers (who were influenced by Platonic and Neoplatonic conceptions of the atemporality of forms) including Augustine, was not a perpetual duration of time but a state of timelessness that was an attribute of God. The most famous name for this kind of eternity which transcended time was nunc stans, which means 'abiding now', or 'now that remains', as opposed to nunc fluens, the 'now that passes'. Milton would have known the terms from numerous sources, and most importantly from St Thomas Aquinas's commentary on Boethius's theology of time: 'Boëtius quod *nunc fluens facit tempus, nunc stans facit æternitatum.*' ('Boethius said the now that passes produces time, the now that remains produces eternity.')[10] Aquinas is paraphrasing Boethius's argument in *De Trinitate*, iv.7.

Boethius actually uses the terms 'nunc quasi currens' and 'nunc permanens', but nevertheless the terms 'nunc fluens' and 'nunc stans' have become associated with his theology due to Aquinas. I use them here, rather than Boethius's original terms, because they have more currency in modern as well as early modern theology and philosophy. According to Boethius, the nunc fluens is the perspective of time afforded to humans, who travel through time linearly and can only perceive one time at a time as present, while the nunc stans is the eternal perspective of God, who perceives all times at once. Boethius summarises the two in his *Consolation of Philosophy*:

> whatever lives in time lives in the here and now, and advances from past to future. Nothing situated in time can at the one moment grasp the entire duration of its life. It does not as yet apprehend the morrow, and it has already relinquished its yesterday. [. . . W]hat does rightly claim the title of eternal is that which grasps and possesses simultaneously the entire fullness of life without end; no part of the future is lacking to it, and no part of the past has escaped it. It must always appear to itself as in the present, and as governing itself; the unending course of fleeting time it must possess as the here and now.[11]

Eternity, for Boethius, is a perspective: it is a question of how things appear, including how the mind that holds that perspective appears 'to itself'. Free will, too, is a matter of perspective. Boethius developed his theory of eternity in order to shift the question of foreknowledge to one of present knowledge, so as to solve the problem of the compatibility of God's omniscience and humanity's free will:

> since God's status is abidingly eternal and in the present, his knowledge too transcends all movement in time. It abides in the simplicity of its present, embraces the boundless extent of past and future, and by virtue of its simple comprehension, it ponders all things as if they were being enacted in the present. Hence your judgement will be more correct should you seek to envisage the foresight by which God discerns all things not as a sort of foreknowledge of the future, but as knowledge of the unceasingly present moment. For this reason it is better to term it *providentia* ('looking forward spatially') rather than *praevidentia* ('looking forward in time'), for it is not set far apart from the lowliest things, and it gazes out on everything as from one of the world's lofty peaks.
>
> Why, then, do you demand that things surveyed by the divine light be necessary, when even men do not pronounce as necessary the things they see?[12]

The nunc stans embraces past, present and future within one eternal 'now' so that God's foreknowledge becomes knowledge; every event is temporally simultaneous with, and thereby causally separated from, God's knowledge of it. Of course, from this perspective events appear not only simultaneous with God's knowledge but with one another, too; and therefore are not only causally severed from God's knowledge but from one another. Temporal continuity, the prerequisite for causation, becomes spatial contiguity, and every moment, not only the eternal observer, 'appear[s . . .] as governing itself'.

It is quite clear that Milton's depiction of the Father in Book 3, viewing 'all things at one view', is derived from Boethius's description of the nunc stans, and especially from his image of God's foreknowledge as a 'gaze out' from a 'lofty peak'. Despite this, there has been relatively little discussion of Milton's use of the nunc stans. Edward W. Tayler has suggested that the 'now' of the Nativity Ode may 'be considered a poetic *nunc stans*', conflating Christmas 1629 with the first Christmas 'as though viewed from the vantage of Eternity'.[13] Some other treatments of Milton's engagement with Boethius have focused not on time but on Milton's use of the consolatio genre in *Comus*, *Samson Agonistes* and Books 11 and 12 of *Paradise Lost*.[14] Critics such as Stephen J. Schuler and William Myers acknowledge the Boethian source of God's 'prospect high' in Book 3, but dispute Milton's wider acceptance of the Boethian theory of eternity (I will address their arguments later in this chapter).[15] Dennis Richard Danielson takes a more nuanced view, acknowledging that Milton does 'present the model of knowledge as vision, which Boethius implies, and he does present God's vantage point as a high place . . . Milton takes the model of *scientia visionis* and gives it a literal as well as conceptual role in his epic'. But Danielson argues that overall '*Paradise Lost* does not embody the most distinctive characteristic of Boethius's treatment – namely, the concept that God's knowledge is actually *scientia*, rather than *praescientia*, because God dwells in an eternal present that transcends our categories of time and tense'.[16] Recently, however, Jefferey H. Taylor and Leslie A. Taylor have argued that '[t]he motif of the Divine Vista pervades *Paradise Lost* and establishes the framework from which Milton's position on predestination brilliantly escapes the complexities of the protracted theological debates and is clearly presented in visual terms that are inescapably Boethian'.[17] What Taylor and Taylor call the 'Divine Vista' is Boethius's 'visual term' of the prospect view, the image of God surveying all time 'as from one of the world's lofty peaks'.

With the exception of Taylor and Taylor's study, the importance of the nunc stans theory for Milton, and specifically for his thinking about free will, has been underestimated or denied outright due, I think, to a misunderstanding of Milton's own conception of the nunc stans. His nunc stans differs subtly from that of his contemporaries but remains faithful to, even as it extends and develops, Boethius's original formulation, specifically that prospect view visualisation. Milton's innovation in his use of the nunc stans theory is the way he picks up Boethius's depiction of God's knowledge as 'gazing out on everything as from one of the world's lofty peaks', and elaborates the image by adapting it to the new form of the prospect poem. Crucially, this visualisation enables both God and Milton to perceive and posit multiple potential relationships between events and moments in time: not just the isolation and spontaneity of every moment, on which both seventeenth-century and twenty-first-century critics of the nunc stans focus, but *also* the linear and causal connections between times. The nunc stans transcends all movement in time, but also accommodates it.

According to Robert Greene, who provides an invaluable overview of the early modern reception of the nunc stans theory, the term 'nunc stans' first appeared in English in 1618, and Greene counts seventy-one printed references to it in the seventeenth century.[18] Most appear in sermons and theological treatises, with particular concentration in the 1650s, but the best-known reference in a work of poetry was in the first book of Abraham Cowley's *Davideis* (1656). Cowley describes Heaven's nunc stans without using the Latin term in the poem itself: 'Nothing is there *To come*, and nothing *Past*, / But an *Eternal Now* does always last.'[19] Sue Starke has argued that Milton learned from Cowley's attempt, and ultimate failure, to blend 'a heavenly [eternal] perspective' with too strict an adherence to classical epic form and linear human history, so these lines on the nunc stans may have held particular resonance for Milton.[20] Milton also would have read Cowley's note to his line on the 'Eternal Now', in which he does use the term 'nunc stans':

> *Eternity* is defined by *Boet. Lib. 5. de Consolat. Interminabilis vitoe tota simul & perfecta possessio.* The whole and perfect possession, ever all at once, of a being without beginning or ending. Which *Definition* is followed by *Tho: Aquin*, and all the *Schoolmen*; who therefore call *Eternity Nunc stans, a standing Now*, to distinguish it from that *Now*, which is a difference of *time*, and is always *in Fluxu*.[21]

Whereas his verses incorporate the nunc stans as an indisputable attribute of Heaven, an accepted concept, Cowley's notes are more cautious: this is one definition of eternity 'followed by' a particular group, the Schoolmen, whose Scholastic methods had dominated European universities in the early seventeenth century but were by the mid-century in sharp decline, and their ideas, including their centuries-old definition of eternity as a nunc stans, subject to attack. The nunc stans was a subject of contentious theological debate in the mid-century. In his *True Intellectual System of the Universe* (1678), Ralph Cudworth complains of 'Atheists' who

> show their little wit, in quibbling upon *Nunc-stans*, or a *Standing Now of Eternity*; as if that *Standing Eternity* of the *Deity* (which with so much Reason hath been contended for, by the Ancient *Genuine Theists*) were nothing but a *Pitiful Small Moment* of *Time Standing still*; and as if the Duration of all Beings whatsoever must needs be like our own.[22]

Whether Cudworth knew of multiple 'Atheists' who contested the nunc stans theory is unclear; here 'Atheists' probably stands for one man, Thomas Hobbes.

In *Leviathan* (1651), Hobbes objected to the definition of eternity as 'the Standing still of the Present Time, a Nunc-stans (as the Schools call it;)', rather than as simply 'an Endlesse Succession of Time'.[23] The heightened concentration of printed references to the nunc stans in the 1650s is mainly due to what Greene has called Hobbes's 'repetitive campaign, waged in six texts, from *Leviathan* in 1651 to *An Answer to a Book* in 1682, to denounce, ridicule, satirise, mock and invalidate nunc-stans', a concept that was for Hobbes representative of disingenuous scholastic metaphysics.[24] The debate between Hobbes and John Bramhall, Bishop of Derry, published in 1656 as *The Questions Concerning Liberty, Necessity, and Chance*, makes clear that free will was a question of time, and particularly of whether God's decree is antecedent to or simultaneous with his foreknowledge. The Bishop takes the Arminian-Boethian view: 'The Knowledge of God comprehends all times in a point by reason of the eminence and vertue of its infinite perfection. And yet I confess, that this is called fore knowledge, in respect of us. But this fore-knowledge doth produce no absolute necessity.'[25] Like Boethius, Bramhall argues that in order to understand free will, humans must strive to imagine, however imperfectly, what God's nunc stans perspective is like: 'the readiest way to reconcile Contingence and Liberty, with the decrees and prescience of God . . . is to subject future contingents to the aspect of God, according to that presentiality which they have in eternity.'[26] Hobbes's main objection is that it is simply impossible to imagine a single point that encompasses all time simultaneously:

> To this I answer, that as soon as I can conceive Eternity to be an indivisible point, or any thing, but an everlasting succession, I will renounce all I have written in this subject. I know *St. Thomas Aquinas* calls eternity *Nunc stans*, an ever abiding now which is easy enough to say, but though I fain would, I never could conceive it.[27]

For Hobbes, eternity was infinite duration and succession, not an absence of duration or succession. And in many of his works Milton appears to agree with this Hobbesian definition. In *De Doctrina Christiana*, he not only does not use the term 'nunc stans' but perhaps hints at the Hobbesian alternative when he defines eternity as 'that which has neither beginning nor end'.[28] He gives the same definition in *Paradise Regain'd*: 'eternal sure, as without end, / Without beginning' (IV.391–2).[29] It is perhaps not surprising, then, that Schuler argues: 'When Milton uses the words "eternal" and "eternity" in his works . . . he always means simply "perpetual" or "unending"; he never uses them to mean absolute timelessness, even when referring to God.'[30] I'm not sure that this is a fair conclusion; Cowley's note to the *Davideis* tells us that 'without beginning or end' could have formed a part of the definition of the nunc stans and did not necessarily signal a rejection of it. But even if we accept this assessment of Milton's treatment of eternity in prose works like *De Doctrina* and *Art of Logic*, just as Cowley's cautious note acknowledging debate does not reflect the acceptance of the nunc stans in his verse, Milton's poetic treatment of eternity is less sceptical than his prose about the Boethian definition. Schuler admits that the prospect image in Book 3 is derived from Boethius, but argues that in both his poetry and prose Milton presents a God who *fore*sees, rather than sees, the future, and that he thereby rejects Boethius's theory of the nunc stans. However, God's capacities both to act in time and to perceive the future *as* future and the past *as* past – Schuler's evidence for Milton's rejection – are not incompatible with the Boethian nunc stans.

When Bramhall visualises the nunc stans, he imagines that God 'comprehends all times in a point'; Hobbes retorts that such a thing is incomprehensible. But a 'point', even 'an infinite point, comprehending all times within it self', is not what Boethius imagines, nor

Milton. This is why Cudworth is so disgusted at misrepresentation of the nunc stans as a '*Pitiful Small Moment* of *Time*'. Boethius imagines the nunc stans perspective as '*providentia* ("looking forward spatially") rather than *praevidentia* ("looking forward in time")', a gaze 'as from one of the world's lofty peaks', and Milton imagines God 'beholding from his prospect high'. These are crucially different spatial figurations from those considered by Bramhall and Hobbes: not every moment condensed to a point, but all moments spread across a map or landscape, existing simultaneously, but distinct. The nunc stans is not one point, but a spread of multiple points, or as the Royalist clergyman Richard Allestree described it, 'an indivisible Infinity of permanent duration, whose every point does coexist to every point'.[31] The image of all time as a spatially extended prospect view affords the nunc stans a flexibility that its detractors, from Hobbes to Schuler, have not acknowledged. Highlighting Boethius's spatial figure of the prospect view, Milton is able to portray a God who perceives past, present and future simultaneously, but who also perceives the temporal relations between events and the unfolding narratives of time. God is able to perceive and be attentive not just to all 'nows' at once, but to the multiple potential relations pertaining between different 'nows'; to 'survey' all times 'at one view' but also to trace the connections between – temporal connections like causation, fulfilment and anticipation – like paths between spatial locations. Such connections are not so clearly visible to the nunc fluens, in which only one moment in time, the present, is ever grasped. This accommodation of sequence and causation within Milton's nunc stans explains why God is described as 'foreseeing' rather than 'seeing', and when God describes the Fall he does so in the future tense, and the Creation in the past tense. God apprehends all times at once and each time as present, but as his language here testifies, he also perceives how each moment or event is past and future in relation to other moments in time. He understands that Adam and Eve are '*yet* the onely two' – that they are at a point in history that is earlier than a later point. Every moment, therefore, appears to God in two ways. Each moment is part of a longer, moving timeline, and derives its meaning and significance from its place in that timeline. And, at the same time, each moment is individual and independent from others in history, deriving meaning and significance from its relation to God's eternal will. Because he can apprehend and experience successive time, God is able to act in time. He carries his actions out in sequence and recognises sequence, even if he also beholds his own actions perpetually and simultaneously with every other event.

God's action in time, therefore, does not contradict Boethius's theory that God perceives all times simultaneously. It is true, though, that God's action in time raises problems for Boethius's use of the nunc stans to understand free will. Boethius's nunc stans, after all, may absolve the foreseeing being from responsibility for wrongs, but it does nothing to absolve the being who creates, controls and intervenes. This is why God's argument that 'if I foreknew, / Foreknowledge had no influence on their fault, / Which had no less prov'd certain unforeknown' (117–19) is so unsatisfactory. It is why the solutions to the free will question offered in contemporary imaginative treatments of the Fall are so absurd. Lucy Hutchinson, in her unfinished long poem *Order and Disorder* (drafted in the 1660s, published 1679) disposes of this problem in neat couplets: 'sinners ... oftentimes / On God himself obliquely charge their crimes, / Expostulating in their discontent / As if he caused what he did not prevent' (V.33–8).[32] Hutchinson's solution only raises the question of *why* God did not prevent their crimes, which Boethius had attempted to answer – God does not foreknow each event but rather knows it, and so cannot be held responsible for not preventing it. The concept of prevention makes no sense from God's perspective. This is not sufficient for Milton, who feels keenly the frustration that God did not send an effective 'warning voice' (IV.1). Peter C. Herman has listed the various points at which Milton clearly shows that God did intervene in ways that might have prevented the Fall, but deliberately made his interventions inadequate. He chained Satan to the floor of Hell, but made chains that would easily break; he made a key to lock the gates of Hell, but entrusted that key to Sin; and so on.[33]

But it is not only his failure to prevent that makes God liable. There is also the ultimate liability of the creator, who has made his creatures with more or less capacity to fall. This seems to have troubled Dryden when he adapted *Paradise Lost* into the opera *The State of Innocence* (1677). In his version of the scene at the end of Book 4 of *Paradise Lost*, in which the angels confront Satan after his foray into Eden, Dryden has Gabriel, Ithuriel and Lucifer engage in an extended debate about freedom. Gabriel admits that God's creatures are 'Made for his use',

> yet he has form'd us so
> We, unconstrain'd, what he commands us do.
> So praise we him and serve him freely best:
> Thus thou, by choice, art fall'n, and we are blest.
> (Act 3, Scene 3)[34]

If God has 'form'd' the angels so that they obey him 'unconstrain'd', has he formed Lucifer so that he, unconstrained, *dis*obeys? There is no answer offered in this dialogue, as the conversation moves on, but in the next scene Dryden's Adam questions the possibility of nondeterminism at length: 'The force unseen, and distant I confess; / But the long chain makes not the bondage less . . . I can but chuse what he has first design'd, / For he before that choice, my will confin'd' (Act 4, Scene 1).[35] Dryden's Adam questions not only the influence of external forces upon his will but the disposition of his will itself, by God who is the first cause at the end of a 'long chain'. But Raphael interprets Adam to refer only to external forces, as he replies: 'Sufficient causes, only work th' effect / When necessary agents they respect. / Such is not man; who, though the cause suffice, / Yet often he his free assent denies.'[36] This successfully makes the point that humans are free to act as they will in any given situation; it doesn't answer the possibility that their will is confined not by circumstance or even influence, but by its internal constitution as 'form'd' by God.

In *Authors to Themselves* Marshall Grossman offers a potential solution. His emphasis on Milton's conception of character as continuously developing might be an alternative to either the spontaneously mutable choice or the fixed identity determined by God:

> Representations of the self within this temporality become less iterative expressions of an original predisposition or humor (Odysseus's cunning or Volpone's slyness would be examples) and more additive conceptions of a temporal development, articulating change within continuity. *Paradise Lost* is not a bildungsroman, but it introduces a relationship of narrative to character that sketches the bildungsroman on the horizon. The notion of self-authorship presented in Milton's narrative reflects and consolidates this change. In it, the human individual is understood to author himself or herself over the course of a lifetime by accumulating judgments and choices and the experiences that follow from them[.][37]

Emphasising the capacity of characters to change, however, does not prevent the reader from tracing that character further back to its original formation, or perceiving the direct intervention of God at each stage of development. In *Paradise Lost* there are numerous references to God's original and ongoing active role in forming the constitution of characters: 'I made him just and right, / Sufficient to have stood, though free to fall' (III.98–9); 'once more I will renew / His lapsed powers' (III.175–6); 'good he made thee' (V.525).

This problem of the God who acts and intervenes in time leads William Myers to complain:

> Milton's God . . . unlike the God of the scholastics, is time-bound, a position that makes his unqualified assertion of divine omniscience and creaturely freedom difficult to sustain. A God who exists outside time, after all, can contemplate past, present and future as on a map or landscape laid out before his immutable consciousness.

Milton, Myers concludes, finds that 'the Boethian conception of God is incoherent'.[38] But viewing times 'as on a map or landscape' is exactly what Milton's God does do, and is in fact what enables him to compare points in time and perceive, more clearly than any being that occupies the nunc fluens, their causal connections. The reason Milton needs his God to perceive both the linear, causal connections between events and their independence from one another is an attempt to resolve this fundamental problem with Boethius's theory, and to develop and extend Boethius's argument, which did not give sufficient attention to the chronological order of events – it is not the rejection of this argument altogether. Boethius developed his theory of eternity as 'the simplicity of [the] present' in order to invest each moment with the spontaneity necessary for self-governance. But Milton saw that God must perceive moments in their horizontal relations to one another because causation is also necessary to free will. If an action is entirely spontaneous to the point of being random, then there is no understanding it except in its vertical relation to Heaven and therefore as a manifestation of God's will imposed upon the actor. But within the linear temporality too, the ultimate cause is of course God. When we trace the causal connections back, we come to God's creation of the continuous character. So it is through a combination of these ways of viewing time that Milton can attribute responsibility to actors but draw up the causal drawbridge before it leads to God.

The fall of Eve is an emblematic example of how the poem navigates between these ways of viewing time in its construction of free will. First, the linear timeline of before-and-after is necessary in order to invest actors with responsibility for their actions. For example, if Eve is to be held responsible for her Fall, she must possess a continuous identity; the Eve who afterwards repents must nevertheless be the same Eve who eats the apple, and the Eve who eats the apple the same Eve who is told by God not to eat it, and who is forewarned by Raphael and her husband: 'For still they knew, and ought to have still remember'd / The high Injunction not to taste that Fruit' (X.12–13). The danger of such continuity is that prelapsarian Eve appears predisposed to fall.[39] In order to counter these awkward implications of linear time, Milton turns to the simultaneity of times that the nunc stans offers, in which each moment can be apprehended as individual, and independent of the past or future, 'governing itself'. So Eve's 'rash' hand picks the fruit in an 'evil hour' (IX.780), and 'rash untried ... sought' to work separately from Adam (IX.860). Adam, at least, can believe that Eve's fall occurred 'on a sudden' (IX.900). But too great an investment in this temporality turns Eve into an innocent creature in whom evil is as it were inserted, willy-nilly, for the sake of enacting some element of God's plan.[40] So as well as asserting the distinctiveness and isolation of the moment in which Eve eats the apple, *Paradise Lost* also shows us how Eve has had experiences, like her dream, that have primed her for the moment in which she succumbs to temptation, and Milton hints at the flaws in prelapsarian Eve's character that made her susceptible.

Reading the Fall is to shift back and forth between the event's decontextualisation and its recontextualisation within a process of degradation. Such a view is possible because through temporal markers that either inscribe continuity ('still they knew') or declare spontaneity ('rash', 'sudden'), we are invited to contemplate the multiple possible relationships between moments in time. We are invited, that is, to take an 'overview' – a prospect view – of the various events surrounding the Fall, and then to perceive it as both (not either/or) a continuous narrative and a collection of discontinuous, isolated moments. This is a perspective that as Bramhall insisted, creatures, even fallen creatures, must try to imagine if they are to approach an understanding of free will. *Paradise Lost* as a whole, then, is a prospect poem, with implications for the reader that I consider more closely in Chapter 3. But Milton utilises the explicit form, inserting as it were miniature prospect poems into *Paradise Lost*, when he and his characters are thinking most deeply about free will. Recognising Milton's use of the prospect poem as a tool for representing time, we can recover the particular generic resources that he draws upon to construct a delicate balance of freedom, responsibility and power.

Bad and Bright Prospects

The two temporal aspects of the nunc stans map onto the two elements of Milton's generic hybrid, his Christian epic. Combining the textual models of classical epic and Scripture required Milton to mediate between the two ways of apprehending time that Erich Auerbach in *Mimesis* (1946) called Homeric and Biblical time. Each moment in biblical history derives its meaning not from its place in the timeline but from above. Each moment in epic history derives its meaning from its contiguous relation forward and back along the horizontal axis. As Tayler puts it, the 'resonant paradoxes' of *Paradise Lost*'s portrayal of time 'cannot be diagrammed or visualized – no straight line or circle will do – but, like the better seventeenth-century conceits, must be apprehended by the eye of the mind'.[41] Boethius's image of the prospect view, however, did offer a visualisation that could at least assist the eye of the mind. It is the under-studied and under-theorised genre of the prospect poem that Milton used to unite and combine epic and Scripture's contrasting apprehensions of time within one vision. Boethius had used the prospect visualisation as a way to lift each moment out of its place in a timeline, but he had not pursued the prospect's capacity to comprehend causal relationships between events. But Milton's contemporaries such as Denham, Marvell and Waller had shown that the prospect poem was able to locate historical events within a spatially extended landscape and yet retain a (somewhat fragile) sense of their place in processes of progress or decline. The prospect poem could both assert historical continuity and upset chronology.

One challenge in comparing *Paradise Lost* directly with other examples of the genre is the difference in scale. *Paradise Lost* is larger both in the scale of its prospect and in its poetic form than the conventional prospect poem. Seventeenth- and eighteenth-century formal prospect poems are generally mid-length poems, with lines numbering in the hundreds rather than thousands. However, *Paradise Lost* does contain within it numerous shorter prospect poems, in which characters assume an elevated position both to survey a spatially extended landscape and to contemplate the relationships between past, present and future. The prospect poem conventionally associates its view with local history as a microcosm of national history; Milton's miniature prospect poems, on the other hand, are Boethian prospects in that the panorama is used to reflect on the question of free will. Focusing in on some of these examples of shorter, explicit prospect views in the poem, we can see how Milton employs the specific tools and features of the prospect poem to justify the ways of God. The prospect poem (1) creates an analogy, implied or explicit, between literal and figurative elevation; (2) assumes a surveying perspective that reorientates power from ownership and control towards knowledge and understanding; and (3) sustains a distance between observer and observed that not only permits but requires and celebrates a level of inaccuracy and idealisation.

The second use of 'prospect' in the poem (after God's 'prospect high') comes later in Book 3, when God's view of Satan takes in Satan's own 'sudden view / Of all this World at once' from the stairs to Heaven, and this view is compared to the 'goodly prospect of some forein land' viewed by a scout from 'the brow of some high-climbing Hill' (III.542–8). The clear verbal echoes of God's own prospect high (God and Satan are both said to 'survey' [III.69, 555]), so soon after that passage, obviously invite direct comparison. We might follow Taylor and Taylor in understanding Satan's prospect view in Book 3 as 'mock-Boethian', an example of 'great visual prospect that can never match the totality of God's providence'.[42] But what is the nature of this 'mockery'? Is it a total Satanic inversion, the prospect poem corrupted – or is it a valid, creaturely attempt to use literal visual prospect as a tool to imagine God's *praevidentia*, a genuine if limited approximation of the nunc stans as Bramhall advocated? Studying the prospect views in *Paradise Lost*, we find examples of both kinds of mock-Boethian-prospect (just as there are both kinds of mock-epic), the immoral inversion (the 'bad eminence') and, like Book 11, the flawed but worthwhile miniature.

There are several obvious examples of the satanic inverted prospect. The fact that in Book 2 the philosophising fallen angels 'apart sat on a Hill retir'd' to reason of 'Providence, Foreknowledge, Will and Fate' (II.557–9) appears to undermine my thesis that in the poem a physical prospect view is a legitimate tool for reasoning on these questions. The prospect is again satanic in Eve's psychedelic toad-induced dream, in which she beholds 'The Earth outstretcht immense, a prospect wide / And various' (V.88–9). Do these prospects suggest that the conflation of literal and figurative heights, so central to the prospect poem, is erroneous? The lines in Book 2 invoke and apparently ridicule the association between 'high' thought and high spaces that Milton had himself invoked at the start of Book 1; but whereas Milton's analogy was figurative, the fallen angels seem to think that sitting on a hill will actually make their 'thoughts more elevate' (558). Similarly, Eve interprets her dream-flight to signify 'high exaltation' in status, an ascent to Heaven (90). We might read *Paradise Regain'd* as an anti-prospect poem in the same way: Satan's main method of persuasion is to treat Jesus to prospect views of cities, and to compare their literal elevation in the landscape to the height of power that Jesus might achieve through rebellion. Literal height, Milton seems to suggest in these examples, the kind of height that defines a prospect poem, has nothing to do with real power or understanding, but is a satanic simulation. Yet in all of these examples, Milton also subtly confirms the correlation between literal and figurative heights. The fallen angels, though on a hill, remain low down in Hell; Eve, though she dreams of flight, is at that moment asleep, low enough for Satan to be described as 'Squat like a Toad' at her ear (IV.800). Their elevations are illusions. And in *Paradise Regain'd*, Satan's defeat is signified by a literal descent, his fall from the spire of the Temple in Jerusalem. These characters are not wrong to conflate literal and figurative heights, but only mistaken in thinking that they are literally elevated at all. The prospect genuinely does offer the opportunity for insight, even for Satan, as long as one's proper relative height and relative lowness are appreciated. Book 4 contains two interpolated prospect poems, both of which feature Satan as the prospector. In the first, the prospect position offers a genuine opportunity to reflect upon time and causation, and Satan uses this perspective to come to a recognition of his own liability by working through and between the two ways of apprehending time that are accommodated within the nunc stans. The second example is a 'bad eminence' rather than a 'bright eminence' because Satan loses his sense of perspective and proportion.

According to Milton's nephew, Edward Phillips, the lines in Book 4 in which Satan addresses the sun were the first part of the poem to be composed. When he placed this passage in his poem, Milton specified that Satan delivers this speech from a prospect position, on the top of Mt Niphates where Satan had landed at the end of Book 3. The astonishing opening to Book 4, then, in which the narrator wishes for 'that warning voice' that could have intervened and prevented the Fall (and which I discuss in more detail in the next chapter), takes place within a miniature prospect poem as well as within the larger prospect poem that is *Paradise Lost*. Satan's address to the sun is a reflection on free will. Instead of reading the landscape below him, he reads the past, present and future:

> Now conscience wakes despair
> That slumberd, wakes the bitter memorie
> Of what he was, what is, and what must be
> Worse; of worse deeds worse sufferings must ensue.
> (IV.23–6)

Satan's speech is Boethian in that it uses a prospect view to stimulate an understanding of time that can clear God of blame, because particular moments and events can be both extracted from and reintegrated into the timeline of chronology and process. These lines, in which the narrator summarises Satan's thoughts, articulate the temporality of continuity, of cause followed by effect. Satan identifies with his past and future selves, and perceives how his 'deeds' in the past (and near future) have shaped and will shape his 'sufferings'. In this way, the future appears determined, but determined by Satan's own actions. But in the address itself, Satan traces the causal connection further back, from his 'deeds' to the character traits that caused him to carry out those deeds.

> O Sun, to tell thee how I hate thy beams
> That bring to my remembrance from what state
> I fell, how glorious once above thy Spheare;
> Till Pride and worse Ambition threw me down[.]
> (37–40)

At first, Satan's prospect position on Mt Niphates seems merely incidental to his speech: a symbol for his contemplation of causation and free will, perhaps, rather than a controlling feature of his logic. But his position directly inspires his reflections: he begins by comparing the sun's higher elevation with his own lost eminence, and recognises (unlike the fallen angels philosophising on the hill in Hell) that his position on a mountaintop is both high and low, relatively speaking. (This is why after his speech we are told that Uriel 'on th' *Assyrian* mount / Saw him disfigur'd' by his agonising reflections [IV.126–7] – this reminds us that any characters' prospect view can be encompassed by that of another, higher character – and all, of course, fall within the view of God's highest prospect.) His position on Mt Niphates, overlooking Eden but beneath the sun and Heaven, is what prompts Satan's repeated use in the soliloquy of the language of highs and lows – simultaneously literal and figurative – as he traces his progress. A literal 'highth recal[s] high thoughts' (IV.95), but Satan's consciousness of his relative lowness is what signifies that this will be a valid prospect view, aware of its limitations but using its view to come to right conclusions.

Having traced the line of causality thus far, from Satan's suffering to his evil deeds to his 'Pride and worse Ambition', the question is then raised: where did this pride and ambition come from? As Satan follows the linear timeline of his own narrative further back, he inadvertently answers this question:

> Ah wherefore! he deservd no such return
> From me, whom he created what I was
> In that bright eminence, and with his good

Upbraided none; nor was his service hard.
What could be less then to afford him praise,
The easiest recompence, and pay him thanks,
How due! yet all his good prov'd ill in me,
And wrought but malice[.]
(42–9)

By the being 'whom he created' Satan refers ostensibly to Lucifer in his 'bright eminence' before he sinned, but we cannot help but identify this instance of 'what I was' with 'what he was' in line 25, which was the being of 'Pride and worse Ambition'. God created a being who, if he was not proud and ambitious to begin with, had the potential to become so: 'all his good prov'd ill in me, / And wrought but malice.' In this light, Lucifer/Satan's actions come to seem an inevitable result of a fundamental flaw in his character that must have been placed there by God.

Satan appears to confront this problem head on, and then to solve it, when he exclaims:

O had his powerful Destiny ordaind
Me some inferiour Angel, I had stood
Then happie; no unbounded hope had rais'd
Ambition. Yet why not? som other Power
As great might have aspir'd, and me though mean
Drawn to his part; but other Powers as great
Fell not, but stand unshak'n[.]
(58–64)

This absolves God's 'Destiny' from the responsibility of creating circumstances that led to Lucifer's fall; but by confirming that it must be Lucifer/Satan's own character, rather than these circumstances, that brought about the Fall, these lines only reinscribe the problem of the origin of that character.

It is in order to solve this issue of origin that we can detect in Satan's speech subtle shifts away from linear, causal, narrative time towards spontaneity. That 'Till' in 'Till Pride and worse Ambition threw me down' is both a process of slowly growing pride and ambition and a sudden catastrophic fall. Like the sudden coming into existence of sin, the appearance of pride and ambition are one of what N. K. Sugimura calls Milton's 'causal time-loops': sin, pride and ambition are their own causes and effects.[43] Satan recalls that in order to believe that he could 'in a moment quit / The debt immense of endless gratitude' (51–2) he had to be 'Forgetful what from him I still receivd' (54). He acknowledges that he had the 'free Will and Power to stand' (66), and yet his 'will / Chose freely what it now so justly rues' (71–2) for no clear reason. Lines such as these convince Claire Colebrook that Satan 'is nothing more than his will, bearing no character that would give ongoing form or sense to his actions'.[44] But the address to the sun is different from Satan's other speeches in the poem, such as his first in Book 1, in which he recalls his fall, and that Langer reads as an account of 'static points in time that are related to each other in the sense that one precedes the other, yet they do not form a causal chain in that the former causes the latter'.[45] In his prospect poem, Satan is able to combine the recollection of spontaneity with a sense of continuity and causation. Diana Treviño Benet has pointed out that different versions of the narrative of the fall of the angels offered by different characters in *Paradise Lost* – Satan, Sin and Raphael – portray the fall as alternatively a 'distinct moment' and a 'traumatic and protracted process'; both possibilities are contained here in Satan's address to the sun, his prospect poem.[46]

The danger is that, if the appearance of pride and ambition in Lucifer's character was spontaneous, then is he really to blame? The poem must return again to linear, causal time in order to justify the punishment that 'deals eternal woe' to Satan (70). So Satan reasserts the continuity of his character into the future:

> But say I could repent and could obtain
> By Act of Grace my former state; how soon
> Would highth recal high thoughts
> . . .
> For never can true reconcilement grow
> Where wounds of deadly hate have peirc'd so deep[.]
> (93–9)

In these lines the ethics of whether 'highth' should 'recal high thoughts' (yes, they should, but only thoughts that are proportionally high – height, literal or figurative, should not delude one into thinking they are or can go even higher) are entwined with the ethics of free will. God's foreknowledge of the continuity of Satan's character justifies the unrelenting punishment, but it also of course reinscribes the problem of God's previous lack of intervention, when he must have known that raising Lucifer to an 'eminence' would raise his 'Pride and worse Ambition'.

God seems responsible whichever temporal perspective is assumed: he is either the ultimate (and foreknowing) origin in a long line of causes and effects, or he has introduced sin into Lucifer's character at a sudden and arbitrary moment in order to construct his greater plan. God is responsible, that is, if we do not combine these temporalities into one paradoxical apprehension of Lucifer/Satan as possessed of both a continuous character and the capacity to change and act spontaneously. The point at which the good Lucifer for which God takes responsibility becomes the sinful Satan for which God does not take responsibility, and the nature and cause of that point of transformation, is by these means obscured. We might question the validity of anything Satan says, but this speech represents a moment of orthodox insight on his part, his coming to an understanding, albeit a paradoxical one, of his own free will.

Book 4 contains two satanic prospect views, both of which stimulate Satan's enquiries into his own culpability, but come to very different conclusions: one correct (within Milton's Christian argument), one incorrect. The second, and Milton's most ambivalent foray into the prospect poem form, is Satan's view from the Tree of Life in Book 4. Here Milton appears to criticise the prospect poem itself, and its limited view:

> Thence up he flew, and on the Tree of Life,
> The middle Tree and highest there that grew,
> Sat like a Cormorant; yet not true Life
> Thereby regaind, but sat devising Death
> To them who liv'd; nor on the vertue thought
> Of that life-giving Plant, but only us'd
> For prospect, what well us'd had bin the pledge
> Of immortality. So little knows
> Any, but God alone, to value right
> The good before him[.]
> (IV.194–203)

For Grossman, Satan's error here is in mistaking prospect for 'the "space before" rather than "the time after"', but that distinction does not fully account for these strange lines.[47] They seem to, but surely cannot, claim that Satan himself (not just Adam and Eve) might have regaind 'true Life' (whatever that would be in Satan's case) by eating the fruit of the tree of life. This troubling reference to Satan's own supposedly proper use of the tree is inserted not to develop some alternative history for Satan, but to draw attention to his limited view. Just as the word 'prospect' refers to and conflates both the position of the beholder and the scene they behold, as well as both space and time, the word 'before' here plays with perspective. The tree is not 'before' Satan once he is perched on it, so presumably the narrator is reflecting on Satan's inability to value the tree as he first approached it; but coming after the lines in which we are told he took up position, these lines read as a reflection upon the limitations of the prospect view itself. They remind us that not only is it difficult to see something for what it is when it is laid out in front of us, but that it is hardest to see that which is right beside or below us. A prospect poem can never get a good look at the elevated space it occupies. *Coopers Hill* does not, and cannot, describe Cooper's Hill. As John Wilson Foster writes, the prospect poem genre was about the limitations of the prospect perspective as well as its expansive capacities:

> A fixed point of view means limitation and partiality. Perspective entails the distortions and shortcomings experienced by the observer of three-dimensional spatial relationships: obstruction, shadowing, foreshortening, optical illusion, and so on. And the poet as observer means that he constructs a world from which he is in some sense shut out.[48]

Satan's achievement in his address to the sun was to recognise his relative lowness as well as his relative height, and to accept that he was 'shut out' from his previous heights. His ability to perceive the proportions of the space around him, including the mountain on which he stood, accurately, was reflected in his ability to reason rightly about time and free will. In Book 4's second prospect poem, we are told at once that Satan's perception of his own prospect position is flawed.

So does his prospect offer a useful view of Eden, which is described in the following 150 lines, all framed within his vision? This framing leads Saskia Cornes to conclude that the description of the 'happy rural seat of various view' is a 'pastoral seduction . . . filtered through a remote, shifty, and satanic optic'.[49] Certainly this prospect is satanic in the most literal sense, but it is 'remote' and 'shifty' only in the sense that all prospect poems are, with their premise of distance and the imprecision that this entails. I don't think we can dismiss as Fishian 'seduction' Milton's use of the prospect poem here, or his use of pastoral. Satan's prospect encompasses the description of Adam and Eve in lines 288–340, the first detailed description we have of them in the poem. And if taking a prospect view of Eden is satanic, why does the unfallen Adam use his gigantic garden wall to take 'prospect large / Into his neather Empire neighbouring round' (IV.144–5)? The prospect still provides the best opportunity to see multiple elements 'at one view' and compare them, a position from which to assess a whole and to see how its parts work in relation to each other.

The problem lies, as in Eve's dream and the philosophising fallen angels, in Satan's misunderstanding of his own status and his capacity to improve that status, a misunderstanding rendered as misapprehension of 'three-dimensional spatial relationships'. Adam uses his prospect of Eden to behold his 'Empire', a miniature version of God retreating to Heaven after the Creation 'to behold this new created World / Th' addition to his Empire' (VII.554–5). But Satan uses his prospect from the tree to survey a world that is not his, and his error is to believe that he can alter his relationship to Eden through invasion:

> yet public reason just,
> Honour and Empire with revenge enlarg'd,
> By conquering this new World, compels me now
> To do what else though damnd I should abhorre.
>   So spake the Fiend, and with necessitie,
> The Tyrants plea, excus'd his devilish deeds.
> Then from his loftie stand on that high Tree
> Down he alights . . .
> (IV.389–96)

As in the address to the sun, the prospector's analysis of his position in relation to the prospect he beholds turns into an analysis of his relative power, which turns into an analysis of free will. But whereas in the former example Satan takes ownership of his own actions but accepts that he does not have power over what he beholds nor the ability to take that power, here the case is reversed: Satan disclaims autonomy but aims to assert authority. The error in understanding his relationship to the landscape turns almost imperceptibly into his error in understanding free will.

The prospect poem is commonly associated with an imperial perspective of both history and the natural world, and the ethical implications of 'surveying' in poetry have been examined by John Barrell and others.[50] The imperial dimension would come to the fore in eighteenth-century formulations of the genre such as Pope's *Windsor-Forest* and Thomson's *Liberty*, but is clearly present in *Coopers Hill* and *Paradise Lost* too. But the power of the prospector over the prospect is of a particular kind. Leah S. Marcus has distinguished between two ways of viewing and organising landscape in seventeenth-century poetry and painting: the 'seigneurial' and the 'cartographic'.[51] In the former kind, the landscape of the Jonsonian country house poem, elements of the landscape are organised around, and subservient to, a particular point 'that provides the "perspective" from which the rest of the landscape is viewed'. In the latter, the 'cartographic' landscape of poems such as Drayton's *Poly-Olbion*, a scene is 'mapped' 'in a way that paid even-handed tribute to all the elements there to be described'.[52] The prospect poem's success, or its failure (depending on your perspective), hinges on the way it combines the seigneurial and the cartographic to produce what Tim Fulford distrustfully calls a 'semblance of disinterest'.[53] It depends on an organising perspectival point, with all that point's implications of ownership and authority; but it also disclaims direct power, either socio-economic or aesthetic, over the landscape. It hints at a qualitative equivalence between the landscape's elements, and pretends to a broad arbitrariness to the order in which it observes those elements, because those elements exist in simultaneity. In other words, the prospector enjoys the freedom to range their eyes at will, and appears to be 'governing' themselves; but the places in the landscape and the events in history that they survey are also distanced from them. In John Dyer's prospect poem *Grongar-Hill* (1726), the speaker stresses that he does not wish to 'covet what I see'.[54] In Thomas Gray's 'Ode on a Distant Prospect of Eton College' (1742, pub. 1747), the surveyor's only power is his knowledge, his awareness of the schoolboys' future compared to their confinement to their innocent present. The elevated prospect position does not make a good prospect poet feel superior but, like Gray's narrator, it makes him feel small. The prospect, 'well used', gives its viewer a more comprehensive understanding, and is not meant to inspire ambition beyond the height they already occupy (which is the mistake of Eve, the philosophising fallen angels and Satan, both when he sits on the tree of life and in *Paradise Regain'd*). This is why Boethius uses the prospect view to shift the question of God's power from one of control to one of knowledge. It is why the prospect poem is such a suitable genre for Milton's God to inhabit, allowing him to claim and disclaim authority over the elements of the landscape that he views, which are events in time.

And it is why Milton uses the prospect view to give Adam an understanding of his own relationship with the future. The most obvious creaturely simulation of God's nunc stans prospect is Adam's vision of the future in Book 11, which takes the form of an extended prospect poem. The last two books are a particularly effective depiction of the combination of temporalities between which Milton is navigating. Within the vision of Book 11 and Michael's prophecy of Book 12 events unfold linearly, and for this reason have been held up as representatives predominantly of linear, historical time. Rosalie Colie has contrasted these books to Book 3, the 'book peculiarly of eternity', arguing that 'Books XI and XII express the long, continuing process of history, the succession of event upon event that is the lot of fallen mankind'.[55] This is true, yet Colie also observes that Adam is 'ultimately granted a limited participation in the divine foreknowledge'.[56] As Stanley Fish has pointed out, even these books of human history have an element of the non-linear temporal perspective. Their transitions and proportions are uneven and awkward, Fish argues, and he suggests that 'the intention is . . . to blunt the sense of continuity one usually associates with a running narrative, and to minimize the importance of the position events happen to occupy on the *continuum* of the story line . . . the reader is directed to the relationships that pertain between them always, not merely in sequence'.[57] Adam is not being told of a likely future that might occur; he is allowed to see it as though it were present and certain, as it really is in God's nunc stans perspective. But he also apprehends that these events will take place in the future, relative to his own present.

Adam's prospect view is a 'bright' one, not a 'bad' one, a miniature version of God's nunc stans rather than a mocking inversion, because he understands that his relationship with what he sees is double. He and his actions are the original cause for what he sees, the 'effects which thy original crime hath wrought' (XI.424); yet he is also unable to alter or intervene in events ('evil he may be sure, / Which neither his foreknowing can prevent' [XI.772–3]). The prospect position, from which he overlooks but which keeps him 'shut out' from the scenes before him, is a spatial rendering of that temporal combination of power and powerlessness. The inversion lies in what Adam takes responsibility for. Whereas God shifts between the temporalities of process and spontaneity in order to take credit for good but not blame for evil, Adam does the opposite. He disclaims credit for the blessing of Abraham ('Favour unmerited by me' [XII.278]), but Michael informs him that the long line of cause and effect does connect his sin with those of Abraham's seed ('sin / Will reign among them, as of thee begot' [XII.285–6]). Similarly, Adam perceives that the Crucifixion comes at its proper time in history, located at the end of a long chronological narrative and therefore linked with his own Fall; yet he also apprehends it as a known and self-sufficient present derived from God's judgement. Reversing historical priority, he takes this future event as an 'example' (XII.572), and acknowledges his 'Redeemer ever blest' (573) (the Son is eternally the Redeemer, even 'before' he has died as Christ in history). When Adam praises the show to Michael –

> How soon hath thy prediction, Seer blest,
> Measur'd this transient World, the Race of time,
> Till time stand fixt: beyond is all abyss,
> Eternitie, whose end no eye can reach[.]
> (XII.553–6)

– he at once disclaims his pretension to share in God's vision of eternity, and expresses gratitude for this vision that is so like eternity. Adam might seem here to define eternity as Hobbesian endless time, but he does not in fact claim that eternity has no end, only that the eye cannot reach it. He imagines eternity as a kind of spatial continuation beyond the extended space of time. Both time and eternity are imagined as prospects, views to be 'seen', spaces to be measured by the eye. The difference lies in scale. Only God's prospect view is elevated enough to take in the horizon of eternity, which contains all times and accommodates them both as a 'transient . . . Race' and as points 'stand[ing] fixt'.

Notes

1. John Denham, *Coopers Hill. A Poeme* (London: Tho. Walkley, 1642), 1.
2. John Denham, *Coopers Hill* (London: Humphry Moseley, 1655), 1. These lines were added to the revised 'B-text' published in 1655.
3. Gordon Teskey, *The Poetry of John Milton* (Cambridge, MA and London: Harvard UP, 2015), 275.
4. Andrew Marvell, *The Poems of Andrew Marvell*, ed. Nigel Smith (Harlow and London: Pearson, 2003), 219.
5. Ann Baynes Coiro, 'The Personal Rule of Poets: Cavalier Poetry and the English Revolution', in *The Oxford Handbook of Literature and the English Revolution*, ed. Laura Lunger Knoppers (Oxford: Oxford UP, 2012): 206–37, 212–13. David Quint, 'Milton, Waller, and the Fate of Eden', *Modern Language Quarterly* 78.3 (2017): 421–41.
6. James P. Driscoll, *The Unfolding God of Jung and Milton* (Lexington: University Press of Kentucky, 1993), 83.
7. Judith Scherer Herz, 'Meanwhile: (Un)making Time in Paradise Lost', in *The New Milton Criticism*, ed. Peter C. Herman and Elizabeth Sauer (Cambridge: Cambridge UP, 2012): 85–101; Amy Boesky, '*Paradise Lost* and the Multiplicity of Time', in *A New Companion to Milton*, ed. Thomas N. Corns (Chichester: John Wiley & Sons, 2016): 408–20; Anthony Welch, 'Reconsidering Chronology in *Paradise Lost*', *Milton Studies* 41 (2002): 1–17.

8. Gary Saul Morson, *Narrative and Freedom: The Shadows of Time* (New Haven: Yale UP, 1996), 43–50.
9. Ayelet C. Langer, '"Pardon may be found in time besought": Time Structures of the Mind in *Paradise Lost*', *Milton Studies* 52 (2011): 169–83 (169). See also by Langer 'Milton's *Aevum*: The Time Structure of Prevenient Grace in *Paradise Lost*', *Early Modern Literary Studies*, 17 (2014); 'Milton's Aristotelian *Now*', *Milton Studies* 57 (2016): 95–117; and '"Meanwhile": Paradisian Infinity in Milton's *Paradise Lost*', *Journal of Literature and the History of Ideas* 19.1 (2012): 1–17.
10. St Thomas Aquinas, *Existence and Nature of God*, ed. and trans. Timothy McDermott (Cambridge: Cambridge UP, 1964, repr. 2006), in *Summa Theologiæ*, 61 vols (Cambridge: Cambridge UP, 2006), ii, 1a.10.2, 138.
11. Boethius, *The Consolation of Philosophy*, trans. P. G. Walsh (1999) (Oxford: Oxford UP, 2008), 110–11.
12. Boethius, *Consolation*, 111–12.
13. Edward W. Tayler, *Milton's Poetry: Its Development in Time* (Pittsburgh: Duquesne UP, 1979), 35.
14. Anne W. Astell, *Job, Boethius, and Epic Truth* (Ithaca: Cornell UP, 1994), 185–210; E. H. Dye, 'Milton's "Comus" and Boethius' "Consolation"', *Milton Quarterly* 19.1 (1985): 1–7.
15. Stephen J. Schuler, 'Eternal Duration: Milton on God's Justice in Everlasting Time', *Milton Studies* 61.1 (2019): 163–85; William Myers, *Milton and Free Will: An Essay in Criticism and Philosophy* (London: Croom Helm, 1987).
16. Dennis Richard Danielson, *Milton's Good God: A Study in Literary Theodicy* (Cambridge: Cambridge UP, 1982), 161.
17. Jeffery H. Taylor and Leslie A. Taylor, *The Influence of Boethius' De Consolatione Philosophiae on John Milton's Paradise Lost* (Lewiston: Edwin Mellen, 2017), 39–40.
18. Robert Greene, 'Thomas Hobbes: The Eternal Law, the Eternal Word, and the Eternity of the Law of Nature', *History of European Ideas* 45.5 (2019): 625–44 (634).
19. Abraham Cowley, *Poems* (London: Humphrey Moseley, 1656), 11.
20. Sue Starke, '"The Eternal Now": Virgilian Echoes and Miltonic Premonitions in Cowley's "Davideis"', *Christianity and Literature* 55.2 (2006): 195–219 (197).
21. Cowley, *Poems*, 33.
22. Ralph Cudworth, *The True Intellectual System of the Universe* (London: Richard Royston, 1678), 645.
23. Thomas Hobbes, *Leviathan* (London: Andrew Ccooke [sic], 1651), 374.
24. Greene, 'Thomas Hobbes', 634. See also Luca Bianchi, '*Abiding Then*: Eternity of God and Eternity of the World from Hobbes to the *Encyclopédie*', in *The Medieval Concept of Time*, ed. Pasquale Porro (Leiden and Boston, MA: Brill, 2001): 543–60.

25. Thomas Hobbes, *The Questions concerning Liberty, Necessity, and Chance Clearly Stated and Debated between Dr. Bramhall, Bishop of Derry, and Thomas Hobbes of Malmesbury* (London: Andrew Crook, 1656), 330.
26. Ibid., 256.
27. Ibid., 257.
28. John Milton, *De Doctrina Christiana*, ed. and trans. John K. Hale and J. Donald Cullington (Oxford: Oxford UP, 2012), in *The Complete Works of John Milton*, ed. Thomas N. Corns and Gordon Campbell, 11 vols (Oxford: Oxford UP, 2008–), viii, 35.
29. John Milton, *The 1671 Poems: Paradise Regain'd and Samson Agonistes*, ed. Laura Lunger Knoppers (Oxford: OUP, 2008), in *The Complete Works of John Milton*, ii, 58. Subsequent references to *Paradise Regain'd* are to this edition, cited in the text by book and line number.
30. Schuler, 'Eternal Duration', 164.
31. Richard Allestree, *Eighteen Sermons* (London: James Allestry, 1669), 98.
32. Lucy Hutchinson, *Order and Disorder* (1679), ed. David Norbrook (Oxford: Blackwell, 2001), 66.
33. Peter C. Herman, '"Whose fault, whose but his own?": *Paradise Lost*, Contributory Negligence, and the Problem of Cause', in *The New Milton Criticism*, ed. Peter C. Herman and Elizabeth Sauer (Cambridge: Cambridge UP, 2012): 49–67.
34. John Dryden, *Plays: Amboyna, The State of Innocence, Aureng-Zebe*, ed. Vinton A. Dearing (Berkeley: University of California Press, 1994), in *The Works of John Dryden*, ed. William Frost and Vinton A. Dearing, 22 vols (Berkeley: University of California Press, 1956–95), xii, 121.
35. Ibid., 124–5.
36. Ibid., 125.
37. Marshall Grossman, *Authors to Themselves: Milton and the Revelation of History* (Cambridge: Cambridge UP, 1987), 15.
38. William Myers, *Milton and Free Will*, 9.
39. For analysis of Eve's simultaneous continuity and spontaneity, see Stephen M. Fallon, 'Narrative and Theodicy in *Paradise Lost*', *Milton Studies* 61.1 (2019): 40–64.
40. I use 'willy-nilly' in its original sense of 'whether (s)he wills it or no', rather than in the modern sense of 'haphazardly' or 'without plan'.
41. Tayler, *Milton's Poetry*, 14.
42. Taylor and Taylor, *The Influence of Boethius*, 58.
43. N. K. Sugimura, 'The Question of "What Cause?": Storytelling Angels and Versions of Causation in *Paradise Lost*', *Milton Studies* 54 (2013): 3–27 (18).
44. Claire Colebrook, *Milton, Evil and Literary History* (London: Bloomsbury, 2008), 16.
45. Langer, 'Pardon may be found', n.p.
46. Diana Treviño Benet, 'The Fall of the Angels: Theology and Narrative', *Milton Quarterly* 50.1 (2016): 1–13 (6, 2).

47. Grossman, *Authors to Themselves*, 77.
48. John Wilson Foster, 'The Measure of Paradise: Topography in Eighteenth-Century Poetry', *Eighteenth-Century Studies* 9.2 (1975–6): 232–56 (239).
49. Saskia Cornes, 'Milton's Manuring: *Paradise Lost*, Husbandry, and the Possibilities of Waste', *Milton Studies* 61.1 (2019): 65–85, n.p.
50. John Barrell, *English Literature in History, 1730–80: An Equal, Wide Survey* (London: Hutchinson, 1983).
51. Leah S. Marcus, 'Politics and Pastoral: Writing the Court on the Countryside', in *Culture and Politics in Early Stuart England*, ed. Kevin Sharpe and Peter Lake (Basingstoke: Macmillan, 1994): 139–59 (142).
52. Ibid., 140.
53. Tim Fulford, *Landscape, Liberty and Authority: Poetry, Criticism and Politics from Thomson to Wordsworth* (Cambridge: Cambridge UP, 1996), 3.
54. John Dyer, *Poems* (London: J. Dodsley, 1770), 15.
55. Rosalie Colie, 'Time and Eternity: Paradox and Structure in Paradise Lost', *Journal of the Warburg and Courtauld Institutes* 23 (1960): 127–38 (131).
56. Ibid., 131.
57. Stanley Fish, *Surprised by Sin* (1967), 2nd edn (London: Macmillan, 1997), 315–16.

Chapter 2

More than Delphic: Miltonic History and Hermeneutics

Between Satan's landing on Mt Niphates at the end of Book 3 and the start of his prospect poem address to the sun in Book 4, Milton inserts a troubling acknowledgement that Adam and Eve could have been warned more explicitly about the approaching danger:

> O For that warning voice, which he, who saw
> Th' *Apocalyps*, heard cry in Heaven aloud,
> Then when the Dragon, put to second rout,
> Came furious down to be reveng'd on men,
> *Wo to the inhabitants on Earth!* that now,
> While time was, our first-Parents had bin warnd
> The coming of thir secret foe, and scap'd
> Haply so scap'd his mortal snare; for now
> *Satan*, now first inflam'd with rage, came down[.]
> (IV.1–9)

In this passage, Milton apprehends each moment – that of Adam and Eve in innocence, the Fall, the age of John the Apostle, the post-lapsarian time in which he writes, the apocalypse – as past, present and future. The two perspectives of time that God enjoys from his nunc stans prospect are condensed into those four words: 'now / While time was'. All times are 'now' and all times are 'while' (that is, meanwhile with one another, simultaneous); yet the tension in these lines comes from the fact that this 'now' is also a past time ('was') in relation both to the Fall and to the seventeenth century in which the poet is stuck. 'The enjambment', Herz writes of 'now / while', 'drops the narrative present now into time already past', placing 'the poet within the text, enabled, he claims, by the Muse to imagine a before as if it were present, and as a result, by force of desire, that is to say, poetry, to attempt to hold back the present'.[1] Milton's initial wish is for the heavenly 'warning voice' which in Chapter 12 of the Book of Revelation warned John that the devil was coming to earth, but the second expression of the wish, 'that now . . .' opens the call out to any warning voice, including that of the poet. But the attempt to hold back the present is futile, and the desire thwarted. Keats's annotation to this passage in his copy of *Paradise Lost* expresses a similar sense of the frustration felt by the 'poet within the text', of the delayed prophet whose warning comes too late:

> A friend of mine says this Book has the finest opening of any – the point of time is gigantically critical – the wax is melted, the seal is about to be applied – and Milton breaks out 'O for that warning voice &[c.]' There is moreover an opportunity for a Grandeur of Tenderness – the opportunity is not lost. Nothing can be higher – Nothing so more than delphic –[2]

The poet's cry is interpreted by Keats as an instance of Milton's 'tenderness' overcoming his higher intellectual aim to justify the ways of God to men. In other words, Milton's wish that people in the past could have known the future is, in Keats's view, the 'highest' achievement in the poem. It is, he writes, 'more than delphic'. What does that mean? Keats uses the term 'delphic' in his poetry to mean 'to do with Delphicus' or Apollo, under which aspect it seems to mean 'divinely inspired'. But 'delphic' also means to do with the Delphic oracle. Milton is delphic in that he is future-seeing by virtue of his retrospective position as a poet writing about history; but he might be 'more than delphic' because he does not simply perceive the future from the perspective of the present, like the oracle, but he perceives that the past was once future. His special prophetic insight is into the fact that every moment once existed and always exists in its own precarious present. The Delphic oracle foresees one determined future; a more than delphic prophet sees the multiple futures that were contained in the past.

But 'more than delphic' might have another, even an opposing, meaning. The oracle spoke in riddles and her prophecies were seldom understood, so 'delphic' can mean 'mysterious and ambiguous'. Elsewhere in his annotated copy of *Paradise Lost*, Keats seems to use the word in this sense to describe Milton's reference to 'the Vales of Heav'n' (I.321): 'It is a sort of delphic Abstraction a beautiful thing made more beautiful by being reflected and put in a Mist.'[3] Milton is delphic in that his prophecy is unheeded by those it concerns, and 'more than delphic' in the extreme extent to which his prophecy is useless, because his own warning voice comes too late and fails to overcome the historical time between himself and his characters. The 'point of time' that Keats identifies as critical is both the thematic 'subject' of time, which we know is essential to Milton's conception of free will, and several 'points of time' in history, understood in configuration: the prelapsarian time when God missed this opportunity to show tenderness, and the time at which Milton writes, when the opportunity for tenderness 'is not lost'. I will return to this Romantic association between Milton and misunderstood prophets like the Delphic oracle and Cassandra in Chapter 8; for now, what matters is Keats's perception of Milton's own frustration at his separation in time from his poetic subjects, his frustration that his own interjection cannot be that 'warning voice'. Milton's ambition to see the past as present and future – his more than delphic insight – is qualified by his confinement to one historic moment, one in which he cannot even be heard, let alone understood – his more than delphic tragedy.

Comparing two accounts of Milton's historical perspective reveals the varied ways in which *Paradise Lost*'s treatment of history can be read. When William Kerrigan describes the prophetic character of the poet-narrator, he does so in spatial terms that recall the nunc stans prospect view of God:

> From the privileged vantage point of eternity [the holy prophet] apprehends the shape of time in a way unavailable to those scientists and historians reasoning within the temporal flux. . . . The prophet, standing outside of history, understands connections between discrete events that cannot be expressed in the mortal formulas of scientific and historical causation.[4]

In Luke Taylor's assessment of Milton as scriptural historian, however, the narrator of *Paradise Lost* does not occupy a Boethian spatial 'vantage point' (Taylor uses the same prospect view term as Kerrigan), but is embedded within the flow of history:

> Milton's truly remarkable commitment to authentic temporality . . . prevents him from taking even the Bible itself as a synchronic whole. Traditional readers move from shadow to fulfillment, from the partial to the whole, from Moses to Christ. This, however, is to view scriptural typology from the outside, spatially, as if from a vantage point where it is already complete. In both *Paradise Lost* and *Paradise Regained*, by contrast, Milton views the Bible from the inside in the temporal process of construction.[5]

Both accounts are true. As a retrospective prophet, Milton is able to see, if not the whole of history, then a long sequence of times from the Creation to the seventeenth century and certainly the partial completion, in the crucifixion, of the biblical stories he retells in *Paradise Lost* and *Paradise Regain'd*. He also recreates the experiences of characters as they move through that history. But Milton's narrator is neither fully 'outside of history' nor fully 'inside' the biblical history that he narrates. He is also always in the seventeenth century. Both his attempts to recover and express the past as a present full of open possibility and his attempts to 'understand [typological] connections between discrete events' – both are perspectives that attempt to overlook or overleap the history that has already been written and that flows in between these events – inevitably slide back into 'mortal formulas of ... historical causation', and a consciousness of the extended timeline of history.

In Chapter 1 I discussed how characters in *Paradise Lost* read time; in this chapter I discuss how Milton's poet-narrator reads history. The irruption of chronology into a desired ahistoricity is tragic for the poet-narrator because it renders him powerless to intervene. But just as Milton's construction of free will requires both sequence and spontaneity, both synchronic and diachronic views of time, so his treatment of history must balance every event's independent eternal significance against its causal significance. The narrator's efforts at reading history are most apparent in his epic similes. These are instances when discrete moments are brought into conjunction, viewed alongside one another as though simultaneous, and comparisons are made apparently to express the real openness of the future from the perspective of the present – only for historical chronology to reassert itself and confirm the pastness of the past. In the similes, characters look to the sky for prophecies, and find inscrutable weather, Keats's delphic mists; but as we linger between times, uncertain futures calcify into determined outcomes, already written in the stars.

As the passage from Taylor above indicates, for Milton history is textual. The same events that are written in time are written in Scripture, and the same hermeneutic methods can be applied to each form of history. The poet-narrator's, and subsequently the reader's, method for interpreting history through the similes by placing events that are ordinarily separated alongside one another, in order to identify varied relations between them, reflects Milton's ideal method for reading Scripture. The similes, that is, are a commonplacing of history. After discussing the similes, I turn to Milton's biblical exegesis as theorised and practised in prose works such as *De Doctrina Christiana* and

Tetrachordon. Seeing the whole as a spatial form, a form that allows us to identify different configurations between parts, is supposedly the best way to read the Bible. Yet Milton remains aware that the truly synoptic perspective, in which everything is simultaneous, must also acknowledge the chronological order of things. Finally, I turn to *Paradise Regain'd*, and Jesus as the ideal reader of both Scripture and history. He exists both 'outside' and 'inside' history, and combines the synchronic and diachronic perspectives into a nunc stans: a prospect view of all times that can still make space for cause and effect.

Reading History: The Similes

The seventeenth-century present of the poem's composition that the narrator alludes to at the start of Book 4 and in his other explicit authorial interventions is not the only additional point in history that Milton introduces into the poem. He invites us to view two or more times 'at one view' in his epic similes. Taking this view, the reader is able to consider the relations between different times, and to ask whether they are linearly and causally connected in a timeline or whether they are distinct, the transitions between them sudden and random except with reference upwards to God's will in Heaven. It is the latter shape of time that the similes seem designed to promote: discrete times are brought into contact in order to illustrate eternal principles that they share. This is the perspective from 'outside' history described by Kerrigan; yet often the very principle expressed is that in any present moment the future remains open and undetermined, which is the perspective from 'inside' history described by Taylor. But as the similes progress, causal connections that bind the two discrete moments emerge, and we begin to apprehend how these moments are fixed in particular chronological relationships with one another, and that the later time invoked represents an inevitable future. The similes are 'more than delphic' because, like Milton crying for the warning voice, they both transcend the linear shape of time and are stuck in it.

Milton expresses the tragedy of chronological history at the start of Book 4 when he wishes to overleap the years in between, but causation over time is necessary in order to invest any moment with ethical and historical significance. Both the spontaneity of a present moment and its causal relations to past and future times (those 'mortal formulas of . . . historical causation') are necessary aspects of God's nunc stans perspective that Milton aims to simulate; the poet-narrator's tragedy is that while he may see time in its dual aspect like

God, unlike God he is bound to his own historical moment and so cannot intervene in past events. Amy Boesky writes of the scene in Book 3, in which Satan sees Jacob's ladder, that 'we are once again occupying a special "now" in which classical, biblical and early modern events slide backwards and forwards, enriching and estranging each other'.[6] The similes behave similarly: we can trace continuity from one time to the other, which enriches the original moment in the narrative with causal power; but this also undermines what is often the ostensible function of the similes, which is to express figuratively a moment of spontaneous choice in the present. For this reason, Milton also shows the two times 'estranging each other', so that we detect discontinuity between the two times, and each appears to be (to quote Boethius again) 'governing itself'.

Milton's similes appear most often at moments of crisis in order to emphasise the risks that different characters face at pivotal moments. A common subject-matter is danger for ships at sea: Satan is compared to Jason and Ulysses dodging rocks and whirlpools (II.1016–20), as well as to the danger itself, Leviathan against whose bulk skiffs founder (I.200–8). The possessed serpent's movements are compared to a ship weaving through veering winds (IX.513–15). In a less obviously threatening variation of the ship trope, Satan in flight is compared to a fleet of trading ships in the distance (II.636–42), but even here a reference to '*Æquinoctial* Winds' (II.637) suggests the theme consistent to these images: ships' and mariners' vulnerability to elemental forces that can be forecast but not foreknown. Thus in Book 4 Uriel comes to warn Gabriel of Satan's approach to Earth,

> swift as a shooting Starr
> In *Autumn* thwarts the night, when vapors fired
> Impress the air, and shews the Mariner
> From what point of his Compass to beware
> Impetuous winds[.]
> (IV.556–60)

In its content the simile expresses a combination of uncertainty and foreknowledge, as the Mariner dreads the coming of the sudden ('impetuous') winds, but is also permitted a glimpse of his compass, allowing him to 'beware' events of the future. But unlike the sailor, the reader cannot possess hope, in this case that Uriel's warning will be sufficient to avert disaster; the flashing glimpse of the Mariner with his compass (an instrument not known in Europe until the Middle Ages) inscribes at this point in the poem a determined, postlapsarian future, even as it expresses hope for safety. This effect led James Whaler to argue that 'Milton is the first epic poet to add to simile the function of prolepsis'.[7]

Perhaps the strangest simile in the poem – 'the most hotly debated simile in *Paradise Lost*', according to John Leonard – similarly balances present uncertainty against historical certainty.[8] And like several of the ship similes, it uses the wind as its image of risk and random chance. In this scene, when characters are poised on the verge of making a choice, Milton demonstrates this sense of precariousness in the moment before decision is made, before outcome is determined by action, by drawing for us a familiar scene of unknowing.

> While thus he spake, th' Angelic Squadron bright
> Turnd fierie red, sharpning in mooned hornes
> Thir Phalanx, and began to hemm him round
> With ported Spears, as thick as when a field
> Of *Ceres* ripe for harvest waving bends
> Her bearded Grove of ears, which way the wind
> Swayes them; the careful Plowman doubting stands
> Least on the threshing floore his hopeful sheaves
> Prove chaff. On th' other side *Satan* allarm'd
> Collecting all his might dilated stood
> . . .
> now dreadful deeds
> Might have ensu'd, nor onely Paradise
> In this commotion, but the Starrie Cope
> Of Heav'n perhaps[. . .]
> (IV.977–94)

The debate over this simile, as Leonard summarises, revolves around whether the plowman ought to be identified with Satan, the angels, the reader or God.[9] In his sense of the doubtful prospect of several possible futures, the plowman is surely meant to stand for the first three of these witnesses. Milton's notorious eighteenth-century editor, Richard Bentley, thought this simile was a pesky intrusion by an editor, because it implied that the angels 'were in a ruffle and hurry'; but it is important that the angels sense just as much risk at this moment as Satan.[10] It is easy for the reader to feel that a plowman beholding his wheatfield has genuinely no foreknowledge of the outcome of his harvest, and we can more easily empathise with his sense of uncertainty, and hence feel the sense of real possibility between two alternatives that Milton tells us was also real when Satan faced the 'Angelic Squadron' and pondered whether to fight.

However, if each of the characters (Satan, the angels and the plowman) feels himself at this point to occupy one present on the brink of several possible futures, the reader is faced with two presents side by side, and must work out their relation. In the relation that we apprehend between them there is much at stake. The simile's ostensible function, to evoke a sense of open possibility at this point in the primary narrative, is only effective if we apprehend these two moments as disjointed, with no causal connection to bind them; if we forget that they are part of one single narrative of history, and apprehend them instead as parallel, simultaneous presents. This perspective locates us simultaneously inside this historical moment (because we sense real possibility) and outside of history itself (because we perceive disjointed moments simultaneously). On the other hand, if we apprehend that this simile is drawn from a *later* time than that of Satan facing the angels, then this serves as a reminder of the certain outcome of the primary narrative: the Fall. Anne Ferry assumes this position when she writes that the 'shifting and divided world which the narrator's similes recall throughout the epic is the world of history stretching between the action of the poem and our own lives'.[11] The plowman is the occupant of a postlapsarian world, all the more overtly for his embodiment of the punishment given to Adam of agriculture, and his likeness to Cain, 'A sweaty reaper' (XI.434). This continuity invests the moment of Satan and the angels with the import of influence, in that their actions in that moment will shape the course of history; but it also renders those actions, from the perspective of the reader if not of the actors, determined. Every articulation of uncertainty in the form of a simile is also an assertion of certainty. For this reason, even while he highlights continuity in the allusion to Cain and agriculture, Milton obscures it in the sheer distance between the two moments in subject-matter and tone, and in the ambiguity over how the components of the vehicle map onto those of the tenor.

The sense of uncertainty about the future that the simile seems to have been introduced to express is further undermined in the subsequent lines, when God places Libra in the sky to tell Satan and Gabriel what will be the inevitable result if they fight. Whereas the weather had represented uncertainty for the plowman, as for the mariners in Milton's ship similes, the sky also contains the stars, the 'celestial Sign[s]' (IV.1011) in which are written known futures. The stars, that is, 'thwart' the uncertainty of the simile's delphic weather just as the 'shooting Starr' flies *a*thwart the night, revealing to the mariner the direction of the impetuous winds.

Milton's repeated use of wind to represent random chance is in part a legacy of Virgil's *Georgics*. The plowman simile is adapted from the 'sudden storm' scene in the first georgic:

> Ev'n when the Farmer, now secure of Fear,
> Sends in the Swains to spoil the finish'd Year:
> Ev'n while the Reaper fills his greedy Hands,
> And binds the golden Sheaves in brittle bands:
> Oft have I seen a sudden Storm arise,
> From all the warring Winds that sweep the Skies:
> The heavy Harvest from the root is torn,
> And whirl'd aloft the lighter Stubble born[.][12]

Milton takes up the nascent genre of the prospect poem in order to articulate the nunc stans perspective of time, and he takes up its cousin-genre of georgic, which was growing in reputation in the second half of the seventeenth century, in order to articulate the unknowability of the future.[13] Milton's ambiguous, inscrutable (delphic) weather also reflects the status of wind in late seventeenth- and early eighteenth-century meteorology: among the 'Arcana' of nature, Daniel Defoe wrote in 1704, 'the Winds are laid as far back as any'.[14] Georgic would remain the genre of choice for exploration of this theme through the eighteenth century, as I discuss in the chapters on Thomson. In all of these texts, by Virgil, Milton, Defoe and Thomson, a question mark remains over whether the weather is random or whether it is caused by God. Milton's winds are impetuous, but they are repeatedly thwarted by the divine starlight of predestination. Chaos, where 'Chance governs all', is characterised by 'warring winds', especially the 'tumultuous cloud' (937) that 'by ill chance' (935) saves Satan from falling. In Book 3 we learn that it is 'devious Air' and a 'violent cross wind' that blows the Fools from Heaven into their Limbo. In both instances the 'sport of Winds' might truly be random or might move with purpose as a tool for divine justice. Milton's wind is contingent in both opposing senses of the word: somehow simultaneously dependent on causes and subject to chance.

Adam knows that his ideal perspective is 'not to know at large of things remote / From use, obscure and suttle, but to know / That which before us lies in daily life' (VIII.191–3). This is not the perspective in which the poem trains its readers. It forces us to keep in view times other than the one that lies before us in the present of the narrative at each moment that we read. Things remote in time are not 'remote in use', 'fume', 'emptiness', 'fond impertinence' (VIII.194–5), but are vital to understanding the present. The poem demands that our 'Mind or Fancie... roave' between times (VIII.188), drawing disparate times together to compare them, even if doing so only reminds us of the gulf in between.

Reading Scripture: Biblical Exegesis

In *Paradise Lost* history, like time, has two shapes: it is a moving timeline, whose parts exist in succession and are linked by cause and effect, and it is a stationary whole, whose parts exist simultaneously and can be placed alongside one another in multiple formations and correlations. In this way, history becomes an image of language, and language of history. The meaning of a word depends upon its relations both to its place in a sequential construction (like a sentence) and to its pre-existing definition and connotations. In structuralist linguistics, every sign exists within a syntagmatic structure and a paradigmatic structure (the two dimensions have often been visualised as horizontal and vertical axes, respectively). For Milton, the activity of reading history in order to interpret events with reference to both structures – its place in a 'horizontal' chronological timeline, and its direct 'vertical' relation to God – mirrors the activity of reading text.

Milton's similes read history through a system of 'commonplacing', taking events that are separate in time and comparing them directly. These events must then be reintegrated into their place in the linear timeline of history, however painful that may be for the historically bound narrator, in order to comprehend their full significance. The same principle applies to Milton's reading of written history. Milton's tracts of biblical exegesis, notably *De Doctrina Christiana* and *Tetrachordon*, are the texts in which his hermeneutic theory is both described and practised most clearly. It is a hermeneutic that combines a sense of the organised linear structure of the text with an aim towards a synoptic perspective – the true interpretation is only visible when we extract pieces of Scripture to compare different parts of the text, but remain alert to the contexts that those pieces had in their original placements.

Scriptural commonplacing, the hermeneutic method of collating different parts of Scripture to compare them side by side, is a practice that dates back to early church fathers including Augustine. Milton cites as his own examples 'some of the shorter Systems of theologians', and declares in the Epistle to *De Doctrina* that, 'following their example', his practice has been 'to distinguish appropriate topic-headings, under each of which I would classify whatever passages of the Bible present themselves for extracting, so that I could recover and use them when I needed to'.[15] The commonplacing practice is based on a particular conception of the work as a static entity whose parts exist simultaneously in time. In the case of written text this is very literally true, but reading 'God's Word' in this way was further justified by Augustine's theory of God's speech in Heaven:[16]

> But how did you speak? Surely not in the way a voice came out of the cloud saying, 'This is my beloved Son' (Matt. 17.5). That voice is past and done with; it began and ended. The syllables sounded and have passed away, the second after the first, the third after the second, and so on in order until, after the others, the last one came, and after the last silence followed. [Your] word is spoken eternally, and by it all things are uttered eternally. It is not the case that what was being said comes to an end, and something else is then said, so that everything is uttered in a succession with a conclusion, but everything is said in the simultaneity of eternity. . . . No element of your word yields place or succeeds to something else, since it is truly immortal and eternal.[17]

(Augustine's account of God's eternity, including his 'eternal' speech, greatly influenced Boethius's theory of the nunc stans.) Milton follows Augustine in acknowledging that 'to human ears' the acts of God 'Cannot without process of speech be told' (VII.176–8), and God's voice must 'sound and pass away' when he speaks with humans directly, such as to Peter in Matt. 17.5. Similarly, God's word must be imagined to 'sound and pass away' if we are to understand its intersection with history – the peculiar line 'Father, thy word is past, man shall find grace' (III.227) is a way of portraying God's judgement as logical and subsequent to human sin even in eternity. But Augustine's theory that God's word does not entail 'order', 'succession', or 'yielding place' enables a hermeneutic of 'extraction', because the original order of things supposedly doesn't matter.

I think that Milton may have had Augustine's theory of God's speech, and his own understanding of its implications for written language, in mind when he made an addition to *Paradise Lost* for the second edition of 1674. Milton divided what had been Books 7 and 10 into two each, creating Books 7 and 8, and Books 11 and 12. In each case, a gap is quite literally opened up on the page, at a natural break in the story. But Milton also fills part of this gap, taking the opportunity to insert new lines at the start of each of the new books he has created.

> The Angel ended, and in *Adams* Eare
> So Charming left his voice, that he a while
> Thought him still speaking, still stood fixt to hear[.]
> (VIII.1–3)

Here we have a hint of the two ways of thinking about time and the two ways of thinking about language to which Milton is committed. The voice is 'ended', and in a linear reading of the poem we are now moving on from those lines before and reading a new book (literally new thanks to Milton's structural revisions); but like the voice of God in Augustine's account, the voice and those past lines are in a way 'still speaking' – not just 'left' in Adam's ear, but on the page and in the reader's mind. Those past lines are 'still . . . fixt', occupying their own time that is both part of a causal timeline and removed from that timeline, the break emphasised in the new break between books. These new lines echo the past lines and reflect back upon them, but cannot rewrite or undo those lines. As a revision, this insertion has hardly any effect on the surrounding poetry. Line 4 (which was l. 641) is revised from 'To whom thus *Adam* gratefully repli'd' to 'Then as new wak't thus gratefully repli'd'; a suggestive and enriching alteration, but one that supplements rather than changes the original, and from which the remaining lines continue unaffected. The interposition seems to have been invited by a gap left open in the earlier version of the poem, but that past version remains intact and unaffected around the interposition, and therefore comes to appear independent of it. The effect is that the past version seems at once altered and unaltered by, at once responsible and unaccountable for, what goes on in that revisionary moment. Whether lines are placed next to each other or separated seems not to matter; a good reader or listener will hold those words that are 'ended' still in their mind.

The commonplacing method of reading the Bible became particularly popular in the early modern period. It accorded with a Protestant emphasis on the necessary interpretative activity of the reading individual, and was facilitated by the printing conventions of English bibles, which since the mid-seventeenth century subdivided chapters into even shorter verses. George Herbert's sonnet, 'The Holy Scriptures (2)', portrays the Bible as a 'book of stars':

> O that I knew how all thy lights combine,
> And the configurations of their glory!

> Seeing not only how each verse doth shine,
> But all the constellations of the story.
> This verse marks that, and both do make a motion
> Unto a third, that ten leaves off doth lie:
> Then as dispersed herbs do watch a potion,
> These three make up some Christian's destiny[.][18]

The last line of this poem refers to the Lutheran notion that a Protestant who discovers how two 'places' in the Bible interpret one another discovers his destiny: the scriptural version of the *sortes virgilianae*, the practice of divining the future by selecting random passages from Virgil, which was used, notably, by Charles I and Abraham Cowley. Dayton Haskin has argued that Milton rejected this notion of biblical reading as too passive and partial, but it is clear that he did respond to the related 'conception of the Book as a vast field, or set of fields, filled with "places" . . . that bear potential relations to one another': in other words, the book as a spatial form, imagined as a prospect of the sky or a landscape.[19] Milton takes up this idea of individual parts, figured by Herbert as stars, which must be collated, and adjusts the emphasis from spontaneous discovery to working through the text, finding out which verse 'marks' another through laborious cross-referencing. The principle is the same: focusing on just one line of the Bible will show us truth, but only a fragment of that truth. The Bible cannot be understood without internal reorganisation: keeping in mind parts that may be 'ten leaves off' (in either direction) from the part being read in the present. The text possesses 'configurations', that is, structural relations between the parts, beyond the simple linear shape in which it is laid out in the book.

In *De Doctrina Christiana*, his personal interpretation of Scripture, Milton describes his method in these terms.

> In this work nothing new is being taught: rather, I seek only, for the sake of the [reader's] memory, to place at his fingertips things which are read in dispersal in the holy books, by bringing them together for convenience into a single body, so to speak, and by distributing them under definite headings.[20]

Milton is making concessions to the needs of his human readers, but attempting to assist them to a more comprehensive understanding 'from the weaving together of the passages'.[21] The implication is that the ideal reader would be able to hold all parts of the Bible in mind at once, in order to perceive the ways in which different parts speak to one another. His method, here and in *Tetrachordon*, is to draw from every part of the Scriptures in order to answer the questions that concern him in the present. Similarly, the title *Tetrachordon* means 'four-stringed', and the 1645 tract consists of Milton's attempts to draw four 'places' in the Bible (spread across Genesis, Deuteronomy, Matthew and Corinthians) together into a coherent argument to justify divorce.

The extracted and reconfigured parts, however, like the moments in history extracted from the timeline by the similes, must be reintegrated into chronological order for a full understanding of their significance. The second chapter of Genesis, Milton writes, in which the Lord declares he will make a help meet for Man, 'is granted to be a Commentary on the first [chapter], and these verses granted to be an exposition of that former verse, *Male and female created he them*'; the 'former verse' is said itself to be 'but a brief touch, only preparative to the institution which follows more expressly in the next Chapter'.[22] The order in which we encounter these verses in the reading text matters. This is true even for different parts of a single short verse: 'He that said, *Male and female created he them*, immediatly before that said also in the same verse, *In the image of God created he him*, and redoubl'd it, that our thoughts might not be so full of dregs as to urge this poor consideration of *male and female*, without remembring the noblenes of that former repetition.' It is important to note that here Milton retains awareness of the internal structure of the verse, and of the experience of the reader who reads linearly, at least at this local level. The very meaning of the verse is derived, in part, from the order of the phrases and the effect that this order has upon the reader: the former statement is made first, so that the 'much inferior' point of sex is not given undue weight. The reader's perception of the 'redoubling' and 'repetition', and their act of 'remembring', is crucial to correct interpretation of this verse.

That phrase in Gen.1.27, 'male and female created he them', is understood in the context of both earlier and later statements. As he faces his exegetical challenge, which is 'the reconciling of those places which treat [of the relevant] matter in the Gospel', it is not possible to discover in *Tetrachordon* or *De Doctrina* that Milton privileges either the earlier or later parts. One former verse is 'a brief touch' in comparison to the later, but in another instance a former statement has greater 'noblenes' than a later 'inferior' point. Often the New Testament appears to be given precedence over the Old, but Milton is anxious to explain that this is a case of supplementation, not replacement: St Paul, for example, 'meant not to thrust out a command of the Lord by a new one of his own, as one nail drives another, but to release us from the rigor of it' (that is, to show that it is a 'permission' in certain contexts, and not a 'command' that pertains always). While the later will often modify the earlier in the reader's experience, the earlier must equally be kept in view in order to understand the later: 'we must take both these together, and then we may inferre completely as from the whole cause.' Truth is not something that gradually accumulates over the course of the reading experience; it is discovered once the 'whole' has been digested, and all the parts can be compared alongside one another *and* retain their place in the text's structure: 'I urge everyone, and particularly set an example of this, that on whatever points they do not feel fully satisfied, they should withhold assent until the evidence of the scriptures prevails.'[23] The reader experiences the text in the chronological order of its parts, and allows this order to exert its influence, and then combines this linear experience of reading with a more synoptic perspective:

> Thus having enquir'd the institution ... from the I Chap of *Gen.* where it was only mention'd in part, and from the second, where it was plainly and evidently instituted; and having attended each clause and word necessary with a diligence not drousy, wee shall now fix with som advantage; and by a short view backward gather up the ground wee have gon, and summ up the strength wee have, into one argumentative head, with that *organic* force that *logic* proffers us. (*Tetrachordon*)

Milton's depiction of remembering your linear reading experience as taking a 'short view backward' – a miniature prospect view – shifts into a strange image of 'gathering up the ground', suggestive of the way a piece of paper or fabric can be scrunched up into a 'head' so that different parts come into contact without losing the structural integrity of the whole. Clauses and words are extracted from their place in the text in order to consider them alongside other clauses and words further off, but their original placement, the original experience of encountering them in a particular order, must be remembered. As David Ainsworth writes of Milton's biblical exegesis, although it consists in an initial act of 'fragmentation of the original scriptural text', it is 'a constructive task' rather than 'an aggressive dismemberment'; it is also a *re*constructive task, remembering and analysing the linear text alongside the new configurations that it creates.[24]

When Milton depicts his ideal reader of Scripture, that reader follows this same hermeneutic method. This reader is none other than the Son himself, who is shown engaging with both the texts and events of Scripture in *Paradise Regain'd*. Jesus describes how he read the Old Testament in order to uncover his own identity: 'I again revolv'd / The Law and Prophets, searching what was writ / Concerning the Messiah, to our Scribes / Known partly' (I.259–62). Jesus 'searches' for relevant texts 'concerning' the subject at hand, and pieces them together to understand his task. Mary carries out a comparable reading method, although she is less confident about drawing conclusions. She assembles her own 'commonplace book' in her memory: 'My heart hath been a store-house long of things / And sayings laid up, portending strange events' (II.103–4).

Jesus in *Paradise Regain'd* is the clearest example of a character 'inside' scriptural history as described by Taylor. He reads the world around him as though it is – as it would become – scriptural text. And because he is living the New Testament in the present before it is written, unaware of its ending, he 'suspend[s] his opinion' on many questions, as Milton advocates in *De Doctrina*. But Jesus combines a sense of his own linear travelling through time with a synoptic, albeit as yet incomplete, idea of the whole.

> And looking round on every side beheld
> A pathless Desert, dusk with horrid shades;
> The way he came not having mark'd, return
> Was difficult, by human steps untrod;
> And he still on was led, but with such thoughts
> Accompanied of things past and to come
> Lodg'd in his brest[.]
> (I.295–301)

Jesus begins with a very partial prospect view. He has no elevation from which to gain a clear perspective of the landscape around him, and no means of distinguishing its features or understanding their interrelations, the 'paths' that would connect them. Whereas the seventeenth-century reader of Scripture can take 'a short view backward [to] gather up the ground wee have gon', Jesus has not marked the way he has come – his past and future are not yet recorded in text. 'But', Milton says, Jesus is accompanied by thoughts 'of things past and to come'. Gregory Chaplin has pointed out the frequency of the word 'now' in the poem (it occurs seventy-five times), but notes that the obsession with 'now' belongs to other characters, not Jesus.[25] His journey 'on' through the desert is counterbalanced by his 'looking round on every side', and as space here is figuring time, the onward movement through history is counterbalanced by his sense of this moment's place in a much larger narrative, although what he knows of this narrative at this point is not divulged. Jesus's reading of his own situation is linear and successive – 'Thought following thought, and step by step led on' (I.192) – but also attempting synopticism – 'O what a multitude of thoughts *at once* / Awaken'd in me swarm' (I.196–7, my emphasis). He considers 'All his great work to come before him . . . How to begin, how to accomplish best / his end' (II.112–14), contemplating the beginning alongside the ending in order to make sense of each part. Satan he can read in full without difficulty, his faith filling in for the unwritten future: 'I know thy scope' (I.494), 'compos'd of lyes / From the beginning, and in lies wilt end' (I.407–8). Jesus's difference from the 'more than delphic' narrator of *Paradise Lost* is his timing: he gets to live through the time he reads, and both gives and hears his own warning voice.

But Jesus's summation of Satan is not entirely fair, as Satan is capable of both speaking and reading truth. In Book 4, Milton reverses Herbert's simile and Satan reads the stars with the same collating hermeneutic that Herbert uses to read the Bible. What Satan reads is technically correct, although he (deliberately) misses the point:

> if I read aught in Heaven,
> Or Heav'n write aught of Fate, by what the Stars
> Voluminous, or single characters,
> In their conjunction met, give me to spell,
> Sorrows, and labours, opposition, hate,
> Attends thee, scorns, reproaches, injuries,
> Violence and stripes, and lastly cruel death;
> A Kingdom they portend thee, but what Kingdom,
> Real or Allegoric I discern not,
> Nor when; eternal sure, as without end,
> Without beginning; for no date prefixt
> Directs me in the Starry Rubric set.
> (IV.382–93)

A reading should be both 'voluminous' and attentive to the 'conjunctions' of 'single characters', that is, it should take in the whole, but respect the various connections between the parts including their chronological order. Satan's reading of Jesus's future is correct, although his nature perverts his conclusions.

Milton's depictions of reading in *Paradise Regain'd* beg the question: are we supposed to apply the same hermeneutic methods to reading this poetry as to reading Scripture? Of course, neither *Paradise*

Regain'd nor *Paradise Lost* is Scripture, and we should not assume that the methods of reading the Bible that Milton advocates in his prose or poetry are the proper ways to read his poems. But many critics have argued that the analogy between the poetry and Scripture is valid, although the conclusions they draw from this vary hugely. The likeness between *Paradise Lost* and Scripture may be taken as confirmation of the poem's homogeneity: Michael Lieb argues that, 'Aligning his poem with the sacred writings, [Milton] would have suggested the kind of hermeneutics most appropriate for his poem, a hermeneutics consistent with that which was to be applied to the Scriptures', and so just as 'Reading the Scriptures becomes for Milton an exercise in the discovery of God's intentions' so we must search *Paradise Lost* for the poet's intended meanings, which are its only true ones.[26] Counterintuitively, the likeness to Scripture may be taken actually to justify the poem's indeterminacy. For Ainsworth, reading Books 11 and 12 of *Paradise Lost* 'involves the same kind of interpretative struggle involved in reading and rereading the Bible'.[27] Joseph Wittreich writes that 'even if Scripture advances one "sense" at a time, it sponsors indeterminacy of reading, Milton thereby establishing a closer alliance between hermeneutics, secular and sacred, scientific and biblical, than is often supposed'.[28] The conclusion that it is most important to draw, I believe, is Kerrigan's: the poem is undoubtedly Milton's 'fullest imitation of the Bible', and it is 'therefore the least centrifugal of his poems. Anticipations find their fulfilments.'[29] Parts are related to others that may be 'ten leaves off', to quote Herbert again. Whether we should frame this as a pattern of 'anticipation and fulfilment' in the linear spread of time, however, is subject to debate. This debate is the subject of the following chapter.

Notes

1. Herz, 'Meanwhile', 87.
2. Keats and Milton, *Keats's Paradise Lost*, 85.
3. Ibid., 12.
4. William Kerrigan, *The Prophetic Milton* (Charlottesville: University Press of Virginia, 1974), 219.
5. Luke Taylor, 'Milton and the Romance of History', *Milton Studies* 56 (2015): 301–29, n.p.
6. Amy Boesky, '*Paradise Lost* and the Multiplicity of Time', 382.
7. James Whaler, 'The Miltonic Simile', *PMLA* 46 (1931): 1034–74 (1034). Whaler adds that there are 'hints of prolepsis' in ancient epic similes, but argues that they are not used as 'a conscious matter of technique' (1071).

8. John Leonard, *Faithful Labourers: A Reception History of* Paradise Lost, *1667–1970*, 2 vols (Oxford: Oxford UP, 2013), i, 355.
9. Ibid., 355.
10. John Milton, *Milton's Paradise Lost. A New Edition, by Richard Bentley, D.D.* (London: Jacob Tonson et al. 1732), 143. Quoted in Leonard, *Faithful Labourers*, i, 359.
11. Anne Ferry, *Milton's Epic Voice: The Narrator in* Paradise Lost (Chicago: University of Chicago Press, 1963, repr. 1983), 81.
12. John Dryden, *Virgil's Georgics*, in *The Works of John Dryden*, ed. William Frost and Vinton A. Dearing, 22 vols (Berkeley: University of California Press, 1956–95), v: *Poems, 1697*, ed. Dearing, Alan Roper and Frost (1987), I.427–35. All subsequent references to the works of Virgil are to this edition and translation.
13. Examples of foundational work on Milton's engagement with georgic include Anthony Low, *The Georgic Revolution* (Princeton: Princeton UP, 1985), 296–352, and Stella Revard, 'Vergil's *Georgics* and *Paradise Lost*: Nature and Human Nature in a Landscape', in *Vergil at 2000: Commemorative Essays on the Poet and His Influence*, ed. John, D. Bernard (New York: AMS Press, 1986): 259–80.
14. Daniel Defoe, *The Storm*, ed. Richard Hamblyn (London, Penguin 2005), 209.
15. Milton, *De Doctrina Christiana, Vol. 1*, ed. and trans. John K. Hale and J. Donald Cullington (Oxford: Oxford UP, 2012), in *The Complete Works of John Milton*, viii, 5.
16. Milton's familiarity with Augustine's writings is demonstrated by Peter A. Fiore in *Milton and Augustine: Patterns of Augustinian Thought in Paradise Lost* (University Park, PA: Pennsylvania State UP, 1981).
17. St Augustine, *Confessions*, trans. Henry Chadwick (Oxford: Oxford UP, 1991), XI.vi(8)–vii(9), 225–6.
18. George Herbert, 'The Holy Scriptures (2)', in *The Complete English Poems*, ed. John Tobin (London: Penguin, 1991, repr. 2004), 52.
19. Dayton Haskin, *Milton's Burden of Interpretation* (Philadelphia: University of Pennsylvania Press, 1994), 1–2.
20. Milton, *De Doctrina Christiana*, 19.
21. Ibid., 9.
22. John Milton, *Tetrachordon, The John Milton Reading Room*, ed. Thomas H. Luxon (Dartmouth: 1997–2017), <https://www.dartmouth.edu/~milton/reading_room/tetrachordon/title/text.shtml> (accessed 5 July 2021), n.p. Subsequent references to *Tetrachordon* in this paragraph are to this edition.
23. Milton, *De Doctrina Christiana*, 7.
24. David Ainsworth, *Milton and the Spiritual Reader: Reading and Religion in Seventeenth-Century England* (New York and London: Routledge, 2008), 81.

25. Gregory Chaplin, 'The Circling Hours: Revolution in *Paradise Regain'd*', in *Milton in the Long Restoration*, ed. Blair Hoxby and Ann Baynes Coiro (Oxford: Oxford UP, 2016), 265–83 (270).
26. Michael Lieb, *Theological Milton* (Pittsburgh: Duquesne UP, 2006), 154, 144.
27. Ainsworth, *Milton and the Spiritual Reader*, 130.
28. Joseph Wittreich, 'Sites of Contention in *Paradise Lost*', in *Milton's Rival Hermeneutics*, ed. Richard J. DuRocher and Margaret Olofson Thickstun (Pittsburgh: Duquesne UP, 2012), 101–33 (107).
29. Kerrigan, *Prophetic Milton*, 229.

Chapter 3

A Full-grown Beauty: Reading *Paradise Lost*

Cowley's lines describing the nunc stans in Book 1 of the *Davideis* are introduced with a reference to the spatial as well as temporal infinity of heaven: 'Nor can the glory contain it self in th'endless space.'[1] In his note to this line Cowley reflects on the relationship between subject-matter and poetic length, acknowledging the three extra syllables: 'I am sorry that it is necessary to admonish the most part of *Readers*, that it is not by *negligence* that this verse is so loose, long, and, as it were, *Vast*; it is to paint in the number the nature of the thing which it describes.'[2] In his 'Life of Cowley' Samuel Johnson objected to this logic affiliating a long line with great space: 'Verse can imitate only sound and motion. ... I cannot discover ... why the *pine* is *taller* in an alexandrine than in ten syllables.'[3] There is an absurdity in the implication that three extra syllables can better represent 'endless space', but this is not the basis of Johnson's objection. By Johnson's logic, poetic length can represent a long length of time (by imitating motion), but not space. Cowley's reference to lines 'painting' space, however, suggests that unlike Johnson he conceives of his poem as a spatial form. This is corroborated by his going on in the note to extract lines from 'divers other places of this *Poem*' to illustrate his principle, reading them independently of their immediate context in the organisation of the poem.[4] The fact that this note immediately precedes the note on Boethius's theory of the nunc stans further suggests that his idea of spatial form builds on this theological groundwork. The nunc stans permits time to be mapped onto space and vice versa; a long time and a wide space implicitly represent one another. While Cowley's '*Eternal Now*' is contained within a neat pentameter line, his theory of the mimetic potential of poetic length applies equally to the length of a whole poem as to a line, so it is no leap to consider that a poem of epic length is for Cowley the fit vehicle for communicating the vast time *and* space that the nunc stans embraces. Every line, every word in the poem is, like every moment or event, both a time and a place in a vast spatio-temporal prospect.

This is the case in *Paradise Lost* too, for both the poet-narrator and the reader. Milton hints, at the opening of Book 7 of *Paradise Lost*, both that his composition was a linear process that took place over time, at each moment fraught with uncertainty and decisions to make, and that it was always a determined finality, each of its parts destined to be as it turned out to be, and all existing simultaneously in his mind if not yet on the page. Similarly, the reader is encouraged to move through the poem linearly, from beginning to end; to foreknow the outcome (which is after all written in the poem's first line, and which Samuel Johnson complained rendered the poem tedious) but to experience a progression towards this outcome as it gradually unfolds over the course of the poem.[5] But the reader of *Paradise Lost* is also encouraged to experience the parts not in sequence but side by side, to think of the end when we are at the beginning, not as a future towards which we are moving, but as a present that is already present and completed without reference to its place in the poem's chronological order. In other words, we are invited to comprehend the poem as a spatial form replicating God's nunc stans prospect view, with all parts of the poem existing simultaneously and speaking to one another in multiple configurations and cross-references; but we are also, again like God viewing time from his prospect high, invited to comprehend the whole as an unfolding narrative, the chronological arrangement of which matters.

Surveying critical responses to *Paradise Lost*, we discover readers shifting between these different conceptions of the poem (as a spatial or temporal form) and different approaches to reading it (synchronic or diachronic). This is not surprising; of course, the majority of Milton's readers, now and since its publication, move instinctively between these reading practices. What is interesting is the way that readers have leaned towards and aligned themselves with one or the other approach, and how they have framed and theorised their approach in terms of authorial power and readerly autonomy. In this chapter I focus on two periods of Milton's reception when readers tended most consistently to one or the other extreme: the Romantic period and the second half of the twentieth century. Even the central and most persistent debate about *Paradise Lost* – whether the poem justifies the ways of God to men, or at least makes a legitimate attempt at justification, or whether its portrayals of God and Satan are fundamentally ambiguous and ambivalent – is bound up with an implicit debate over how to read the poem as a whole.

Here my exploration of Milton's treatment of time enters the territory of reception history, and therefore inevitably finds itself in the wake of John Leonard's magisterial two-volume *Faithful Labourers: A Reception History of* Paradise Lost, *1667–1970*. Leonard, working through specific iterations of the various debates that have divided readers, similarly argues that underlying many of these contests is the question of how to read the poem, and that, quoting T. S. Eliot, '*Paradise Lost* does ask to be read "in two different ways"'.[6] The two different ways Leonard distinguishes are 'rapid' and 'slow', replacing Eliot's distinction between reading for the 'sound' and reading for the 'sense'. These two 'kinds of attention' do result in a different perspective on structure, in that the quick reading gives more emphasis to larger units, privileging for example the paragraph over the line, whereas the slow reading encourages dwelling on each individual line.[7] I would reframe this slightly: the question of pace is not the initial or crucial distinction, but the secondary effect of a particular conception of the structure of the whole as either synchronic or diachronic. Emphasising the chronological order of the poem and the linear reading experience slightly fosters the rapid reading, whereas emphasising the independence of each part from its place in the order of the poem fosters the slow reading, encouraging as it does the extraction of parts for particular attention.

Romantic Readers

All readers, inevitably, approach the poem both as a compilation of parts, all existing simultaneously and each available for potential extraction, and as a linearly unfolding narrative whose parts must be encountered in chronological order. Thus the Richardsons, Jonathans Sr and Jr, in their *Explanatory Notes and Remarks on* Paradise Lost in 1734, write about how in reading *Paradise Lost* 'we Treasure up a Collection of Fine Imaginative Pictures', but also how the poem 'Aims at a More Noble and More Extensive Moral [. . . and] leads the Mind towards it by the Way of Pleasantness'.[8] The commonplacing hermeneutic of collecting treasures (with its implicit conception of the poem's parts as static and simultaneous in the use of 'pictures') is balanced against a sense of linear progress through the text. There is no attempt to privilege one reading habit over the other.

In the Romantic period, however, a 'commonplacing' hermeneutic that reads *Paradise Lost* as a spatial form whose parts exist independently from one another begins to gain ascendancy. And in spite of its resemblance to biblical hermeneutics, generally the non-linear 'commonplacing' reading has been associated with the Romantic and post-Romantic heterodox (or even Satanic) readings. We have already seen Keats's description of a long poem as a 'Region . . . where [the reader] may pick and choose'. Keats's phrase suggests the readerly autonomy implied by this kind of reading. The reader is not constrained by the order in which the author has arranged the text. The appeal of such an approach, which appears to enfranchise the reader at the expense of Milton the poet, is clear for Keats, whose fraught relationship with his predecessor is well known, or indeed for a reader like William Blake, who wants to claim that the Romantic reader has better sight of the poem than Milton himself had, and that Milton didn't always know what he was doing. Milton is not exactly rendered powerless in these readings, but he is cast in a particular and slightly passive role: that of the prophet divinely inspired in a moment, rather than the labourer constructing his work over time. It has long been noted that Milton had, in Lucy Newlyn's words, a 'dual status' in the Romantic period, 'first as a historical figure, actively involved in politics . . . and second as the oracular vehicle for timeless truths'.[9] As I argue in Chapter 8, it is the former 'historical figure' that most captures Wordsworth's imagination, but when it comes to reading and interpreting *Paradise Lost* a majority of Romantic-period commentators develop the latter view. Charles Lamb's famous response to seeing the manuscript of 'Lycidas' captures this Romantic ideal:

> There is something to me repugnant, at any time, in written hand. The text never seems determinate. Print settles it. I had thought of the Lycidas as of a full-grown beauty – as springing up with all its parts absolute – till, in evil hour, I was shown the original written copy of it, together with the other minor poems of its author, in the Library of Trinity, kept like some treasure to be proud of. I wish they had thrown them in the Cam, or sent them, after the latter cantos of Spenser, into the Irish Channel. How it staggered me to see the fine things in their ore! interlined, corrected! as if their words were mortal, alterable, displaceable at pleasure! as if they might have been otherwise and just as good! as if inspirations were made up of parts, and those fluctuating, successive, indifferent![10]

It is one thing to imagine a very short lyric poem 'springing up' fully formed, another to imagine a mid-length lyric like 'Lycidas' doing so, and yet another to imagine an epic poem coming to be in this way, but nevertheless Romantic readers repeatedly try. Percy Shelley offered a more temperate version of Lamb's fantasy of composition, and one that is not only plausible but encouraged by *Paradise Lost*: 'Milton conceived the Paradise Lost as a whole before he executed it in parts.'[11] The poet, that is, may be bound to carry out his labour through a long expanse of time, but he may have been determined (whether by his mind or by some external inspiring Spirit) that it should, and how it should, be executed. It is notable that Lamb too, although he is appalled at the idea of 'inspirations' being 'made up of parts', acknowledges that even in his fantasy the poem itself has parts, although they sprang up simultaneously and 'absolute'. He laments a manuscript's implication that parts are 'displaceable at pleasure', but it is the possibility that *Milton* may have displaced them at his pleasure that is so upsetting. 'Print settles' a poem into a particular configuration, but we know that Lamb himself was happy to extract and rearrange the parts. In a poem, his sister, Mary Lamb, recalled the days when they would read Milton together: 'And you would . . . Find me out the prettiest places, / The poetic turns, and graces.'[12] Having sent Coleridge some volumes of Milton, Lamb advised him: 'If you find the Miltons in certain parts dirtied and soiled with a crumb . . . or peradventure a stray ash of tobacco . . . look to that passage more especially: depend upon it, it contains good matter.'[13] The way the conception of the text as a spatial form whose parts exist simultaneously facilitates a slower reading is clear in Lamb's descriptions of reading Milton. 'In Milton', he wrote, 'you love to stop, and saturate your mind with every great image or sentiment; in Homer you want to go on, to have more of his agreeable narrative.'[14]

On one hand, this idea of *Paradise Lost* as an absolute simultaneous whole encourages readers to contemplate the full length of the poem in their interpretations. The ideal Romantic reader of *Paradise Lost* is a *re*reader who feels the presence of the end at the beginning and, moreover, vice versa. Thus Whaler, echoing Shelley in his conception of the poem: 'Inasmuch as Milton composed with all parts of his completed poem in view, one need not be surprised at similes which are fully interpretable only through a knowledge of the completed fable.'[15] There is a flipside to this hermeneutic's 'knowledge of the completed' whole, however. Readings that approach the poem as a spatial form are able to compare different parts directly, side by side; but they are also empowered to extract parts wholesale, as they perceive meaning to be derived vertically, inherent in the part rather than dependent on the part's place in a larger, linear whole. William

Hazlitt wrote that 'The two first books [of *Paradise Lost*] alone are like two massy pillars of solid gold'.[16] 'Alone' here has a double meaning: the first two books have this worth *even* if we take them on their own; or perhaps *especially* if we take them on their own. Byron wrote that 'Milton's Paradise Lost is, as a whole, a heavy concern; but the first two books of it are the very finest poetry that has ever been produced in this world – at least since the flood'.[17] The poem as a whole is nearly too heavy, whereas the first two books are 'massy' enough to stand alone.

We can see why Jonathon Shears characterises the Romantic and post-Romantic reading by 'the misalignment of multiplicity and singularity, parts and wholes'.[18] That is, Romantic readers and their post-Romantic followers 'are consistently attracted to indeterminate features in the text in order to privilege them ahead of Milton's stated purpose',[19] and they forget 'the teleological imperative of Milton's argument'.[20] As the Lamb and Shelley quotations above testify, Romantic readers were more aware of the difference between 'parts' and 'wholes' than Shears gives them credit for; the key is that they conceive of the 'whole' not as a linear one but as a 'beauty . . . with all its parts absolute' at once. Of course, a non-linear reading would not necessarily lead to a Satanic interpretation – it would allow a reader to consider the orthodox Christian parts of the poem as 'absolute' too – yet this seems to be the preferred hermeneutic method of those who seek to make such an interpretation. By inviting direct comparison between parts of the poem that seemingly contradict one another, it allows them to emphasise the inconsistencies and ambiguities between the parts, and then to 'privilege' the earlier parts of the poem in which Satan appears most attractive and convincing.

The Romantic conception of *Paradise Lost* as a region in which to wander, whose parts exist simultaneously and therefore can be enjoyed in any order, seems to mimic God's nunc stans perspective of time. Yet as I argued in Chapter 1, God's nunc stans in Milton's hands accommodates perception of the chronological order of time and sequences of cause and effect. This may be just one of many shapes of time perceptible to God, one of the many ways in which moments in history can speak to one another, but it is not to be disregarded.

Long-distance Runner Readers

In 1945 Joseph Frank coined 'spatial form' as a literary-critical term to describe modernist art (although as we have seen, this conception of literature is much older). It wasn't long before Milton criticism staged a backlash against this and other formalist theories. In his essay 'Syntax and Music in "Paradise Lost"', included in Frank Kermode's 1960 essay collection *The Living Milton*, Donald Davie argued that understanding Milton's elaborate syntax

> become[s] possible only with the recognition, by poet and reader alike, that language and therefore the arts of language operate through and over spans of time, in terms of successive events . . . It is a perception about language which much of the most influential modern criticism – working as it does through spatial metaphors, talking of 'the figure in the carpet', of tensions balanced and cancelling out inside structures – seems expressly designed to obscure.[21]

A few years later in 1963, Christopher Ricks, in *Milton's Grand Style*, agreed with Davie's assessment of modern criticism. He added that 'The skills and beauty of the epic poet will be those of the long-distance runner, rather than of the boxer. Our pleasure will not be that of surprise, of jolt and jerk, but of anticipation and of suspense, felicities controlled by larger rhythms.'[22] In the 1960s, in Milton criticism at least, spatial forms were out, and the linear reading process over time was in.

The most (in)famous articulation of this hermeneutic approach is Stanley Fish's 1967 *Surprised by Sin: The Reader in Paradise Lost*. The poem's 'method', according to Fish, 'is to provoke in its readers wayward, fallen responses which are then corrected by one of several authoritative voices (the narrator, God, Raphael, Michael, the Son)'.[23] As we read the poem, we are met first with one (Satanic) meaning, then, later, another alternative (Christian) meaning, which apparently overwhelms the first. In this reading, when we come across a meaning 'early', we must remember it, but we must also allow it to pass away in the flow of time if we later find a meaning that is superior or preferable; we must not exactly forget the past meaning, but we must allow our understanding of the poem to change and develop as we read. This is not a new response to *Paradise Lost*; Andrew Marvell described a similar process of reading the poem over time and changing his mind, although he did not ascribe the initial 'doubt' to a deliberate effect by Milton: 'the Argument / Held me a while misdoubting his Intent . . . Yet as I read, soon growing less severe . . . But I am now convinc'd.'[24] Linda Gregerson sums up *Surprised by Sin*'s impact in the 1960s: 'What Fish added fifty years ago to specifically poetic analysis was a *fresh* insistence upon the poem's existence in time. The poem is not a thing we take in as a "whole," but rather as a succession of spatio-temporal parts and momentums' (my emphasis).[25]

Fish approaches the poem almost as though it were a speech act, in which one part 'has sounded and passed away' (to quote Augustine) to be superseded by something else which is later and therefore, for some reason, better. Arguably the Fishian school of reading does claim to take in the poem as a 'whole', but only from the retrospective vantage point of the poem's end, from which perspective the deceptive early books are both safely distant and seen in their true light. However, if it does not exclude the 'Satanic' parts of the poem from its consideration, by submitting them to and defining them by the poem's Christian claims, and often specifically by the later books, this approach hierarchises certain parts of the poem over others as dominant, more important, or somehow *more* true. Wittreich calls this 'sequential principle' '[o]ne of the most provocative and, simultaneously, misguided claims of late-twentieth-century Milton criticism' (instead of privileging later books over early ones, Wittreich identifies his own hierarchy of voices in the poem).[26] The Fishian disciple Robert McMahon makes the boldest statement of this kind of reading: for McMahon, 'parts are not of equal value' in the poem, because '*Paradise Lost* is not a static entity. It must be read in time, and it presents itself in a certain sequence . . . temporal sequence is designed to emphasize the climax.'[27] For McMahon, therefore, the meanings that receive 'greater emphasis simply by being later' in our reading experience are the poem's dominant ones (for example, the biblical mode is of more value than the classical).[28] Oppositions in the poem, he writes, can be 'felt fully as oppositions: they may be found complementary, but the later can also be seen to qualify or correct the earlier'.[29]

There will be exceptions to such a broad generalisation, but it does seem that the synchronic view of the poem and its associated 'commonplacing' reading is favoured by readers who question the efficacy of Milton's Christian argument, whereas the diachronic view and its associated linear reading is favoured by those who accept or seek to accept it. In *Milton's Scriptural Reasoning*, for example, Phillip J. Donnelly aims to understand the contradictions in the poem as functioning within a religious worldview, but in a way that does not dissolve these contradictions in hierarchy. Donnelly 'corroborates the recent emphasis upon interpretive openness in Milton's writings, but [his] analysis goes beyond the New Milton Criticism by setting Milton's poetic strategies in the context of his biblicism'.[30] The indeterminacy of *Paradise Lost* arises, Donnelly argues, from

Milton's 'attempt to imitate biblical form', which presents its truth in incomplete, imperfect parts, but when these parts are viewed together produces one whole truth.[31] Clearly I agree with Donnelly's identification of 'biblical form' in the poem; I only hesitate at his optimism that an overall moral doctrine does emerge from the various contradictions when the poem is viewed as a whole. (The triumphant meaning he identifies is 'the human apprehension of divine love'.)[32] In order to identify this emergent doctrine Donnelly tends toward the Fishian retrospective method of reading, with his theory that meaning emerges through a linear process of 'revelation' in which later books modify earlier ones.[33]

Ricks described the poet of a long poem as a long-distance runner. For Fish, the reader of a long poem must be a long-distance runner too, committed (at least in theory) to reading continuously from beginning to end. Compared to Keats's Romantic wandering, this is a hermeneutic that emphasises hard work, but also a strange passivity, as the reader submits to the experience that has been prearranged for them by the poet. Since Fish, it has been harder for readers to claim, or even aspire, to know the whole of *Paradise Lost* as they read. Critics who initially express sympathy with or desire for a Romantic synchronic conception of the text waver at the implications for readerly power. R. A. Shoaf, the only critic to have advanced an extended comparison between the way we read *Paradise Lost* and God's nunc stans perspective, discusses the case of puns and metaphors: 'In a pun or metaphor, the simultaneity of meanings gives us a feeling of the access of power (the overcoming of time): we feel we know more, faster, than we feel we do in ordinary discourse.'[34] But Shoaf concludes that this view of the whole is impossible, and that the attempt is sinful presumption on the part of the reader, an illusory 'simulacrum of divine knowing' that makes us forget our limitations. 'Rather than affect such pride, we must be humble before the necessity of sacrifice, purify ourselves by the trial that is by contraries, sorting and separating and cutting out the meanings that are heard in the word (and that herd in the word).'[35] Gale H. Carrithers and James D. Hardy also begin by asserting: 'It is impossible to know about the beginning of *Paradise Lost* until the end is understood – and the reverse is true as well. The reader cannot know the parts without knowing the whole – and again the reverse is true.'[36] Yet they qualify their advocacy of knowing the whole: 'the end and the beginning can never be truly seen *together* or sung through *completely* [. . . because] completeness and simultaneity are attributes of God, not of persons': 'the God's-eye view is presumptive rather than knowable.'³⁷ This doubt causes them to turn to the notion of a linear reading, even after they have expounded its inadequacy.³⁸ They conclude that, although it idealises the non-linear reading, *Paradise Lost* 'enacts the becoming implied in work and journey'.³⁹ Trial, work and journey – these are qualities of the linear reading experience, in stark contrast to the image of Lamb enjoying his supper and pipe as he lingered over his favourite passages.

Shoaf is right that the poem's simulation of the nunc stans can only ever be a simulacrum, but I do not agree that this simulacrum is necessarily sinful, and that it must be rejected. Key is the recognition that God's nunc stans incorporates both synchronic and diachronic views of the whole. *Paradise Lost* portrays both earthly and celestial beings aspiring to this perspective and Milton repeatedly endorses such an effort as the best route to understanding – whether in the case of God surveying time, characters figuring out their own free will, the poet-narrator reading history or Milton himself reading Scripture. It might seem obvious to say that lots of readers do this, but having seen the potential implications of either extreme method, we might renew our appreciation for those readings that consciously and explicitly make use of both approaches in their attempt to interpret the whole.

He in Whose Hand All Times and Seasons Roll

It speaks to the difficulty of apprehending a poem the length of *Paradise Lost* as a whole with 'all its parts absolute' that one of the most Romantic modern readings of Milton discusses not *Paradise Lost* but Milton's shorter epic, *Paradise Regain'd*. In a similar way that I relate the reading of *Paradise Lost* to depictions of temporal perspective within the poem, Ryan Netzley has compared the experience of reading *Paradise Regain'd* to Jesus's perspective as it is depicted in that poem, and understands this perspective as bound up with theological theories of time. *Paradise Regain'd* is, of course, a very different poem from *Paradise Lost*. Its shorter length invites greater confidence that the structure of the whole can be apprehended. 'His subject is indeed confined, and he has a narrow foundation to build upon', Thomas Newton writes of *Paradise Regain'd* in 1749, using a conventional image of spatial form: 'but he has raised as noble a superstructure, as such little room and scanty materials would allow.'⁴⁰ As a result it is lyrical immanence, rather than epic narrative, that Netzley places alongside the reader's sense of the completed whole. 'The brief epic ... explicitly eschews the teleological notion of reading', Netzley argues: 'If the reader already knows where a poem is going, then reading merely reaffirms what is already the case'. Instead, he proposes that reading *Paradise Regain'd* is not a process with a 'recognizable payoff', but rather 'a state of rapt attention, in this case to the immanent presence of words as well as an already regained and granted paradise'.[41]

Netzley's description, I would suggest, actually describes the experience of reading *Order and Disorder* more than *Paradise Regain'd*. It is not only that *Order and Disorder* cannot offer a 'payoff' for the reason that it is unfinished. Hutchinson's poem as a whole, albeit an unfinished whole, replicates in its larger structure the equilibrium of her couplets. Although it follows the chronology of Creation from Genesis, there is no narrative impetus or suggestion of cause and effect. As suggested by the title – a pair of opposed nouns, without the implicit narrative implied by the verbs/adjectives 'lost' and 'regained' – the poem is organised as a collection of balanced juxtapositions. It eschews the linear logic of either narrative or justificatory argument in order to embrace the seemingly arbitrary relations between events in time. For example, just as Eve was created from Adam's rib, 'So from the second *Adams* bleeding side / God form'd the Gospel Church, his mystique Bride' (III.467–8); does that 'So' express a causal, intentional or coincidental relationship? It doesn't matter: 'mystique' and 'mystery' (V.67, 279) form the basis for thematic and structural connections in the poem. Milton's long poems, on the other hand, are more insistent on the importance of the linear unfolding of the text.

I agree with Netzley that a reading of *Paradise Regain'd* inevitably involves awareness of the completion of the poem, of paradise that is 'already regained and granted' in both history and eternity. But Netzley's argument overstates the rejection of teleology in the poem. As I argued in Chapter 2, the poem endorses a similar hermeneutic method to *Paradise Lost*, through its depiction of Jesus's own acts of reading. The poem is interested in the chronological order of events: 'how to begin, and how to accomplish best his end' (II.113–14). Hence Milton's construction of the poem as a debate, in which Jesus's responses to Satan both follow the latter's specific arguments – picking up on, revolving, and redirecting Satan's precise words – and invoke principles derived from above:

> Raign then; what canst thou better do the while?
>   To whom our Saviour answer thus return'd.
> All things are best fulfil'd in their due time,

> And time there is for all things, Truth hath said;
> If of my raign Prophetic Writ hath told,
> That it shall never end, so when begin
> The Father in his purpose hath decreed,
> He in whose hand all times and seasons roul.
> (III.180–7)

Jesus's words only make sense in the contexts both of Satan's immediately preceding challenge and of eternal 'Truth', written elsewhere and informing Jesus's answers. Just as Christ's reign must be seen both to 'begin' at a specific time and season and to be already complete from eternity, so we must read Jesus's words as simultaneously contingent on this present dialogue, determined by texts written long before, and bestowed upon him independently of either of these factors by God.

It is easy to see why readers, faced with numerous seemingly irreconcilable meanings in Milton's poems, choose to hierarchise those meanings by privileging particular parts of the poem through the development of a particular apprehension of the shape of the whole and the kind of reading experience that they deem necessary. This is even more tempting in the case of *Paradise Lost* than *Paradise Regain'd* due to its sheer unmanageable length. Critics have located what they identify as the most important or *truest* meaning at various points in *Paradise Lost*. J. R. Watson, for instance, locates it in Books 6 and 7; for Anne Ferry, it is the parts where/when the poet writes as a historical personage.[42] Even the New Milton Critics, who aim to take a holistic view in the understanding that ambiguity is central to *Paradise Lost* and part of its meaning, arguing that alternative meanings are not there to be sifted through and either accepted or rejected, inevitably give greater credence to the paradoxical moments of the poem rather than the explicit statements of doctrine. The most frequent claims for priority, however, are for the early or the late books.

One model for a reading that self-consciously combines the synchronic and diachronic hermeneutics in an attempt to comprehend the whole is David Quint's *Inside Paradise Lost*. Quint comes to a similar conclusion to Donnelly, that the 'message' of the poem is the recognition and endorsement of love, but finds that this message inheres in individual parts as well as emerging through the poem's varied patterns. He proceeds by reading the 'poems within the poem', searching for the 'verbal arrangements and thought structures that bind together – in widening configurations – episodes, individual books, motifs that run through the larger poem' in ways that require foreknowledge as well as memory.[43] Quint pithily sums up the Romantic 'commonplacing' approach to the poem in his introduction: 'Some assembly is required.'[44] He reads the poem 'from its inside out', for example, identifying thematic links that connect Books 5 and 6, 4 and 7, 3 and 8, 2 and 9, and the beginning and end of the poem: this is both an exercise in readerly reassembly, an affront to the linear construction of the poem, and a tribute to Milton's 'concentric and symmetrical scheme', attributing to the poet an astonishing oversight and control of his vast work.[45] Quint attends to Milton's authorial assembly ('the cunning of Milton's plotting'), his arrangement of the poem and to effects like succession and repetition, as well as to readerly reconfigurations.[46] But although Quint traces the way a reader's sympathies shift through a linear reading, the process is presented as additive, confirmatory rather than corrective.

Milton encourages us to experience *Paradise Lost*, as well as *Paradise Regain'd*, as both a progressively unfolding timeline and a non-linear space containing all its parts simultaneously through the same fundamental method by which he gives us the same experience of history: by drawing together disparate parts or 'times', then confounding the relation between them. Gregerson has written on how, in *Paradise Lost* and other long poems, 'a broken surface, a failed plot line, a conspicuous imperfection or authorial intervention . . . announces the poem's artificial status and disrupts the illusion of wholeness'.[47] But these broken surfaces also draw our attention to the fact that we can perceive the whole, by dint of the fact that we can perceive its brokenness. Anthony Welch views (some of) the poem's ambiguities as performing a function that is related to time, arguing that Milton incorporates chronological inconsistencies into his poem in order to draw our attention to our flawed conception of time; that he deliberately presents an impossible chronology in order to show us how temporal narrative cannot accommodate the eternal.[48] But I would modify this claim, and suggest that the inconsistencies and self-contradictions are actually functioning to draw our attention not to our inability to approach eternity, but to our capacity to come remarkably near to it, and to simulate in our perspective of the structure of the poem God's own perspective of the structure of time, which is inherently paradoxical. When we compare different parts, we find that they represent both a continuously developing sequence, and a discontinuous collection of parts each possessed of its own independent meaning, and complete and full in itself. This is achieved even at the most local level of syntax. Milton's famously convoluted sentences speak simultaneously of the irrelevance of conventional syntax – they almost imply that words can make sense in any order – and of the importance of his own particular syntax in the creation of subtle and precise meaning. The same is true of the larger plot of Milton's poem. The events of his narrative occur out of chronological order, suggesting that the whole of a narrative can be understood without the need for a strictly linear experience of events, but at the same time Milton has created a new and meaningful order in his plotting of that narrative.

Those lines from Book 3, in which God beholds Adam and Eve from his prospect high, are dense with reflexive references:

> On Earth he first beheld
> Our two first Parents, yet the onely two
> Of mankind, in the happie Garden plac't,
> Reaping immortal fruits of joy and love,
> Uninterrupted joy, unrivald love
> In blissful solitude[.]
> (III.64–9)

Milton goes out of his way to put us in mind of other parts of the poem: 'Reaping immortal fruits of joy and love', for instance, takes us back to Book 2 when we met Death (a reaper), and back to the 'Fruit' of the first line of Book 1, as well as forward to the plucking of the fruit (a kind of reaping) in Book 9, and then further forward to when death is depicted as the dropping of ripe fruit: 'So maist thou live, till like ripe Fruit thou drop / Into thy Mothers lap' (XI.545–6). We simply cannot read and understand these lines without reference to other parts of the poem. On the one hand, perceiving the 'past, present, and future' of the poem in these lines brings to view the changes that the meanings of the words used here undergo over the course of the linear reading experience. The chronological reading takes us from these 'immortal fruits' through to the 'false Fruit' of the Tree of Knowledge (IX.1011), and then to a 'ripe Fruit' that is death (the direct product of the 'false Fruit'), but death softened; finally, we come full circle, from the 'immortal fruits' of prelapsarian Paradise to the fruits of the next paradise:

> New Heav'ns, new Earth, Ages of endless date
> Founded in righteousness and peace and love
> To bring forth fruits Joy and eternal Bliss.
> (XII.549–51)

The repetition here of the language of Book 3 – 'love', 'fruits', 'joy', 'bliss' – invites us to compare the passages and to perceive how our understanding of these words has changed over the course of reading. The chronological reading has enacted for the reader the discovery of the happy Fall, and makes sense of a troubling word in the Book 3 passage, 'immortal' – viewed in the context of the coming of Christ, the 'fruits of [God's] joy and love' truly are immortal, for all that they will be 'interrupted'.

But to what extent is it necessary to view the parts in this order in order to apprehend these meanings, which are, after all, eternal attributes of God's plan? Arguably, all these nuances to the word 'fruit' are visible within this passage from Book 3 even taken alone, or particularly when the 'part' is extended to embrace the rest of Book 3, in which the Father will summarise the events of the Fall and the Son will offer himself. These meanings were even visible in *Paradise Lost*'s opening lines. We apprehend from those lines in Book 3, through their relation to other parts that invite comparison, the future time of our reading experience, but we also apprehend how each part relates to a scheme of meaning that was present from the outset. We are shown the poem in its entirety both as an unfolding narrative and as a commonplace book in which parts are connected by their participation in the shared larger category of God's (and Milton's) plan.

This double apprehension of time is typological. This term has been used, incorrectly I think, to describe only the linear, successive reading. Grossman, using it to characterise his own linear reading, defines 'typological hermeneutics' in this way: 'Meaning is not traced to another scene, to an atemporal world in which universal truths are universally enforced, but rather to a historically situated action. The locus of meaning is no longer elsewhere, but later.'[49] 'The sequential reading of the poem', he argues, 'respects and thematizes this representation of semantic deferral as a narrative form.'[50]

But typological temporality has a more complex structure, as testified by Auerbach's completely opposite understanding of it:

> a connection is established between two events which are linked neither temporally nor causally – a connection which it is impossible to establish by reason in the horizontal dimension (if I may be permitted to use this term for a temporal extension). It can be established only if both occurrences are vertically linked to Divine Providence, which alone is able to devise such a plan of history and supply the key to its understanding. The horizontal, that is the temporal and causal, connection of occurrences is dissolved; the here and now is no longer a mere link in an earthly chain of events, it is simultaneously something which has always been, and which will be fulfilled in the future; and

strictly, in the eyes of God, it is something eternal, something omnitemporal, something already consummated in the realm of fragmentary earthly event.[51]

For Milton, meaning is both 'deferred until the eschaton', dependent upon the fulfilment of God's plan in its proper time in history, and 'something eternal . . . already consummated'. Such an apprehension of time is the necessary condition for an understanding of free will, of history, of Scripture and of *Paradise Lost*.

Notes

1. Cowley, *Poems*, 11.
2. Ibid., 32.
3. Samuel Johnson, 'Cowley', in *The Lives of the Poets*, ed. John H. Middendorf (New Haven, CT: Yale UP, 2010), in *The Yale Edition of the Works of Samuel Johnson*, ed. Robert DeMaria, 23 vols (New Haven, CT: Yale UP, 1958–), xxi, 3–84 (81).
4. Cowley, *Poems*, 32.
5. Samuel Johnson, 'Milton', in *The Lives of the Poets*, xxi, 99–205 (194–5).
6. John Leonard, *Faithful Labourers*, i, 193.
7. Ibid., 6.
8. Jonathan Richardson [father and son], *Explanatory Notes and Remarks on* Paradise Lost (London: James, John and Paul Knapton, 1734), clx, clxi.
9. Lucy Newlyn, Paradise Lost *and the Romantic Reader* (Oxford: Clarendon Press, 1993, repr. 2001), 37.
10. Charles Lamb, from *London Magazine* (October 1820), in *The Romantics on Milton*, 298.
11. Percy Shelley, 'Preface to Laon and Cythna' (1818), in *The Romantics on Milton*, 530.
12. Charles Lamb and Mary Lamb, *Works of Charles and Mary Lamb*, ed. E. V. Lucas (London and New York: Macmillan, 1903–5), v, 15. Quoted in J. Milton French, 'Lamb and Milton', *Studies in Philology* 31.1 (1934), 92–103 (92).
13. Charles Lamb, *Works*, vi, 249. Quoted in French, 'Lamb and Milton', 94.
14. Charles Lamb and Mary Lamb, *The Letters of Charles and Mary Anne Lamb: 1809–1817*, ed. Edwin W Marrs, Jr (Ithaca and London: Cornell UP, 1978), iii, 23.
15. Whaler, 'Miltonic Simile', 1042.
16. William Hazlitt, 'On Shakespeare and Milton', in *Lectures on the English Poets*, in *The Selected Writings of William Hazlitt*, ed. Duncan Wu, 9 vols (London: Pickering & Chatto, 1998), ii, 206–7 (223).

17. George Gordon Byron, *Selected Letters and Journals*, ed. Leslie A. Marchand (Cambridge, MA: Belknap Press of Harvard UP, 1982), 100.
18. Jonathon Shears, *The Romantic Legacy of Paradise Lost* (Aldershot: Ashgate, 2009), 18.
19. Ibid., 18.
20. Ibid., 207.
21. Donald Davie, 'Syntax and Music in "Paradise Lost"', in *The Living Milton*, ed. Frank Kermode (London: Routledge, 1960): 70–84 (74).
22. Christopher Ricks, *Milton's Grand Style* (Oxford: Oxford UP, 1963), 48.
23. Stanley Fish, 'Preface to the Second Edition', *Surprised by Sin*, x.
24. Andrew Marvell, 'On Mr. Milton's Paradise Lost', *The Poems and Letters of Andrew Marvell*, ed. H. M. Margoliouth, 3rd edn, 2 vols (Oxford: Clarendon Press, 1971), i, 138.
25. Linda Gregerson, 'The Poem as Thinking Machine', *Milton Quarterly* 52.1 (2018): 317–23 (318).
26. Joseph Wittreich, *Why Milton Matters: A New Preface to His Writings* (New York: Palgrave Macmillan, 2006), 32.
27. Robert McMahon, *The Two Poets of Paradise Lost* (Baton Rouge: Louisiana State UP, 1998), 8.
28. Ibid., 8.
29. Ibid., 10.
30. Phillip J. Donnelly, *Milton's Scriptural Reasoning: Narrative and Protestant Toleration* (Cambridge: Cambridge UP, 2009), 7.
31. Ibid., 7.
32. Ibid., 174.
33. Ibid., 75.
34. R. A. Shoaf, *Milton, Poet of Duality* (New Haven: Yale UP, 1985), 62.
35. Ibid., 63–4.
36. Gale H. Carrithers and James D. Hardy, *Milton and the Hermeneutic Journey* (Baton Rouge: Louisiana State UP, 1994), 25–6.
37. Ibid., 72.
38. Ibid., 3.
39. Ibid., 49.
40. Thomas Newton, 'The Life of Milton', in *Paradise Lost. A Poem, in Twelve Books. The Author John Milton. A New Edition, with Notes of Various Authors, by Thomas Newton, D. D.*, 2 vols (London: J. and R. Tonson and S. Draper, 1749), i (vol), xliii.
41. Ryan Netzley, 'Reading, Recognition, Learning, and Love in *Paradise Regained*', in *To Repair the Ruins: Reading Milton*, ed. Mary C. Fenton and Louis Schwartz (Pittsburgh: Duquesne UP, 2012), 117–45 (128, 142).
42. J. R. Watson, 'Divine Providence and the Structure of *Paradise Lost*', *Essays in Criticism* 14 (1964): 148–55; Anne Ferry, *Milton's Epic Voice*.
43. David Quint, *Inside Paradise Lost* (Princeton: Princeton UP, 2014), 1–2.
44. Ibid., 2.
45. Ibid., 234–5.

46. Ibid., 218.
47. Linda Gregerson, *The Reformation of the Subject* (Cambridge: Cambridge UP, 1995), 3–4.
48. Welch, 'Reconsidering Chronology'.
49. Grossman, *Authors to Themselves*, 34.
50. Ibid., ix.
51. Erich Auerbach, *Mimesis: The Representation of Reality in Western Literature*, trans. Willard R. Trask (Princeton: Princeton UP, 1953, repr. 2003), 73–4.

Part II

Thomson

Chapter 4

Shade Softening into Shade: Georgic Causation in *The Seasons*

James Thomson has been called the 'characteristic Miltonic poet of the eighteenth century'.[1] His 'indebtedness [to Milton] is a commonplace', but identifying the Miltonic quality of *The Seasons* is difficult and must pursue subtle lines of connection.[2] I propose that Milton's use of the long poem to explore the role of God either as a first, original cause or as an immanent, immediate cause, and his use of the prospect poem framework to hold these two possibilities in suspension has implications for the development of the long poem in the eighteenth century, for the emergent popularity of non-narrative genres and for Thomson's own treatment of time in *The Seasons*.

I begin by outlining what I take to be the key intellectual historical and generic contexts for Thomson's thinking about time: the contemporary debate over the capacity of natural philosophy to identify 'secondary' causes within nature, without recourse to the 'first cause' of God; and the fashionable georgic mode that offered a model for writing about time as at once a continuous process and a succession of disjointed, isolated moments. This is followed by a discussion of how Thomson's temporality manifests at the level of content, in his more overtly georgic passages as well as in exemplary passages of natural description. In the next chapter I will consider two variations on Thomson's usual subject of natural description, both of which seem to demand a more clearly linear apprehension of time: the interpolated tales, and the depictions of the poet in the process of composition. I will argue that these parts, too, are structured so as to give a sense of movement, but to question the straightforward and continuous direction of that movement. In the final chapter of this section, as I did with *Paradise Lost* in Chapter 3, I turn to the reader's experience of time as it is shaped by the poem's structure.

Readers over three centuries have disagreed over whether *The Seasons* behaves as an 'unfolding' timeline or as a space or picturesque canvas in which to wander and from which to extract.

In this way I hope to contribute to two dominant strands in recent Thomson criticism: ecocritical approaches to *The Seasons*, and studies of its use of genre, particularly its relation to georgic and its status as a long poem (Sandro Jung and Kwinten Van De Walle's edited collection, *The Genres of Thomson's The Seasons*, the only recent book-length study of *The Seasons*, focuses on these questions of genre).[3] I argue that Thomson based his particular binary temporality on a georgic model found in Virgil's *Georgics*, Milton's *Paradise Lost* and contemporary eighteenth-century formal georgic poems; and that he developed this temporality in order to accommodate competing contemporary conceptions of nature's processes, and a typically georgic combination of confidence and humility in the capacity of humans to understand the natural world.

In the 'Hymn' at the end of *The Seasons*, Thomson reflects on both the subject and the form of his poem:

> A simple Train,
> Yet so delightful mix'd, with such kind Art,
> Such Beauty and Beneficence combin'd;
> Shade, unperceiv'd, so softening into Shade;
> And all so forming an harmonious Whole;
> That, as they still succeed, they ravish still.
> (21–6)

The movement of the seasons and, Thomson implies here, of *The Seasons*, is successive and continuous, each 'Shade' – whether a moment in time or a part in the poem – 'softening into [another] Shade'. Thomson describes a world that is in smooth and constant change, and his poem reflects this in a form that rolls organically from one topic to another. But we find in *The Seasons* that pulling against his sense of constant movement is his sense of the present as a moment that might be not only dwelled in but dwelled upon, and that he might hold 'still'. Here in the Hymn the word 'still' has its temporal meaning of 'continuously', and under this aspect expresses the constant movement of 'succession'. It also has a spatial meaning of 'stationary', under which aspect it suggests quite the opposite: that the movement of the cycle has been paused. The binary georgic temporality that I identify in *The Seasons*, based like Milton's around a distinction between stillness and movement, is structured as follows:

1. In place of Milton's apprehension of the movement of time as linear and historical, Thomson apprehends not the line of history but the circle, or cycle, of the seasons. The glimpse of 'one unbounded SPRING' (Wi.1069) at the end of the poem is a glimpse beyond what concerns *The Seasons*; within the remit of the poem, winter will not end in an eternal spring, but in another spring that will lead to another summer. Our experience of this cyclical time at the local level is linear, as suggested by the word 'Train' in the 'Hymn', and Thomson conveys this sense of time through his descriptions of nature in constant process: always moving, growing, decaying. Every event in nature appears to follow organically from that which preceded it, and lead organically to that which follows.
2. But this cyclical temporality means that logical organisations depending on concepts like 'before' and 'after' are unsettled, because every point in the cycle is both a beginning and an ending, as the seasons 'inexhaustive flow continual round' (Sp.479). Milton's linear history allowed for a clear pattern of cause and effect. Thomson's cycle allows for processes of growth and decay, but every event and every moment appears as (potentially) both the cause and the effect of every other. Thomson conveys this sense of time by discomposing the 'train' and the principle of 'succession', and creating the impression that every individual 'shade', or moment, is somehow independent, disjointed from the rest. Like Milton's Plowman, paused in the present before multiple unknown futures, the narrator of *The Seasons* is never sure what is coming next.

Milton developed a spatial rendering of all of time based on the theological concept of the nunc stans, in which past, present and future are stretched out as though on a canvas, each point in time analogous to a point in space, and he communicated this idea through the form of the prospect poem. Eric Gidal has argued that both of Thomson's major works, *The Seasons* and *Liberty*, are prospect poems, 'composing a range of moral and visual tableaux within topographies of seasonal or historical progress', and Ingrid Horrocks has described how *The Seasons* 'is imagined through a series of "prospect" views from aristocrats' rural estates'.[4] For Thomson, the Boethian–Miltonic prospect view of time was available not only in God's hypothetical perspective but in the prospects of the British countryside that he enjoyed, and of foreign scenes that he imagined. His 'Plains immense' that 'Lie stretch'd below . . . And vast Savannahs' (Su.690–2) echo not only Eve's dream of 'The earth outstretched immense, a prospect wide / And various' (V.88–9), but also Adam's vision of the future 'Stretcht out to the amplest reach of prospect' (XI.380), and Jesus's in *Paradise Regain'd*, from 'a Mountain at whose verdant feet / A spatious plain out stretch't' (III.253–4). Unlike Milton's characters, however, Thomson's narrator does not see the past, present and future of *history* in his prospects, but rather the past, present and future of the seasonal cycle: not just the next season to come, but the same season as it will be and has been.

When we examine Thomson's depictions of the eye's encounters with nature, we find that Thomson obscures whether the dimension in which he moves is time or space, and therefore whether the eye is taking in an extended scene in one moment – 'Here let us sweep / The boundless Landskip' (Su.1408–9) – or whether he is moving through time – 'the Morning shines . . . Unfolding fair the last Autumnal Day' (Au.1165–6) – and whether he is perceiving nature as it changes over time or as it varies across space. This is not a radical claim, and it has been observed by numerous critics. W. B. Hutchings has argued that '[t]he poetry of *The Seasons* strives for a formal equivalence, in the temporal mode of language, of what nature presents both simultaneously (as in a single scene of landscape) and successively in the cyclical roll of the seasons'.[5] That is, Thomson's descriptions of natural processes successfully convey a sense of three-dimensional space, and in turn his descriptions of 'single scene[s]' successfully incorporate a sense of nature changing over time. This point seems so evident that it is sometimes made in passing, even in parentheses, as when Ralph Cohen observes that Thomson often offers an alternative to or reversal of a particular image: 'the same scene or action is treated from another point of view in order to expand the range (space and time).'[6]

But I want to push this point further than it has been pushed, because there are serious implications here for Thomson's conception of time and causality. The effect of this temporal/spatial ambiguity that Thomson introduces is not only to make it difficult to say where one moment in time ends and the next begins, but to question the continuous flowing movement that would seem to bind one moment to the next. One feature of nature is described, and then another; but if we can't be sure whether the poet's eye moves across space or records changes through time, then those features may have existed a moment before or after one another as time flows on successively, or they may exist simultaneously with one another; but if simultaneous with one another, then they may just as well be separated by a gulf of time, since the processes of cause and effect that would connect them are undone. Cohen hints at this possibility, but does not pursue its implications, when he refers to Thomson's portrayal of 'the changing variety of nature, its rich responsiveness to different elements at different moments, its limited transitory quality within recurrent cycles'.[7] The seasons' recurrent cycles mean that things can turn out differently within different iterations of each season: this is the hope and the fear of georgic. The same 'scene or action' may indeed be 'treated from another point of view', as Cohen argues is one of the principal motions shaping the organisation of *The Seasons*; but, more drastically, Thomson may describe a similar 'scene or action' that occurred, with variation, in a different year entirely. At how local a level does this ambiguity occur? In this chapter I will demonstrate how passages in different books of the poem, verse paragraphs that follow one another, and even contiguous lines, are both causally connected to one another through the language of process and radically disjointed from one another through the language of simultaneity, spontaneity or self-sufficiency. What this means is that even though in nature's recurrent cycles shade softens into shade, nature still has the capacity to surprise us.

Causation and the 'Book of Nature'

Readings of *The Seasons*, and of Thomson's more overtly political and historiographical poems like *Liberty* and *Britannia,* as poetic expressions of a progressive 'Whig history' are no longer fashionable.[8] In the twenty-first century both the notion of 'Whig history' itself and the straightforwardness of Thomson's own Whiggism have been questioned.[9] Kevis Goodman has offered a more nuanced account of the way *The Seasons* registers 'the noise of history or, more accurately, the presentness of ongoing history beyond lived experience'.[10] Goodman's interest in the poem's 'recognition of the problem of presentness' is focused on the question of the historical present rather than the philosophical question of the temporal present and its relation to past and future.[11] *Liberty* and *Britannia* are more clearly about history, and utilise the conventional frame of the prospect poem and its shift from spatial extension to historical progress. Thomson's magnum opus *The Seasons*, however, is concerned less with history than with how the nonhuman world and its human, nonhuman and even non-living inhabitants exist in and through time. (Goodman shows how Thomson's description of microorganisms as 'unseen People' is a reference to an occluded imperial history; from an ecocritical perspective, it is important to remember that they are also really microorganisms.)[12] They do so in ways, Thomson suggests, that can apply at any point in history since the Golden Age and before the eternal spring at the end of time; in the cycle of the seasons, distinguishing the historical present from the past becomes less urgent. The many prospect views that feature in *The Seasons* do not open into historical vistas, but into more and more natural description, the elements of which lack almost any definition in terms of either spatial or temporal placement and whose relationships with one another remain ambiguous.

There have been few attempts to read Thomson's poem in the light of early eighteenth-century philosophies of time. In Sitter's account of 'the shift . . . from spatial to temporal theodicy, from proportion to process', he locates Thomson somewhere in the middle of this shift, alongside Young and Akenside but different from Pope. Thomson is 'literally between the generation of Gay and Pope . . . and that of Gray and Collins', and is therefore negotiating between the two traditions.[13] The picture is complicated further because Thomson was not only negotiating between spatial and temporal figurative models, like the Great Chain of Being and the Book of Nature, but also between multiple available ways of thinking about time. The change in the philosophy of time between Milton and Thomson that is best known and most celebrated today is Newton's development of his theory of 'Absolute, true, and mathematical time', laid out in 1687 in his *Principia*. Absolute time, according to Newton, 'in and of itself and of its own nature, without reference to anything external, flows uniformly and by another name is called duration'. Newtonian absolute time has no punctuation or texture, no particular moments that are raised above others. Its structure is linear, regular, and organised independently of the events that take place within it: the 'order of the parts of time is unchangeable . . . All things are placed in time with reference to order of succession.'[14] The dominant narrative of philosophy of time in the eighteenth century is therefore that of 'a shift in the epistemological grounding of time itself', 'a new understanding of time as an absolute "flow" – a dynamic quantity independent of the events that it had theretofore only measured'.[15]

However, the cultural currency of Newton's theory of time in the first half of the eighteenth century should not be overstated. 'Relative, apparent, and common time is any sensible and external measure (precise or imprecise) of duration by means of motion; such a measure – for example, an hour, a day, a month, a year', Newton acknowledged, 'is commonly used instead of true time'.[16] This kind of time, of course, is the remit of Thomson, whose poems appear if anything to reject the concept, or at least the relevance, of absolute time. When Thomson discusses time in his 'Poem Sacred to the Memory of Sir Isaac Newton' (1727), his image of 'The noiseless Tide of Time, all bearing down / To vast Eternity's unbounded sea' does hint at Newton's absolute time 'flowing equably' (although the tide is a perplexingly cyclical image).[17] However, in the following lines, which were a likely source for Wordsworth's lines on Newton in Book 3 of *The Prelude*, Thomson makes clear that this is a tide that Newton 'stem'd alone'. He then describes how Newton 'rais'd / His lights at equal distances, to guide / Historian, wilder'd on his darksome way' – a reference not to Newton's theory of absolute time in the *Principia*, but, as Walter Keith Thomas and Warren U. Ober have suggested, to Newton's *Chronology of Antient Kingdoms Amended*.[18] The rest of the poem is dominated by images of neither absolute time nor chronological human history, but of natural time, recurrent and repetitive rather than linear: 'Oft had [the planets] roll'd / O'er erring man the year', before Newton worked out how their course was directed by gravity, for example. It's unsurprising that Thomson was not heavily influenced by Newton's abstract temporality. As Marjorie Hope Nicolson has shown, Newton's *Opticks* provided more fruitful inspiration for poets of nature.[19] More recently, Philip Connell has demonstrated the pervasive influence on *The Seasons* of Newtonian physico-theology, showing how Newton's argument from design converged with Whig political interests in the period and in Thomson's poem.[20] I want to pursue this line of investigation, suggesting that this aspect of Newtonian natural philosophy also influenced Thomson's conception of time, more than did Newton's own theories of time. Recently Courtney Weiss Smith has described the implications of Newton's theory of gravity, in particular, for a wider debate in the seventeenth and early eighteenth centuries around causation in nature.[21]

Milton, as I discussed in the first section of this book, was interested in cause and effect as it operated in and between divine and creaturely will. Thomson is interested in cause and effect as it operates between physical bodies in the natural world. This was the subject of heated philosophical debate in the seventeenth and eighteenth centuries. What was the relation between the 'secondary', 'intermediate' or 'natural' causes of effects and events in the natural world, more and more of which natural philosophers were discovering, and the 'first cause', God's influence? Had God designed the universe and set it running like a clock or other mechanical device, all its 'secondary causes' functioning without his direct involvement, as Leibniz, Locke and sometimes Boyle argued, adapting the Aristotelian idea of 'powers' inherent in objects? Or was God's immediate will and continuous intervention required to keep the system running at every moment, as in the occasionalist or concurrentist theories argued by Malebranche, Berkeley and sometimes Boyle, and taken to its extreme in the Cartesian claim that God actually recreates the world at every moment?[22] Edward Young appears to articulate the first position in *Night Thoughts* when he describes God as 'First Father of effects, that progeny / Of endless series!' (IX.2220–1), whereas William Cowper articulates the second position in *The Task* when he writes that matter must be 'impell'd / To ceaseless service by a ceaseless force' (VI.218–19).[23]

Newton himself remained agnostic about the cause(s) of the forces he described in nature. But as Smith has shown, the lack of an obvious 'natural' cause for gravity suggested to many of Newton's contemporaries that God's will was an immediate requirement for gravity to work at every moment; God was no longer a 'distant first cause', but 'constantly at work in both the material world and human hearts'.[24] Both Smith and Connell point out that this notion of God's constant working presence is expressed repeatedly in Thomson's poetry. In the 'Poem Sacred to the Memory of Sir Isaac Newton', God 'fills, sustains, and actuates the whole'. Similarly, in 'Spring' God is a 'Spirit' and 'Energy' that 'pervades, / Adjusts, sustains, and agitates the Whole' (853–5). Gravity itself is listed in the poem to Newton as one of those 'few causes' that governs a huge 'scheme of things, / Effects so various, beautiful, and great'.

But Thomson is equally interested in tracing the role of secondary causes in natural processes of growth, change and decay. His competing interests in secondary causes and the first cause are expressed in the paean to Reason that ends 'Summer': 'up-tracing, from the dreary Void, / The Chain of Causes and Effects to HIM, / The World-producing ESSENCE, who alone / Possesses Being' (1745–8). Thomson wants to keep the first cause in sight, and stress God's presence, but also to trace and do justice to the 'Chain of [secondary] Causes and Effects' in nature; to affirm that natural bodies do indeed have causal power. The image of a chain leading back posits God as an original rather than a persistent cause, and it is notable that the expression 'World-producing', which could refer to an original or a perpetual act of creation, was altered from the original 'all-sustaining', which suggested a more occasionalist scheme. In these lines Thomson appears to confirm momentary intervention and reject it in one breath.

There is a further complexity in that even if God is accepted as a 'distant first cause', as Smith puts it, and the causal power of objects is retained, the question remains as to *how* distant? In this way the ontological debate over the causes of natural events spills into an epistemological debate for natural philosophers in the period. The 'main Business of Natural Philosophy', wrote Newton, 'is to argue from Phaenomena without feigning Hypotheses, and to deduce Causes from Effects, till we come to the very first Cause, which certainly is not mechanical'.[25] In other words, natural philosophers should resort to the first cause only when they have exhausted natural mechanical explanations, as many believed was the case with gravity. God may continually sustain his 'few [immediate] causes' like gravity, but he permits nature to carry out other processes according to the causal logic with which he has invested it. Defoe, for example, wrote that God is the 'Continual' as well as the 'Original' 'Guide of [Nature's] Executive Power', but we only 'enquire after God . . . where we find Nature defective in her Discovery, where we see Effects but cannot reach their Causes; there 'tis most just, and Nature her self seems to direct us to it, to end the rational Enquiry, and resolve it into Speculation'. The origin of the winds is one of those mysteries, he claims, in which 'the deepest Search into the Region of Cause and Consequence, has found out just enough to leave the wisest Philosopher in the dark . . . [Nature] tells you, *It is not in Me, you must go Home and ask my Father*'.[26] In *The Seasons*, God as the spirit and energy that 'adjusts, sustains, and agitates the whole' is introduced not at an arbitrary moment to imply that God's will is immediately present in every natural event, but when Thomson asks a question about an unknown cause in nature: what 'Instructs the Fowls of Heaven' to sing? 'What, but GOD?' (851–2).

The problem is: how does the natural philosopher know that he or she has arrived at the first cause, and hasn't only come up against the limitations of human perception and understanding, or even only the limitations of contemporary science? Robert Boyle, eulogised by Thomson as he 'whose pious Search / Amid the dark Recesses of his Works, / The great CREATOR sought' (Su.1556–8), summarises this problem:

> in the book of nature, as in a well-contrived romance, the parts have such a connection and relation to one another, and the things we would discover are so darkly or incompleatly knowable by those, that precede them, that the mind is never satisfied till it comes to the end of the book . . . And yet the full discovery of nature's mysteries is

so unlikely to fall to any man's share in this life, that the case of the pursuers of them is at best like theirs, that light upon some excellent romance, of which they shall never see the latter parts.[27]

The seeming gap in the causal timeline – the 'darkness', as both Boyle and Defoe picture it – may be filled not by God, but by some unknown secondary cause. Where nature diverges from our expectations and experience, this may not be a miracle, but rather an effect of hidden natural causes in a natural system so complex. From the mid-seventeenth century the source of necessity in nature shifted, as Sean Silver writes, from 'Divine fiat to the complex interbraiding of physicalist forces . . . referring an event to a concurrence of [unknown but, increasingly, theoretically knowable] causes instead of a categorically unknowable design'.[28] 'Scrutinous Philosophy looks deep', Thomson writes, 'With piercing eye, into the latent cause', and is distinguished from the 'mystic faith' of the vulgar ([1730] Su.1130–2). 'Latent', 'unseen', and 'secret' secondary causes pervade *The Seasons*, from the 'vast eternal Springs' that feed the great rivers, but 'lie conceal'd / From mortal Eye' (Au.773–5), to the mysterious origin of frost: 'What art thou, Frost? And whence are thy keen stores / Deriv'd, thou secret all-invading Power[?]' ([1730] Wi.671–2). At such moments, when he alludes to contemporary scientific debates, Thomson is willing to consider that a lack of evident cause is due not to arrival at the first cause but to the limitations of human knowledge, at least in the historical present.[29]

The Seasons, then, makes an intervention in a contemporary debate that may not appear at once to be a question of time, but is focused upon questions and definitions of causation that the poet therefore addresses through their construction and portrayal of temporality. God's constant presence adjusting and sustaining the whole at every moment implies a breakdown of the causal timeline: each moment may as well be removed from the succession as it bears no necessary connection to the moments preceding or succeeding it. David Hume would later take this theory to its logical conclusion when the causation debate culminated in his rejection of any connection between events at all, whether by God's will or by their own natures. A nightmarish version of this temporality in which 'Time is dealt out by particles' (I.367) also appears in another long poem of the period, Young's *Night Thoughts*. The impossibility of knowing the future is felt as an imprisonment in the perpetual 'now' of the present: 'Where is tomorrow? In another world' (I.375).[30] Young's treatment of the idea of isolated, disjointed moments brings into relief Thomson's own far more optimistic approach. Thomson suggests the 'sustaining' immediacy of God through his depiction of isolated moments, independent or suddenly divergent from those before and after, and of events with multiple possible outcomes. However, there is always the possibility that it is not God, but hidden secondary sources, that brought about the divergence or the unexpected outcome. To give due consideration to secondary causes, known and unknown, Thomson must also stress the ongoing flow of time, in which one moment leads organically and necessarily to the next in a continuous process.

To articulate this dual perspective of time, Thomson develops a georgic temporality based on Virgil's *Georgics*, georgic moments in Milton's poetry, and contemporary formal georgic poems. Georgic is the genre in which the poet's desire to 'trace the secret Cause' is counterbalanced by their awareness of the limitations of human knowledge of natural causes (Dryden, *Virgil's Georgics*, II.699). It is the genre in which past empirical observation of cause-and-effect relationships does not guarantee the necessity of that relationship in the future.

Georgic Time

The narrative of Milton's overbearing influence enervating the epic mode for eighteenth-century poets is familiar. Less appreciated is the extent to which Miltonic energies and techniques were channelled, successfully, into the newly fashionable georgic mode in the first half of the eighteenth century. Georgic was the eighteenth-century genre in which blank verse was the dominant verse form, and it was the genre that produced the greatest number of readable long poems in the period. Eighteenth-century georgics have been widely maligned, but in recent years critics have begun to rediscover and argue for the artistic and political fascination of poems such as John Philips's *Cyder* (1708), William Somervile's *The Chace* (1727), and James Grainger's *The Sugar-Cane* (1764).

The most popular georgic poem of the century (arguably the most popular poem of the century in any genre), and the only one that didn't completely lose its canonical status in the twentieth century, was Thomson's *The Seasons*. Perhaps one reason that this poem was relatively tolerated, if not widely celebrated, in the twentieth century was because it is not as overtly didactic as other formal georgics of the period. Its relation to the georgic genre has been a question of particular interest in recent years as critical interest in the poem has grown. On the one hand, Rachel Crawford calls it 'the fundamental georgic poem of the [eighteenth] century and perhaps the most fundamental English georgic of all time'.[31] On the other hand, many have pointed out the need to recognise 'that the polymorphous structure of the long poem relies not on the exclusive use of a single genre. Rather, it is underpinned by a continuous series of generic modulations.'[32] I am arguing that one way in which it is helpful to understand *The Seasons* as georgic is in its construction of time. In its conception of time *The Seasons* has more in common with Virgil's *Georgics*, the georgic moments of *Paradise Lost* and eighteenth-century formal georgic poems than it does with the contemporary 'philosophical' long poems that it resembles in other ways, like Mallet's *The Excursion* (1728), Young's *Night Thoughts* (1742–5), or Akenside's *The Pleasures of Imagination* (1744).

Thematically, georgic is the ideal genre in which to explore debates around first and secondary causes in the natural world. In perhaps the most frequently imitated passage of Virgil's *Georgics*, the *beatus ille* passage in Book 2, the poet asks the Muses to grant him knowledge of nature: lunar cycles, eclipses, tides and 'what Cause delays / The Summer Nights, and shortens Winter Days' (II.683–4). But he then adds that 'if my heavy Blood restrain the Flight' of his understanding, his 'next Desire' is a quiet country life (685–8). A few lines later he declares again, 'Happy the Man, who, studying Nature's Laws, / Thro' known Effects can trace the secret Cause' (698–9) ('Felix, qui potuit rerum cognoscere causas'), but then returns quickly again to the simple country life: 'And happy too is he, who decks the Bow'rs / Of Sylvans' (702–3). Juan Christian Pellicer has called the Virgilian *beatus ille* 'Thomson's poetic keynote, to which he repeatedly turns throughout the articulation of *The Seasons*'.[33] Thomson translated Virgil's passage in his preface to the first edition of 'Winter' (1726), and adapted it to close 'Autumn' (1235–373).

Georgic also offered a model for exploring the relationships between causes and effects in form and structure. Milton's georgic Plowman, standing doubting before his waving fields, is inserted to illustrate Satan and the angels' uncertainty about the result of their potential combat, although this is undermined by both the proleptic nature of the simile and the subsequent appearance of Libra, placed in the sky by God to foretell the determined outcome should they engage. Georgic allows Milton to do this because it occupies a present that is poised on the brink of multiple hypothetical futures. Georgic is 'ever on the move', as David Fairer puts it, 'responding to local conditions, shifts in the weather, and difficulties and predations of various kinds; it is a world in process whose rewards are hard won'.[34] But it proceeds through that process in isolated moments of seeming stasis, like the moment at which Milton's Plowman 'doubting stands', from which the farmer or narrator faces various hypothetical futures. Georgic takes its energy, its forward momentum through the cycle in acts of attempted control, from the perpetual possibility of surprise, and nature's capacity to diverge from what is predicted. As Fairer notes, unlike 'the repetitions of pastoral . . . georgic's routines are seldom free of specific pressures and constraints: new challenges and disturbing contingencies are always waiting to disrupt the pulse of life'.[35] The action of the georgic labourer is based on past experience, but the georgic world itself is spontaneous and surprising. 'Let him forecast his Work with timely care', writes Dryden a few lines after the storm scene, choosing a significant word with no direct correlation in Virgil's passage (I.352). The labourer must fore*cast*, but not fore*know* the results of his labour: 'A thousand Accidents the Farmer's Hopes / Subvert, or cheque; uncertain all his Toil.'[36]

This articulation (in both senses of that word) of time as a series of distinct moments of presentness is exemplified by the moving 'now' of georgic. Book 2 of John Philips's *Cyder* (1708) moves from 'Learn now' (162), to 'And now' (315), to 'Now also' (329), to end on another 'And now' (645). William Somervile's *The Chace* (1735) has multiple 'nows', among them 'Now golden Autumn' (II.51), 'All now is free as Air' (II.57), 'Now gently put her off' (II.147), 'Now the poor Chace / Begins to flag' (II.258–9), 'All now is joy' (II.292), 'Now the loud trumpet sounds a charge' (II.473), and so on.[37] On the one hand, these 'nows' signify a progressive narrative, each new 'now' following naturally and seemingly inevitably from the last. On the other, they mark each moment as distinct. They can as easily be read not as a continuous process, but as a series of separate hypothetical futures, imagined from the perspective of the farmer waiting for the outcome of his labours, or of the poet writing in his study.

We see this combination of process and stasis near the opening of 'Spring', when Thomson articulates a series of moments of suspension within the moving cycle, developing a perspective that is limited to the present, but which can forecast (but not foreknow) the future.

> FORTH fly the tepid Airs; and unconfin'd,
> Unbinding Earth, the moving Softness strays.
> Joyous, th' impatient Husbandman perceives
> Relenting Nature, and his lusty Steers

> Drives from their Stalls, to where the well-us'd Plow
> Lies in the Furrow, loosen'd from the Frost.
> . . .
> Meanwhile, incumbent o'er the shining Share,
> The Master leans, removes th' obstructing Clay,
> Winds the whole Work, and sidelong lays the Glebe.
>
>   WHITE, thro' the neighbouring Fields the Sower Stalks,
> With measur'd Step, and liberal throws the Grain
> Into the faithful Bosom of the Ground.
> The Harrow follows harsh, and shuts the Scene.
> (Sp.32–47)

These lines are an adaptation of a passage in Virgil, and seem to make particular use of some of the language in Dryden's translation:

> While yet the Spring is young, while Earth unbinds
> Her frozen Bosom to the Western Winds;
> While Mountain Snows dissolve against the Sun,
> And Streams, yet new, from Precipices run.
> Ev'n in this early Dawning of the Year,
> Produce the Plough, and yoke the sturdy Steer,
> And goad him till he groans beneath his Toil,
> 'Till the bright Share is bury'd in the Soil.
> That Crop rewards the greedy Peasant's Pains,
> Which twice the Sun, and twice the Cold sustains,
> And bursts the crowded Barns, with more than promis'd Gains.
> But e're we stir the yet unbroken Ground,
> The various Course of Seasons must be found . . .
> (I.64–76)

Virgil's original passage used the future conditional tense, describing when he, the speaker, would have the bull plough, but Dryden translates this into the dominant georgic tense of conditional imperative. In both cases the passage describes a hypothetical present, and it is followed by a hypothetical successful future of 'crowded Barns', available if the peasant is patient enough to allow two years' growth. But then the poem draws back to that moment of poise or pause: the ground is 'yet unbroken' ('ignotum . . . aequor' in the Latin, or 'unknown ground' before it is cut).

Thomson's version of the passage includes the same sense of an ongoing process of nature's 'relenting', 'unbinding', 'moving', the sense of motion and growth for which his poem has been celebrated; he also incorporates a sense of the past in the image of the 'well-us'd Plow'. But Thomson has not only borrowed Virgil's imagery of natural processes.

As Milton did in his Plowman simile, Thomson borrows Virgil's closing off of the present into a distinct poised moment, from which the future is 'yet' unknown. Thomson's human figures appear relatively undistracted by anticipations of the autumn harvest – his husbandman is 'impatient', but seemingly only to get ploughing, not for those crowded barns. Both scenes of ploughing and sowing are closed into self-containment: 'Winds the whole Work, and sidelong lays the Glebe', 'The Harrow follows harsh, and shuts the Scene.' This kind of pictorial framing has led critics such as John Barrell, Nick Groom, and Michael Genovese to criticise Thomson's version of georgic as removed from the harsh reality and risk of agricultural work; he is a gentleman observer without investment in the outcome of the labour he describes: the distant narrator of a prospect poem rather than a real georgic labourer.[38] Without defending the social philosophy of *The Seasons*, I suggest that this impulse to 'shut the Scene' emerges not (only) from a desire to avoid the less picturesque elements of georgic work, but from a view of time that is fundamentally georgic, in that it draws a line between the experienced present and the unknown future.

In the cycle of agricultural work, of course, no work is ever truly 'wound up'. As Stephen Duck points out in *The Thresher's Labour* (published in 1730, the same year as the full *Seasons*), if the labourers 'think no toils to come, nor mind the past',

> the next Morning soon reveals the Cheat,
> When the same toils we must again repeat,
> To the same Barns again must back return,
> To labour there for room for next year's Corn.[39]

Or as Thomson put it, 'with to-morrow's Sun, their annual Toil / Begins again the never-ceasing Round' (Au.1233–4). Ploughing and sowing are followed by a harvest, whether good or bad, and the labour that accompanies it. To separate in causal terms the acts of ploughing and sowing from the harvest is to render them literally fruitless. But there must be temporal separation in order to perceive the potential risk that is central to georgic. The scene is 'shut' here in 'Spring' in order to articulate the same state of present unknowing as that in which Milton's Plowman stands in Book 4, and Virgil's narrator stands before the 'yet unbroken Ground': looking forward, but unable to do more than hope for good conditions and a good harvest. Thomson continues:

> BE gracious, HEAVEN! for now laborious Man
> Has done his Part. Ye fostering Breezes blow!

> Ye softening Dews, ye tender Showers, descend!
> And temper All, thou world-reviving Sun,
> Into the perfect Year!
> (Sp.48–52)

Here, as frequently in *The Seasons*, 'Heaven' refers both to the ultimate first cause whose 'grace' is stated as the requirement for a good harvest, and to the secondary causes of weather and climate listed in the lines that follow. Thomson does not attempt to predict the results of this labour as explicitly as Virgil does; instead, he moves on to a reflection of the worthiness of the plough as a theme, such as 'the rural MARO sung' (55). Several lines later he invites Britons to 'Let AUTUMN spread his Treasures to the Sun' (67), but there is no suggestion of a causal relationship to the scene of ploughing and sowing that we have just read. That 'Scene' was 'shut'.

However, this time in 'Spring' lingers in the memory and perhaps in its actual physical effects, when in 'Autumn' we return to a similar georgic scene at a different point in the seasonal cycle:

> Before the ripen'd Field the Reapers stand
> ...
> Behind the Master walks, builds up the Shocks;
> And, conscious, glancing oft on every Side
> His sated Eye, feels his Heart heave with Joy.
> (153–64)

Clearly this is a partner piece to the ploughing and sowing scene of 'Spring', with perhaps the same 'Master' following behind. And like that passage, the scene is followed later by a religious inversion and a moral reflection on the pride of the rich. But any causal connection drawn with the passage in 'Spring' is, possibly, the stuff of imagination only. This harvest is just one of the possible potential futures that was forecast in that time. 'Spring' looks forward to a harvest, but perhaps not this harvest, which could be occurring elsewhere, years later, or even years before. 'Autumn' carries the memories of ploughing and sowing, but perhaps not that ploughing and sowing we saw in 'Spring'. In this way the autumnal scene appears as the product of labour in spring, but also strangely divorced from any particular knowable spring.

While Thomson's harvest passage seems to be defining itself against Milton's Plowman scene in its comparative complacency, like the Plowman scene it is a version of that sudden storm passage in *The Georgics* when Virgil reminds us that even this moment of harvest only appears to be 'secure of Fear'. Virgil describes the moment, or moments, 'Ev'n while the Reaper fills his greedy Hands', that a sudden storm can arise and destroy the crops. This possibility is coded in Thomson's poem in the lines that follow the reaping scene, acknowledging other possible outcomes in other years in the form of a moral reflection on charity:

> Think, oh grateful think!
> How good the GOD of HARVEST is to you
> . . . The various Turns
> Of Fortune ponder; that your Sons may want
> What now, with hard Reluctance, faint, ye give.
> (169–76)

The usual causal correspondence between sowing and harvesting, the reassuring cyclical process represented by agricultural work and celebrated in the earlier claim that 'ALL is the Gift of INDUSTRY' (141), is undermined by the presence of God in both of these episodes from 'Spring' and 'Autumn': while labour is a necessary precondition for a good harvest, it seems that God has the ultimate say. But we also see in these passages the difference in the role that God plays in Thomson's poem compared with Milton's. In 'Spring', the invocation 'BE gracious, HEAVEN!' momentarily unsettles the causal and affective power we can read into the labour depicted previously. But there is some room for manoeuvre in that, in *The Seasons* generally, Thomson's God signifies not certainty but uncertainty, which is the more georgic perspective. Here in 'Autumn' the God of harvest is arbitrary. We are told how good he 'is' at this present time, not how good he was or will be at another time. There is no suggestion that charity will be rewarded by a good harvest, only the faint possibility that it may encourage future charity in return. God is introduced to limit our sense of human autonomy in the face of the 'various Turns / Of Fortune', but in such a way as to give value to industry rather than undermining it. Unlike Adam and Eve working for the sake of it in Eden, these labourers cannot foreknow what storms or floods God (or Nature) will send between the time of sowing and the time of harvest, so they must work harder to store up against catastrophe.

By rendering ambiguous the relation between the ploughing/sowing scene in 'Spring' and the harvest scene in 'Autumn', Thomson is able to suggest that it is God's spontaneous intervention that produces the harvest in autumn, *and* that nature's bounty is the result of a combination of natural and cultural causes: favourable weather and good farming. Fairer may be correct in his assertion that 'Being simultaneously a georgic and a deistical theodicy, Thomson's *Seasons* is characterised by a tension between daily human necessities and the divine scheme', but Thomson manages to elide that tension because theodicy and determinism are constantly counterbalanced by the possible impact of 'secondary causes' including human (and animal) industry.[40] This coexistence of first and secondary causes may account for the critical disagreement over the centrality of God to *The Seasons*. For Blanford Parker, 'The least important and the least representative qualities in Thomson are those of moral generalisation, classical abstraction and Christian theodicy. The existence of organic and moralising elements points in the end to the inefficacy of teleological morality in an empirical poem.'[41] Dustin Griffin claims that 'Few readers of *The Seasons* would claim that the theodicean element is more than intermittently present'.[42] But there have of course been many readers who have argued for the centrality and importance of God to *The Seasons* as a 'unifying' force, among them Patricia Meyer Spacks, Ralph Cohen, Richard Terry and John Sitter.[43] In Thomson's georgic scheme, God is perpetually present as a first cause who may also be intervening at every moment to bring about the events of the present; but at every moment he is also perpetually deferred behind endless possible secondary causes. As in *Paradise Lost*, he is both present and absent in every human action and in every natural occurrence.

The Coming of Spring

It is one thing to argue that the temporal and therefore causal relation between 'Spring' and 'Autumn' is unsettled in Thomson's georgic scenes. After all, these books are separated by hundreds of lines. But Thomson also experiments with the same effect locally, too, at the scale of lines within a single scene. By rendering the relationship between individual events ambiguous, Thomson is able to depict flowing, continuous processes in which moments follow others in succession, but also a disjointed series of images that may exist simultaneously or may be separated from one another by longer stretches of time. This is not only the case in passages with overtly georgic themes, but in his passages of natural description. The ploughing and sowing scene in 'Spring' is itself the culmination of, as well as a sudden shift from, a series of images of the coming of Spring that opens the poem, and the strange temporality of motion and stillness is established in these opening lines before Thomson then makes the clear association with the georgic genre.

At the opening of *The Seasons*, nature's processes seem to be both present and future:

> COME, gentle SPRING, Etherial Mildness, come,
> And from the Bosom of yon dropping Cloud,
> While Music wakes around, veil'd in a Shower
> Of shadowing Roses, on our Plains descend.
> (Sp.1–4)

This opening is an odal invocation to a personified Spring, and therefore occupies the temporality of lyric: a suspended moment of utterance. Motion is registered as it is in a landscape painting, by its signs and effects in a single moment (we can perceive even in a single moment that a cloud is in the process of 'dropping', for example, if it appears low and dark over the land). But these lines also invite the reader to visualise the literal natural event onto which Thomson has superimposed the personified Spring: the descent of rain from 'yon dropping Cloud'. For Thomson, a natural event like rainfall is a process occurring over time, each component falling naturally in succession as it is brought about by the previous, as well as a series of disjointed phenomena that can occur simultaneously and therefore separately.

To convey this dual temporality, Thomson makes it impossible to define the temporal relation between the time in which the cloud is 'dropping', and the times in which spring is 'coming' and 'descending'. These times are shown to be both successive and simultaneous, both momentary and possessed of duration. The entreaties 'Come' and 'descend' are already temporally ambiguous. On the one hand, they look forward to a future coming and descent; on the other, they may be beseeching Spring to continue coming and descending, rather than to begin. After all, at the instant that Thomson entreats Spring to 'come', 'Spring' the poem has already begun. That is, it may already be raining, and Thomson is not so much thinking of the future as describing the present. In either case, these lines could be describing a process over time – from the moment of Thomson perceiving the coming of Spring, to that of 'yon dropping Cloud', to that of the rain descending – or it could describe a single moment in which these actions are simultaneous – Spring comes as the rain descends from the cloud as it drops.

Certainly the (quite literal) line between the dropping and the descending is ambiguous. 'While Music wakes around' suggests both possibilities, that the descending follows the dropping in time or that it occurs at the same time. This adverbial phrase has a zeugmatic dual reference. Grammatically, it modifies Spring's descent, but the music might also be waking 'while' the cloud is dropping. If the 'while' looks in both directions, then the dropping and descending may be temporally continuous (that is, the duration of the music's waking extends through time to cover both times) or they may be temporally simultaneous, both occurring in one present 'While Music wakes'. One of Thomson's eighteenth-century commentators, John More, pointed out a further temporal disorientation in these opening lines: the roses are imagined at the beginning of spring, but these flowers 'are not certainly quite so early in our island'.[44] Not only do these lines imagine roses unnaturally early in the season, they even appear simultaneously with, if not before, the rainfall that would allow them to grow and blossom.

As the poem moves on to an address to the Countess of Hertford, it is still not clear whether what we see are successive stages in the process as spring progresses in its coming, or whether we remain in the same liminal moment, registering the effects of movement and change on the present scene but not actually perceiving movement and change in the temporal dimension. As Cohen points out, 'The poet does not connect the two formal addresses' to Spring and Hertford, 'but they are joined analogically'.[45] As Jung puts it, Thomson's 'desire to approach the season from a multi-dimensional perspective that explored spring both spatially and temporally, as well as associatively' results in a 'lack of subordination of some parts to others . . . reflected in the imbalance between description and self-conscious address. Discourses exist next to each other but are not clearly related to each other.'[46]

Thomson goes on:

> AND see where surly WINTER passes off,
> Far to the North, and calls his ruffian Blasts:
> His Blasts obey, and quit the howling Hill,
> The shatter'd Forest, and the ravag'd Vale;
> While softer Gales succeed, at whose kind Touch,
> Dissolving Snows in livid Torrents lost,
> The Mountains lift their green Heads to the Sky.
> (Sp.11–17)

As in the previous verse, it is possible to read these lines in two ways. We can read them as the expression of a movement through time, from the period when 'Winter passes off' through that when 'softer gales succeed', and finally when the snows have disappeared from the mountaintops. This reading perceives the mountains lifting their green heads *after* the snows have been 'lost'; there has been a passage of time between the present-tense 'Dissolving' and the present-tense 'lift'. But as Parker notes, 'the direction of Thomson's mind is always toward a greater and greater elaboration of the spatial view'.[47] The lines, as well as seeming to describe a process over time, describe a movement across space, from hill to mountain to marsh, and the introduction of this dimension makes it possible that the eye is perceiving different elements of an extended landscape that exist at one single moment, its wide perspective made possible by an implied prospect view position. Hence Albert Cook's summary of Thomson's natural description as an 'act of picturing a single scene, as though Thomson were fulfilling a contract for a landscape that could be hung'.[48] Hertford's eye is invited to perceive not 'when' winter passes off, but 'where', and as with the dropping cloud Thomson turns this temporal movement into a spatial one, with winter moving not into the past but 'Far to the north'. The passing off of winter may be perceived in an instant: 'surly Winter' at the brink of disappearance. Winter's call to his 'blasts', and their obedience and exit may be a linear process of before-and-after, or it may be a call similar to 'Come' in the first line of 'Spring': simultaneous with the obeying. Equally we may perceive the 'softer gales' succeeding 'while' winter is still in the process of passing off – the two are, for a moment, simultaneous. The 'Dissolving snows', though 'lost', may be being lost rather than already lost; there is a point, after all, when the green heads are visible even while snow is still pouring away. This sense of instantaneous simultaneity is enhanced when we read these lines against their source in Virgil. The two lines that led into the ploughing scene were rendered by Dryden as 'While Mountain Snows dissolve against the Sun, / And Streams, yet new, from Precipices run', and in the Latin is even further condensed into a single image, 'gelidus canis cum montibus umor / liquitur', or 'when from snowy peaks the run-off / flows'.[49]

We can also compare Thomson's ambiguous renderings of temporal and spatial relations with the clearly defined transitions in *The Excursion* (1728), by Thomson's friend David Mallet. In Book 1 Mallet covers very similar ground to Thomson, describing scenes of nature over the course of a summer's day, but there is a striking difference in technique. Mallet is careful to distinguish between his temporal and spatial movement. The first half of Book 1 is dominated by his rapid progress through the passing day, far quicker than Thomson's equivalent progress in 'Summer'; Mallet scarcely pauses to register the spatial expansion of the scene. Then in the second half of the Book, once night has been reached, he turns from nature's variation over time to its variation over space, and uses spatial markers to make explicit the dimension in which he is now moving: 'Far on the Left', 'Behind me', 'at near Distance'.[50] There is a comparison of British and foreign scenes, by which point the temporal narrative of the passing day has receded entirely. In the light of Mallet's very different treatment of time and space in his otherwise similar long poem of natural description, Thomson's habit of blending temporal and spatial movement within single passages and images appears to be a positive method rather than a lack of clarity or symptom of haphazardness.

As 'Spring' continues, the spatial and temporal organisation of the scene remains ambiguous.

>   AS yet the trembling Year is unconfirm'd,
>   And WINTER oft at Eve resumes the Breeze,
>   Chills the pale Morn, and bids his driving Sleets
>   Deform the Day delightless: so that scarce
>   The Bittern knows his Time, with Bill ingulpht,
>   To shake the sounding Marsh; or from the Shore
>   The Plovers when to scatter o'er the Heath,
>   And sing their wild Notes to the listening Waste.
>   (Sp.18–25)

We have just read a description of Winter passing, but here he 'resumes the Breeze'. This may mean simply that he has returned, or, more disturbingly, it may mean that the previous lines didn't necessarily occur before these in time. The eves and morns described here could occur before winter appears again to pass off, or they could occur simultaneously with that scene, since we have relocated from the hills and mountains to the marsh and waste. At this point in the unconfirmed year, this scene and the previous one of winter's passing off occur and reoccur in cycles. The birds share the reader's confusion over whether winter has passed, is passing, or is yet to pass. Thus, Thomson makes it impossible for the reader to locate the point at which one present 'shades' into the next and becomes a new moment; at least until the next verse paragraph:

>   AT last from *Aries* rolls the bounteous Sun,
>   And the bright *Bull* receives him. Then no more
>   Th' expansive Atmosphere is cramp'd with Cold;
>   But, full of Life and vivifying Soul,
>   Lifts the light Clouds sublime, and spreads them thin,
>   Fleecy, and white, o'er all-surrounding Heaven.
>   (Sp.26–31)

'At last ... Then no more' marks a decisive break in time, as the sun has moved from Aries to Taurus. It is a turning point, a new moment when the dropping clouds reverse their motion and begin to lift. But the strange temporality of the previous lines has implications for the way we read this transition too. We can easily read this 'At last' as the next stage in the gradual process of spring's coming; now spring is arrived and confirmed. But, again, Thomson disrupts this flowing movement of time by offering an alternative possibility. The preceding description of spring's coming may be understood as a time of development leading towards this point; or it may appear as a single, stationary moment, or a collection of disparate moments, with change registered not through time but across space. If the former, the entire passage is a continuous process through time, from winter's passing off to the confirmation of spring. If the latter, then the transition from the moment when 'the trembling year is unconfirm'd' to the time 'At last' is not a gradual, organic development but a sudden and inexplicable leap forward, and this new moment 'At last' loses its dependence upon the previous moment described in lines 1–25. Like Milton's slippery use of 'Till' at IV.40, which I analysed in Chapter 1, Thomson's 'At last' is one of those connectives of questionable signification that he uses frequently to obscure the temporal and logical connection between passages in his poem. The complexity of others such as 'while', 'or', 'hence', and of course the georgic 'now', has been discussed extensively by critics.[51] Like these words, here 'At last' works to assert continuity and discontinuity simultaneously.

Why would Thomson create this effect? He does so to make an important point about cyclical time, in which there is no 'At last' and in which winter's cold is never 'no more'. This new time may occur at a specific point in the cycle, the start of spring, but it can occur at any iteration of the cycle. By suggesting that this moment might be discontinuous with the moment described in the preceding lines, Thomson emphasises that the two could be the descriptions of entirely separate years; the scene that occurs 'At last' may even have happened *before* the scene preceding it in Thomson's poem. By scrambling the causal timeline, Thomson hints at the gradual processes of secondary causes, but also at the possibility of other causes intervening, which were not perceived in the moments before. The introduction of 'Heaven' at the end of the passage hints at the first cause that may have introduced 'Life and vivifying Soul' to the atmosphere from seemingly nowhere. On the other hand, 'Atmosphere' was a scientific term coined only around a century earlier, and was widely thought of as a sphere in which multiple secondary causes worked in ways unknown to humans, a sphere 'where we see Effects but cannot reach their Causes', in Defoe's words. This moment in spring appears as the inevitable culmination of winter's gradual passing off in the previous lines. But it also appears as, in Boyle's words, 'incompleatly knowable' by those moments that precede it, since those that precede it are themselves an incoherent collection of disparate and interchangeable events.

These lines are followed by the overtly georgic scene of ploughing and sowing, but this opening to 'Spring' already establishes a georgic temporality, in which we are invited to 'trace the secret Cause' but also to accept our inability to fully understand the causal relationships between different elements in nature. Given the ways in which Thomson disorders the sense of continuity and succession in these opening verses, I think it fitting that I have discussed them out of order, beginning with the georgic scene of sowing and only then turning back to the 'coming' of Spring: after all, that scene of sowing can occur only after winter passes off within the seasonal cycle, but it has occurred many times before any particular scene of winter passing off that Thomson and the Countess of Hertford might behold.

Loosening the 'Train' of 'Shade ... softening into Shade', counterbalancing the impression that the poem gives of nature in constant, continuous movement by seeming simultaneously to present scenes of self-contained presence, Thomson can emphasise the non-linearity and repetitiveness of cyclical time, in which each iteration of the cycle has the potential to be different. Holding a moment still, and then questioning its causal relation with the next or preceding moment, Thomson retains the possibility that the present moment was brought about not by the lines that preceded it, but by God's immediate intervention *or* by multiple hidden secondary causes. As I discuss in the next two chapters, Thomson managed the structure of his long poem in order to reflect this paradoxical combination of continuous process and momentary stasis, by writing a poem in which 'no one can guess what incongruity is coming next'.[52]

Notes

1. Dustin Griffin, *Regaining Paradise: Milton and the Eighteenth Century* (Cambridge: Cambridge UP, 1986), 179.
2. David Reid, 'Thomson's Poetry of Reverie and Milton', *SEL* 43 (2003): 667–82 (667).
3. Sandro Jung and Kwinten Van De Walle, ed. *The Genres of Thomson's The Seasons* (Bethlehem: Lehigh UP, 2018).

4. Eric Gidal, 'Prospect and Form in the Eighteenth-Century Progress Poem', *Ricerche di Storia dell'arte* 72 (2000): 21–8 (23). Ingrid Horrocks, '"Circling Eye" and "Houseless Stranger": The New Eighteenth-Century Wanderer (Thomson to Goldsmith)', *ELH* 77.3 (2010): 665–87 (668).
5. W. B. Hutchings, '"Can Pure Description Hold the Place of Sense?": Thomson's Landscape Poetry', in *James Thomson: Essays for the Tercentenary*, ed. Richard Terry (Liverpool: Liverpool UP, 2000), 35–66 (45).
6. Ralph Cohen, *The Unfolding of The Seasons* (Baltimore: Johns Hopkins University Press, 1970), 19.
7. Ibid., 19–20.
8. See for example R. D. Havens, 'Primitivism and the Idea of Progress in Thomson', *Studies in Philology* 29.1 (1932): 41–52; and William Levine, 'Collins, Thomson, and the Whig Progress of Liberty', *Studies in English Literature, 1500–1900* 34.4 (1994): 553–77.
9. For a reappraisal of Whig history see, for example, Annabel Patterson, *Nobody's Perfect: A New Whig Interpretation of History* (New Haven and London: Yale UP, 2002); on the complexities of Thomson's Whiggism see Philip Connell, 'Newtonian physico-theology and the varieties of Whiggism in James Thomson's *The Seasons*, *Huntington Library Quarterly* 72.1 (2009): 1–28 (4), and Dustin Griffin, *Patriotism and Poetry in Eighteenth-Century Britain* (Cambridge: Cambridge UP, 2002), chapter 3.
10. Kevis Goodman, *Georgic Modernity and British Romanticism: Poetry and the Mediation of History* (Cambridge: Cambridge UP, 2004), 64.
11. Ibid., 41.
12. Ibid., 60.
13. Sitter, *Literary Loneliness*, 91.
14. Isaac Newton, *Philosophiae Naturalis Principia Mathematica*, trans. I. Bernard Cohen and Anne Whitman (Berkeley: University of California Press, 1999), 410.
15. Grant, *Beating Time*, 93.
16. Newton, *Principia*, 408.
17. James Thomson, *Liberty, The Castle of Indolence, and Other Poems*, ed. James Sambrook (Oxford: Oxford UP, 1986), 11. Subsequent references to Thomson's poem on Newton are to this edition.
18. Walter Keith Thomas and Warren U. Ober, *A Mind for Ever Voyaging: Wordsworth at Work Portraying Newton and Science* (Edmonton: University of Alberta Press, 1989), 108.
19. Marjorie Hope Nicolson, *Newton Demands the Muse: Newton's Opticks and the Eighteenth-Century Poets* (Princeton: Princeton UP, 1946).
20. Connell, 'Newtonian physico-theology'.
21. Courtney Weiss Smith, *Empiricist Devotions: Science, Religion, and Poetry in Early Eighteenth-Century England* (Charlottesville: University of Virginia Press, 2016), 78–90.
22. For a thorough account of the controversy, see Walter Ott, *Causation and the Laws of Nature in Early Modern Philosophy* (Oxford: Oxford UP, 2009), and for Boyle's ambiguous position pp. 152–6.

23. Edward Young, *Night Thoughts on Life, Death, and Immortality* (London: William Tegg & Co., 1859), 328; William Cowper, *The Poems of William Cowper*, 242.
24. Smith, *Empiricist Devotions*, 90.
25. Isaac Newton, *The Opticks* (New York: Dover, 1979), 369.
26. Defoe, *The Storm*, 11–12.
27. Robert Boyle, *The Works of the Honourable Robert Boyle*, 5 vols (London: A. Millar, 1744), iii, 428.
28. Sean Silver, 'Contingency in Philosophy and History, 1650–1800', *Textual Practice* 32.3 (2018): 419–36.
29. Alan Dugald McKillop discusses the contemporary debates around the origin of river water and the nature of frost in *The Background of Thomson's Seasons* (Minneapolis: University of Minnesota Press, 1942), 77–85 and 60–1.
30. Young, *Night Thoughts*, 18.
31. Rachel Crawford, 'English Georgic and British Nationhood', *ELH* 65 (1998): 123–58 (126).
32. Alfred Sjödin, 'The European Georgic and the Politics of Genre: Johan Gabriel Oxenstierna and *The Seasons* in Sweden', in *Genres*, ed. Jung and Van De Walle, 185–99 (187).
33. Juan Christian Pellicer, 'The Articulation of Genre in *The Seasons*', in *Genres*, ed. Jung and Van De Walle, 119–35 (121).
34. David Fairer, 'The Pastoral-georgic Tradition', in *William Wordsworth in Context*, ed. Andrew Bennett (Cambridge: Cambridge UP, 2015), 111–18 (111).
35. David Fairer, '"The Year Runs Round": The Poetry of Work in Eighteenth-Century England', in *Ritual, Routine, and Regime: Repetition in Early Modern British and European Cultures*, ed. Lorna Clymer (Toronto: University of Toronto Press, 2006): 153–71 (163–4).
36. John Philips, *Cyder. A Poem in Two Books* (London: Jacob Tonson, 1708), II.46–7.
37. William Somervile, *The Chace, a Poem* (1735) (London: G. Hawkins, 1749), *Literature Online*, 25, 26, 30, 35, 36, 45 [accessed 18 July 2015].
38. John Barrell, *English Literature in History*, 61, and *The Idea of Landscape and the Sense of Place 1730–1840* (Cambridge: Cambridge UP, 1972), 58–9; Nick Groom, *The Seasons: An Elegy for the Passing of the Year* (London: Atlantic, 2013), 221; Michael Genovese, 'An Organic Commerce: Sociable Selfhood in Eighteenth-Century Georgic', *Eighteenth-Century Studies* 46 (2013): 197–221 (205).
39. Stephen Duck, *The Thresher's Labour*, ed. E. P. Thompson and Marian Sugden (London: Merlin Press, 1989), 11.
40. Fairer, 'The Year Runs Round', 162–3.
41. Blanford Parker, *The Triumph of Augustan Poetics* (Cambridge: Cambridge UP, 1998), 159.

42. Griffin, *Regaining Paradise*, 190.
43. Patricia Meyer Spacks, *The Varied God: A Critical Study of Thomson's The Seasons* (Berkeley: University of California Press, 1959); Cohen, *Unfolding*; Richard Terry, '"Through Nature shedding influence malign": Thomson's *The Seasons* as a Theodicy', *Durham University Journal* 87 (1995): 257–68; John Sitter, 'Eighteenth-century Ecological Poetry and Ecotheology', *Religion and Literature* 40.1 (2008): 11–37. Although these critics disagree over the extent to which the poet can share in God's harmonising vision, they all argue for the importance of *the idea* of this vision to the poem. Spacks uses 'unifying' on p. 40, Cohen on p. 3, and Terry on p. 267.
44. John More, *Strictures, Critical and Sentimental, on Thomson's Seasons* (London: Richardson and Urquhart, 1777), 34. On the identity of More see Ralph Cohen, *The Art of Discrimination: Thomson's The Seasons and the Language of Criticism* (London: Routledge & Kegan Paul, 1964), Appendix II, 508–12.
45. Cohen, *Unfolding*, 12.
46. Sandro Jung, 'Epic, Ode, or Something New: The Blending of Genres in Thomson's *Spring*', *Papers on Language and Literature* 43.2 (2007): 146–65 (161).
47. Parker, *Triumph of Augustan Poetics*, 148.
48. Albert Cook, 'The Transformation of "Point": Amplitude in Wordsworth, Whitman, and Rimbaud', *Studies in Romanticism* 30.2 (Summer 1991): 169–88 (180).
49. Virgil, *The Georgics: A Poem of the Land*, trans. Kimberly Johnson (London: Penguin, 2009), 6–7.
50. David Mallet, *The Excursion. A Poem. In Two Books* (London: J. Walthoe, 1728), 22, 23, 26.
51. For example: John Dixon Hunt discusses 'while' in *The Figure in the Landscape* (Baltimore: Johns Hopkins UP, 1976), 106; David Reid discusses both Thomson and Milton's use of 'or' in 'Thomson's Poetry', 673; I have discussed 'hence' in 'The Golden Age and Iron Times: Pastoral and Georgic in "Spring"', in Jung and Van De Walle ed. *Genres*, 139–63 (156–7); Cohen discusses the use of 'now' in 'Winter', *Unfolding*, 249, and Christopher R. Miller discusses its difference from 'then' in 'The Lyric Self in *The Seasons*', in Jung and Van De Walle ed. *Genres*, 61–81 (70).
52. Bonamy Dobrée, *English Literature in the Early Eighteenth Century, 1700–1740* (Oxford: Oxford UP, 1959, repr. 1968), 484.

Chapter 5

The Broken Scene: Thomson's Tales

Nature possesses variety both spatially and temporally, which allows Thomson to obscure the dimension in which he is moving, rendering the temporal relation between the elements of nature that he describes ambiguous. In spite of *The Seasons'* important status as a non-narrative long poem, however, it does contain passages that more overtly embrace narrative and therefore seem to depend upon a linear timeline of before-and-after, and to depict a process that is clearly a movement from one point in time to another rather than (though sometimes in addition to) across space. In this chapter I will examine those parts of *The Seasons* that do appear to depend on narrative time. I look first at the interpolated tales, the stories of people undergoing change, and then in more detail at one specific tale, the Damon and Musidora piece in 'Summer'.[1] I show how it encouraged its own reception – in the form of illustrations, adaptations and even authorial revisions – as a collection of isolated images as well as an unfolding narrative. The poem contains other depictions of its own processes of inspiration and composition, too, which I examine in the final section of this chapter. As we will see, even in these seemingly narrative or quasi-narrative parts of the poem, the onward progression of time is complicated by pauses and returns, so that identifying where the change, turn or development occurs is more difficult than it first appears. Thomson develops a picturesque treatment of narrative in order to accommodate sentimental tales within *The Seasons* without affront to his non-narrative form.

The most obviously narrative parts of the poem are the interpolated tales; Celadon and Amelia (Su.1169–222), Damon and Musidora (Su.1269–370), and Palemon and Lavinia (Au.177–310) are the most extended narratives, but there are also the miniature tales, such as those of the man struck by lightning ([1727] Su.771–87), the desert caravan covered by a sandstorm (Su.959–79), the horseman in the bog (Au.1145–64) and the swain frozen to death (Wi.276–321). It is necessary to address these to see how they fit into Thomson's conception of cyclical time, in which no moment can truly be said to come 'before' or 'after'. Even in these moving narratives, Thomson finds ways to hint at the isolation of each moment. For all their overt emphasis on movement through time, upon closer analysis these tales do not function so differently from the passage that opens 'Spring', in which the sense of continuous flowing through time is counterbalanced by the possibility that we are reading the description of one extended moment followed ('At last') by another moment, whose precise relation to the former is unclear.

Each narrative tells a story that takes place over time, and involves a change that is a point of no return: death, declaration or discovery. Such moments of schism clearly distinguish past from future and cannot be rendered simultaneous. Time must be apprehended in its successive chronological shape. However, the point of no return – like the 'At last' in the opening of 'Spring' – itself frequently possesses an ambiguous relation to what precedes or follows it. This is clearest in the cases where the turning point is derived not from human activity but from natural causes, such as the lightning bolt that kills Amelia, the snowstorm that freezes the shepherd, the sandstorm that covers the caravan or the will-o'-the-wisp that leads the horseman astray in the bog. As Thomson makes clear in the Amelia episode, such events may be forecast but cannot be foreknown. They are random, even more so than the strange gusts of wind that blow through *Paradise Lost*, which as I suggested in Chapter 2 do contain hints of ethical determinism. In *The Seasons*' stories, 'not always on the guilty Head / Falls the devoted Flash' (Su.1170–1). The Amelia episode in particular disturbs Jonathan Bate's over-simplification that 'Thomson celebrated the variety of the seasons, but the thrust of his argument was that the weather itself has a fundamental order, a concord in its discord; disorder resided in the morality of the observer and was accordingly a matter of human agency'.[2] By 1730, Thomson had removed a passage preceding the Celadon and Amelia episode that related lightning too explicitly to the will and justice of God.

This randomness means that, within each tale, there is a point before the crisis when the outcome remains unknown; this is the georgic present that I outlined in the previous chapter. There is a gap, inexplicable and inexpressible, between the moment when Celadon finishes speaking – '"'Tis Safety to be near thee sure, and thus / To clasp Perfection!"' (1213–14) – and the moment when

Amelia is struck – 'From his void Embrace, / (Mysterious Heaven!) that moment, to the Ground, / A blacken'd Corse, was struck the beauteous Maid' (1214–16). The narrative leading up to this point has been progressive, as we are shown 'The succession of the lovers' different mental states (anxiety, terror, reassurance)', but even these are distinct enough to be held apart, as Jung holds them here.[3] Jung characterises the structure of the tales as follows: 'The progressive structure of the narrative . . . culminates in the observer's arrested gaze.'[4] It is indeed possible to read the Celadon and Amelia tale as a progressive narrative leading up to the point of petrification. But as well as a continuous process ending in a single frozen moment, it is also possible to read each of the tales as a series of frozen moments of 'arrested gaze', which have only an arbitrary connection with one another. The moment before the lightning strikes Amelia, the instant in which Celadon clasps Amelia 'thus', is a moment of still pause as surely as the moment afterwards. And the 'evil Hour' (1190) in which the entire narrative takes place – the phrase, of course, taken from Milton's description of the Fall of Eve (*PL*, IX.780) – in turn separates the time of the walk from the time before it. Katarina Stenke writes, 'In a sense, the "evil Hour" signals the start of the narrative, just as Adam and Eve's expulsion from Eden initiates postlapsarian history. However, it also interrupts or "ruffles" a smoothly flowing stream of earlier experience.'[5] The period of Celadon and Amelia's walk before the lightning strikes is described by Thomson as an 'eternal *Eden*' (1194), which the eighteenth-century commentator John Scott complained was ridiculous: 'It was surely . . . a glaring oversight, to call a momentary scene of delight an "*eternal*" Eden.'[6] But within Thomson's georgic temporality, the 'momentary' picturesque present might feel 'eternal' to those who dwell within it, as they feel the passage of time slow down and pause in their absorption in one another and the world around them. Furthermore, given the random nature of lightning in this episode, in itself that moment still contained the possibility that their happiness would have persisted.

What the discontinuity implied by the sudden, unforeseen transformation offers is a series of moments at which things might turn out differently, instead of a sense of inevitable progress towards a climax. The story could have happened, and indeed could happen again, and turn out in a completely different way. The same moment of 'eternal *Eden*' might be experienced by another couple, either at the same moment elsewhere, or at the same point in summer in another year, and their love story might be uninterrupted by lightning. 'Winter', for example, features two shepherds, one of whom freezes to death in the snow (Wi.320–1) while the other 'pensive seeks / His pining Flock, or from the Mountain-top, / Pleas'd with the slippery Surface, swift descends' (757–9). Of the former swain, Denys Van Renen remarks that 'if the reader wants him to be a sacrificial figure in order for his death to mean something, the poet withholds this catharsis'.[7] David Fairer observes that 'There are two shepherds, two fates; but instead of being ironically juxtaposed they are both absorbed into the sublime "mysterious Round"'.[8] Thomson includes alternatives to several of his episodes. The lightning may have struck not Celadon and Amelia but the shepherd who preceded them in the 1727 version of 'Summer'. The clearest example of this sense of open possibility within each narrative is the horseman scene. Thomson developed this scene from Milton's simile comparing Satan to a will-o'-the-wisp in *Paradise Lost* (IX.634–42): 'as when a wandring Fire . . . Which oft, they say, some evil Spirit attends . . . Misleads th' amaz'd Night-wanderer from his way / To Boggs and Mires' (IX.634–41). Thomson's horseman, or rather, horsemen, meet the same fate as Milton's night-wanderer sometimes, but 'at other Times' escape.

> The Wild-fire scatters round, or gather'd trails
> A Length of Flame deceitful o'er the Moss;
> Whither decoy'd by the fantastick Blaze,
> Now lost and now renew'd, he sinks absorpt,
> Rider and Horse, amid the miry Gulph:
> While still, from Day to Day, his pining Wife,
> And plaintive Children his Return await,
> In wild Conjecture lost. At other Times,
> Sent by the *better Genius* of the Night,
> Innoxious, gleaming on the Horse's Mane,
> The Meteor sits; and shews the narrow Path,
> That winding leads thro' Pits of Death, or else
> Instructs him how to take the dangerous Ford.
> (Au.1152–64)

The intervention of nature is no longer traceable to God; no cause is given for the 'Wild-fire', though Thomson attributes the saving meteor to an obscure '*Genius* of the Night' (recalling and inverting Milton's 'evil Spirit' in his corresponding passage). Each weather event in this passage creates a hinge at which the seasonal cycle, though continually ongoing, offers variety at each iteration. In offering these alternative 'other Times', Thomson carries out a kind of 'sideshadowing', a technique named and defined by Morson:

> Whereas foreshadowing works by revealing apparent alternatives to be mere illusions, sideshadowing conveys the sense that actual events might just as well not have happened. . . . Along with an event, we see its alternatives; with each present, another possible present. Sideshadows conjure the ghostly presence of might-have-beens or might-bes. While we see what did happen, we also see the image of what else could have happened.[9]

The key difference is that, in Morson's examples (drawn mainly from novels), the sideshadowed alternative emphatically did not happen. Thomson's alternatives did happen, will happen and are happening elsewhere.

Even death, therefore, is always just a possibility in *The Seasons*. In 'Spring', we see a mother bird losing her offspring: 'Th' astonish'd Mother finds a vacant Nest' (718). In the next lines we are shown the alternative, happening elsewhere simultaneously or perhaps for that same mother in another year: 'wide around the Woods / Sigh to her Song, and with her Wail resound. // BUT now the feather'd Youth the former Bounds, / Ardent, disdain' (727–30). This means that Jung's analysis of the climaxes of these tales, that at these points 'The image is completed', is also subject to qualification.[10] We are invited to read each tale in this way; in the episode of the frozen man, 'On every Nerve / The deadly Winter seizes; shuts up Sense' (Wi.317–18), in the same way that the harrow 'shuts the Scene' in 'Spring'. But we are also invited to see that the cycle is still ongoing. In the vignette of the 'all-involving Storm' in 'Summer' (972), in which a desert caravan is covered and preserved by a sandstorm, Thomson brings us back to the moving world by moving not (or not only) through time, but across space: at the same time as this caravan is petrified, and beyond this moment, 'In *Cairo*'s crouded Streets, / Th' impatient Merchant, wondering, waits in vain, / and *Mecca* saddens at the long Delay' (977–9).

Elsewhere Thomson does introduce a sense of specific historical time. The passage on the prison reforms carried out by the Jail-Committee in 1729 briefly locates the poem in history (Wi.359–88), and there is the case of Miss Stanley, who appears as a ghost in later versions of 'Summer', 564–84, locating this time at a point in a summer after her death in 1738. But even these passages assume a note of timelessness, drawing morals to apply across the ages: 'the wintry Blast of Death / Kills not the Buds of [Stanley's] Virtue; no, they spread . . . Thro' endless Ages, into higher Powers' (Su.581–4). And prison reform is an ongoing search for the timeless virtues of 'Liberty' (365), 'Mercy' (378), and 'Truth' (385), which transcend 'this rank Age' (382). Goodman argues that *The Seasons* registers 'the noise of history or, more accurately, the presentness of ongoing history beyond lived experience', and that Thomson's seeming attempts to suppress the historical present are in fact recognitions of that present's complexity and difficulty.[11] I believe this is to misjudge the accomplishment of *The Seasons* and indeed the temporality of georgic generally. While Goodman is right to question whether georgic really aims to obscure history and the historical present, and identifies moments when it 'turn[s] up' the complexities of the present as 'affective residue' that cannot be accommodated within the georgic cycle, Thomson repeatedly insists on the capacity of nonhuman nature to reintegrate the historical present into an ahistorical scheme.[12] Thomson's invocation of Newton's theory of refracted light, for instance, locates his description of the rainbow in the eighteenth century, but not the rainbow itself (204–17). Cohen writes that 'Thomson uses scientific terms and scientific knowledge to supersede or extend the knowledge of the past, thus making his poem temporally continuous'.[13] And yet this is followed by the swain who 'wondering views the bright Enchantment bend . . . and runs / To catch the falling Glory' (213–15). The swain may be located at any spring in history, and indeed the truth of Newton's theory is true at all past as well as future times, even if unknown. After the rainbow, 'Still Night succeeds, / A softened Shade', and the poem returns to its ahistorical sense of the cycle (217–18). The repetition of nature overwhelms the progress of history.

Damon and Musidora

For Thomson, change can be apprehended as part of a process of organic growth but simultaneously as the creation of something entirely distinct. Of all the interpolated tales, the one that best expresses this binary temporality at the levels of both content and structure is the 'Damon and Musidora' scene in 'Summer'. The reason this is such a rich tale to analyse in terms of temporality is that, in addition to its themes of sudden and gradual character development, the passage itself has given rise to numerous reimaginings and retellings, by both Thomson and subsequent readers and illustrators.

The Seasons was always, in Pat Rogers' words, a 'composition of planned growth', but it continued to develop even after it had evolved from the 405-line *Winter* in 1726 to the complete set of four *Seasons* in 1730.[14] *The Seasons* was then itself substantially revised for a new edition of 1744, then brought out with further emendations in 1745 and 1746. After Thomson's death it was revised by his friend and patron Lord Lyttelton, who for instance excised the drinking scene in 'Autumn' for the posthumous edition of 1750. In addition, many of its scenes, especially the interpolated tales, were re-visioned by artists for illustrated editions well into the nineteenth century. James Sambrook suggests that it is 'unlikely that [Thomson] would have carried out his extensive revisions for the 1744 edition without at least an *ex gratia* payment from his publisher, and it is certain that he needed money in 1743, when he had hopes of marrying'.[15] But even if he had financial motives for having his poem give repeat performances (repeat performances of his play, *Sophonisba*, brought him more money than did his copyright sales for *The Seasons*), revision also created an extra dimension in which the poem's thematic and structural concerns about time could be further explored.[16] Thomson's revisions reflect his understanding of time, as later versions of *The Seasons* seem to grow out of the earlier, but also stand alone and self-sufficient, as if the 1730 *Seasons* was the record of one year, and the 1744–6 *Seasons* the record of another, or even of the same year elsewhere.

Cohen declares that his book *The Art of Discrimination* 'attempts to return "process" to criticism, by applying the study of the poet at work ... to the interpretation of the poem'; he argues that 'revision provides a clue to the poet's verbal uses, his philosophical views [. . . and] to his organization. For all critics who pursue "understanding", such supports seem essential'.[17] Although the kind of 'understanding' Cohen is most concerned with in *The Art of Discrimination*, and also in *The Unfolding of The Seasons*, is contextual – in terms of Thomson's influences and his growing learning – not aesthetic, Cohen does give tantalising hints of the kind of meaning that might inhere in revision, as when he suggests that

> the changes in the poem itself enact [Thomson's] conception of variation and extension . . . the revisions can be interpreted as an unconscious reflection of the conscious temporal distinctions the poet makes. Moving back and forth in time to emphasize the continuity of tradition . . . the poet develops even in his method of composition a procedure that expresses his deepest beliefs.[18]

Continuity is central to Thomson's revisionary method; but the 'temporal distinctions', even between textual versions, are not so clear. As the reader's mind moves 'back and forth in time' between the versions, we apprehend both an ongoing, continuous process connecting the versions, and sudden transformations that question the relation between them. We are obliged to ask whether the versions represent two moments that are part of one process, or two moments that are discontinuous and may therefore occur either many years into the future or even many years in the past, or are perhaps meant to be apprehended as simultaneous alternatives, occurring in the same moment at different places.

There are revisions that seem deliberately to obscure both their original version and their nature as revision. They in fact depend for their meaning upon forgetfulness of their past selves. Take for instance the lines 'in restless Change revolv'd, / Our drooping Days are dwindled down to nought, / The fleeting Shadow of a Winter's Sun' ([1738] Sp.377–9). After 1738, Thomson revised these lines to read 'with inward-eating Change, / Our drooping Days are dwindled down to Nought, / Their Period finish'd ere 'tis well begun' ([1744–6] Sp.333–5). These lines in both versions describe 'Change' negatively, but they enact change in a way that is more ambiguous. The second version contains the 'Shadow' of its own past self in the form of a self-rhyme: 'well begun' with 'Winter's Sun'. We discover a pleasurable continuity when we notice the rhyme that links these different versions of the same line, and it undercuts the despondency of their content: the 'Period' of the first lines has not finished, but has been carried forward in the revision if only in a 'fleeting Shadow'. And yet this is not a couplet, in which both rhyming lines remain visible side by side, along with the rhyme that joins them. This is an 'inward-eating' rhyme: it has only been achieved by the replacement, not the complement, of one line with its rhyme-word. The first version's 'Period' is 'finish'd ere 'tis well begun' in the most literal sense: if we are reading these lines expecting to find 'The fleeting Shadow of a Winter's Sun', we will discover that line annihilated before it is even written. *The Seasons* is a blank verse poem: in this revision it nods to the possibility of rhyme, but only to insist upon the effacement of that rhyme. Just as his transitions between passages can be read both as natural, organic developments with a kind of logic and as drastic transformations into something totally irreconcilable with the past, so Thomson's revisions can be understood as participating in a linear unfolding, as the earlier gives rise to the later that takes its place, but they also hint at a point of irreversible breakage with the past.

Thomson's revision of the Damon and Musidora episode in 'Summer' enacts this principle. It would be easy to account for Thomson's revisions to this episode with commercial explanations. It was one of the most popular parts of the poem, according to Wordsworth who observed that 'in any well-used copy of the Seasons the book generally opens of itself with the rhapsody on love, or with one of the stories (perhaps Damon and Musidora)',[19] and to Hazlitt, who judged that the most popular episodes, the ones frequently anthologised in 'books of extracts, do not convey the most formidable idea of [Thomson's] genius or taste; such as Palemon and Lavinia, Damon and Musidora, Celadon and Amelia'.[20] Cohen puts it most bluntly: 'Musidora represents the vulgarity of popular taste.'[21] This critical snobbery is one of the reasons why, as Jung writes, 'In scholarly terms, the interpolated episodes have gone largely unnoticed'.[22] But Thomson's revision to this episode was meaningful. We find in the revision the same sense of time that is described within the tale: a careful balance, between natural growth on the one hand, and on the other sudden transformation into something wholly new.

The best-known version of the Damon and Musidora story, the one to which Wordsworth, Hazlitt and Cohen refer, is the revised version that first appeared in 1744. Damon suffers from (he believes) unrequited love; he spies the object of his affections, Musidora, bathing naked in a pool and is inspired by the sight to make known his feelings. He leaves a note for her, informing her of his love and that he has retreated in order to stand guard while she bathes. She finds the note, is stirred to reciprocal passion, and replies by carving a note into a tree informing Damon that one day he might have the right to see her unclothed. The original version had appeared in the 1730 edition of *The Seasons* (the original 1727 *Summer* has no Damon and Musidora story), and was rather different from the later, revised version. In 1744 we are told 'young DAMON sat, / Pensive, and pierc'd with Love's delightful Pangs' (1271–2). In 1730, he had been troubled by a different problem: 'DAMON sat, / Thoughtful, and fix'd in philosophic muse . . . the force of beauty scorn'd, / Firm, and to false philosophy devote' (981–5).[23] Damon of 1730 is the prisoner not of love but of stoic philosophy. Musidora does not appear and inspire him to declare his love; rather three women, Musidora along with Amoret and Sacharissa, appear, and their physical beauty softens Damon's hard, philosophic temper: 'the stoick now no more, / But man deep-felt' (1006–7). Both versions of Damon 'drew / Such draughts' of beauty to the soul ([1730] 1031–2; [1744] 1331–2), but in 1744 these draughts 'o'erwhelm his raptur'd Thought / With Luxury' and inspire him to make known his love (1333–4), whereas in 1730 they 'put his harsh philosophy to flight, / The joyless search of long-deluded years' (1033–4), and finally, 'MUSIDORA fixing in his heart, / [beauty] Inform'd, and humaniz'd him into man' (1035–6).

It would be possible to read the 1744 version as a straightforward sequel to the 1730 version, in which Damon, having 'fixed his heart' on Musidora, reveals his love to her (after this time catching her bathing alone). It is also possible to trace a continuous narrative between the two versions, not just of Damon's growth into love, but of the poem's own development from immaturity to maturity. The text itself undergoes the process that is described in the tale: the softening and maturation of harsh philosophy into love. Just as Damon in 1730 grows out of his stoicism and into love, a love that is imperfectly realised in this early version, so the passage grows out of its occupation with a philosophical moral and into a full celebration of love and a more effective (although still creepy) love story. The passage itself, and both Damon and Musidora, are 'humaniz'd' (1744). Damon's ambition to win Musidora – 'if an infant Passion struggled there, / To call that Passion forth' (1284–5) – articulates the passage's own achievement; the 'infant Passion' that Thomson 'struggled' to make convincing in the 1730 version has been called forth and has flowered in 1744.

Reading the versions as parts of an ongoing process of authorial development, those moments (such as the description of Amoret) that do 'struggle' in 1730 become the promising seeds of their later maturation,

> While, like the CYPRIAN goddess, AMORET,
> Delicious dress'd in rosy-dimpled smiles,
> And all one softness, melted on the sense.
> ([1730] 1000–2)

The abstraction of the form of this woman, dressed in multiple 'smiles', 'melted' into 'one softness', hardly communicates a physical body at all, and yet it is this physical body that is meant to carry such affective power. What these lines do communicate is the process by which Amoret will become the 1744 variant's Musidora: she and the other women will be 'melted' together into 'one softness'; their three 'smiles', their physical qualities as described by Thomson, will combine to 'dress' one figure.

On the other hand, each version not only stands perfectly well on its own, but may in fact reward a reading that considers it alone, because viewing the two as parts of one larger narrative – whether of Damon and Musidora's relationship or of Thomson's treatment of the theme of love – also diminishes the integrity of each. The earlier version is held at bay by the self-sufficiency of the later because as a love story it is clearly unsatisfying. In 1730 neither Damon nor the reader is afforded any real intimacy with the women, who are all subsumed into one ideal form, 'the plunging fair' (1021), 'the statue that enchants the world' (1018). Only at the last minute does Damon settle on one of the three women. Remembering Damon's more general lust and impersonal selection of Musidora as the focus of that lust undermines the later version's claim to be about real, personal, mutual love. In turn, while the discomfort of the first version's depiction of Damon and Musidora's relationship would be tempered by the reader's awareness of the passage's more satisfying future, at the same time the effect of the 1730 passage's philosophic moral would be diminished. Most eighteenth-century critics regarded the revised version as an improvement over the original, but in recent years alternative judgements have been offered, such as Sebastian Mitchell's cynical comment:

> by 1744, when Thomson was substantially revising *The Seasons*, he recognized that the episode's central appeal lay in its unqualified salaciousness; and in an act that would have its corollary in the trimming of the moralizing inscription from an erotic print, he removed all of its commentary.[24]

It might be advantageous, by most tastes, to lose 'the moralizing', but it is hard to take seriously the 1730 version's very real point about the inhumanity of stoic philosophy when we look forward to the transformation that the passage will undergo.

The difficulty of reconciling the two versions is exemplified in the case of the tale's first illustration, by William Kent (Figure 5.1). In 1730 the complete composite poem *The Seasons* was printed in quarto, by the author-printer Samuel Richardson for Andrew Millar.[25] It featured illustrations for each season by William Kent, engraved by Nicolas Henri Tardieu. Kent's design for 'Summer' depicts, beneath the personified season in her chariot, the original Damon story. Damon sits with his book (presumably a volume of stoic philosophy), peering round the shrubbery to spy not one, nor three, but in fact four naked women. Their individual identities in Thomson's original version are so weak and fluid as to allow Kent to expand them into four figures, just as Thomson melts them into

Figure 5.1   William Kent, 'Summer' in James Thomson, *The Seasons* (London: Andrew Millar, 1730). Reproduced from a copy in the author's collection.

one, figuratively in 1730 and literally by 1744. This image was to be reproduced repeatedly throughout the century.[26] Kent's design did have to be revised, however, to match Thomson's revisions. When it appeared with the new version of *The Seasons* in 1744, Damon still holds a book (now transformed into the source for his love-note, perhaps), but three of the women have been erased to leave just the seated Musidora, now staring up at an empty space where a companion's face had been.[27] But also visible, very faintly, are the outlines of disembodied arms, not completely successfully turned into creases in the piece of fabric above Musidora's head, and an extra foot next to hers. The ghost of the 1730 version lingers in this image as it lingers in the poetry of 1744. Here it is an unpleasant presence, disembodied remnants of what had once been whole. The real lineage of what looks now like a piece of drapery must be forgotten if we are to accept the integrity of the revised image.[28]

Damon and Musidora were re-visioned by numerous artists in various media, and this is due not only to the appealing nudity in the episode but to its temporal quality. Like the other interpolated tales, the Damon and Musidora tale is characterised by a sense of movement composed of moments of poised stillness. In 1744 Musidora possesses 'busy Thought', experiences 'a softer Train / Of mixt Emotions' (1361, 1254–5); she undergoes her own emotional realisation and growth to parallel Damon's. And yet even these suggestions of movement are caught in freeze-frame: 'As if to Marble struck, devoid of Sense / A stupid Moment motionless she stood' (1345–6). In 1730 'DAMON sat . . . fix'd', then there is another pause to view the naked women as 'fair expos'd they stood', and finally a few shots of the women in the water, 'now beneath the wave . . . now with streaming locks . . . Rising again' (981–2, 1015, 1028–31). In both the poem and the illustrations, we are told there is movement, but are permitted to savour the visual moment, preserved for us in an engraving like 'the Statue that enchants the World' ([1744] 1347). If the inclusion of nude women were not enough to ensure this episode's appeal to illustrators, this technique of structuring the story in both versions as a sequence of captured images must have done the business.

After Kent's first illustration, which featured Damon at its centre as did the 1730 version of the tale, later illustrations almost always have Musidora at the centre of the composition, often posed as the Venus de' Medici. Through illustration the same tale, even the same moment within the tale, is repeated with subtle variation. Nineteenth-century illustrations, in which Musidora is more likely to be clothed, bring in a variety of poses from other points in the tale, such as her discovering Damon's letter, or carving her reply into the tree (Figure 5.2). An 1847 edition of *The Seasons* brought together illustrations by twelve different artists, including an illustration of Damon and Musidora by John Calcott Horsley (designer of the first

The Broken Scene: Thomson's Tales 129

Figure 5.2 Richard Westall, 'Summer', engraved by John Romney, in James Thomson, *The Seasons* (London: John Sharpe, 1825). Reproduced from a copy in the author's collection.

Christmas card) (Figure 5.3). Horsley has Damon top-left (politely averting his gaze) and the usual nude Musidora at centre, but there is also a clothed female figure at top-right. Although owing to her lighter hair we might take her for the ghost of the rejected Amoret or Sacharissa, presumably she is Musidora again. In a medieval pictorial tradition, a different space in the picture represents a different moment in time, but its temporal relation to the central image is

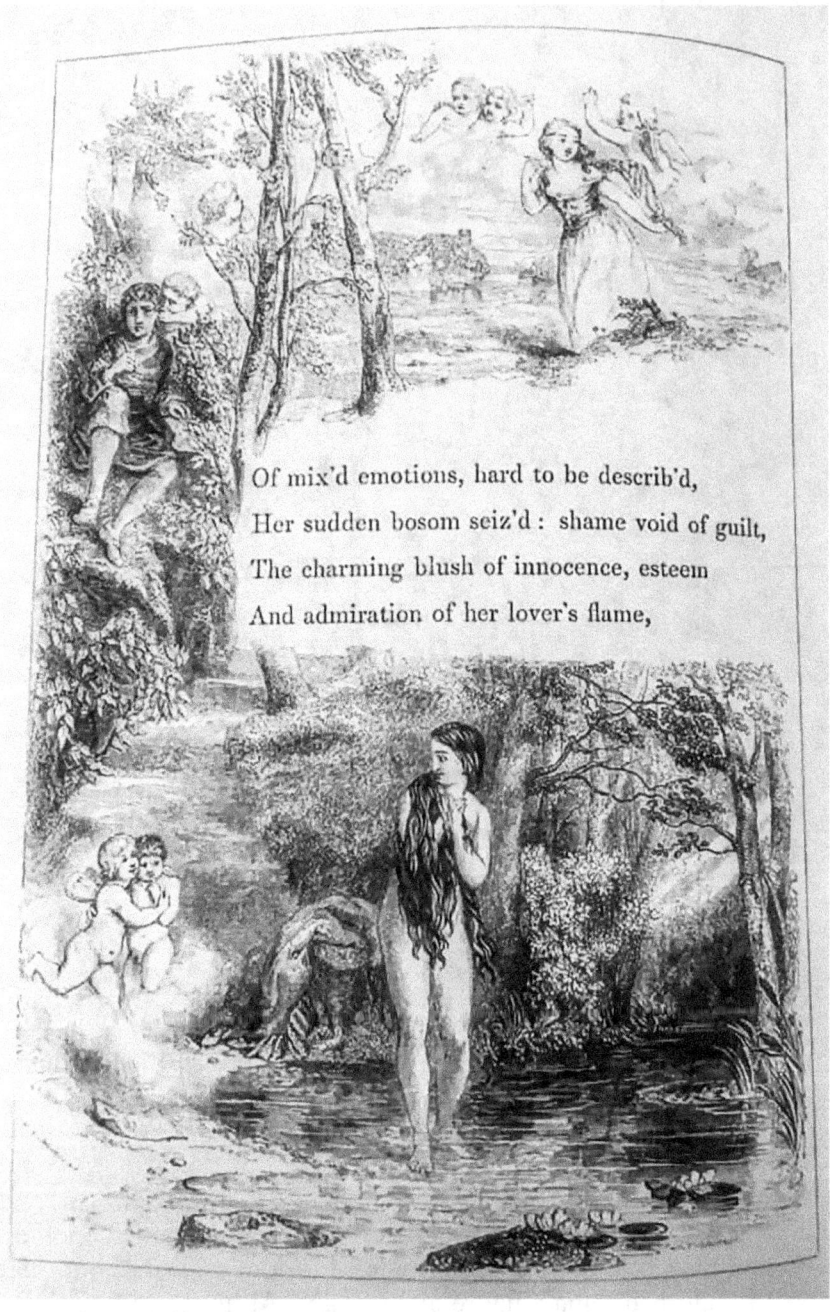

Figure 5.3 John Calcott Horsley, 'Musidora', engraved by J. Thompson, in James Thomson, *The Seasons* (London: Longman, Brown, Green, and Longmans, 1847). Reproduced from a copy in the author's collection.

obscure: is this Musidora earlier in the tale (on her way to bathe), or later (on her way to discover the letter)?

While Horsley's illustration surrounds the text of the poem, the most common placement for illustrations is on the page facing the episode in verse. They appear as a visual parallel: the same tale occurring simultaneously, but in a different place. Sometimes they are a little further away, on the title page to 'Summer': the implication of this placement is that the same things can occur, perhaps with variation, in any summer. Damon and Musidora would also appear on 'porcelain, fans, furniture, watchcases, embroidered silk, and painted fabrics'.[29] In these forms they are extracted not only from *The Seasons* but from the context of the rest of the tale, and they occupy a moment that, while it is clearly part of some longer process, might be part of a number of different processes, a moment within any number of different stories occurring at different times or at the same time and with multiple possible outcomes.

It was, according to Hannah Sullivan, 'over the course of the eighteenth century [that] the meaning of the word *revision* had shifted slightly, from retroactive change made by *anyone* (including the kinds of changes we would call edits or interpolations) to change made by the original author'.[30] Thomson knew that his poem would after his death be susceptible to alterations by his literary executor, Lord Lyttelton, and by his publisher, Andrew Millar, who owned the copyright of *The Seasons* and controlled the poem's production and appearance until his death in 1768, and who added illustrations to his editions in order to raise their price.[31] Thomson wrote a poem that would not be affronted by such future revision and re-vision, but would be fulfilled. The Damon and Musidora story, in both its versions, is about the power of love and beauty when it is caught and revealed in forms that we can observe and hold – a love-note, an inscription on a tree, a human body, an ancient statue, a version of a poem. These static images of love and beauty have the power to set in motion developments that can bring about the reciprocation of love, and the creation of new art, whether an illustration or Musidora's response carved into a tree. The nature of those developments remains uncertain until they are fulfilled in the present. Each pause allows us a moment of uncertainty; at each point of stillness, we don't know for certain what may come next. To this the different versions, with their different outcomes, stand testament: the sight of a naked woman might inspire Damon to throw off his stoicism, whereas at another time it might cause him to declare his love. Musidora's message, 'The Time may come', reiterates the sense that this story is not over, yet the future remains unknown. Each version and each moment in the tale is its own 'eternal *Eden*', from which point things might go badly or well. Thomson's revision is the ultimate expression of the possibility that things might have been, and still might be, different.

His Unpremeditated Strain

In Thomson's acts of revision we see the imprints of the poet who acts and changes, and changes his mind, across time; but we also question the continuity of that process as well as the importance of its chronology. In its content, too, *The Seasons* depicts the poet as someone who thinks and acts across time, as he wanders through fields (or as he imagines doing so), but also as someone who receives inspiration *and* composes his poetry instantaneously. Thomson makes it unclear whether even the process of composition is extended over time or whether it takes place in a single moment. Whereas Milton emphasised the work in and duration of the process of writing a poem, from the point of inspiration's visitation in the night to the next day's composition and the repetition of this process over many nights and days, Thomson was interested in the possibility of spontaneous composition that might in theory take place while he was still in the presence of nature. In his natural description, as we saw in Chapter 4, by obscuring or confounding the logic and causality of its movement, Thomson makes it impossible to tell how a process is spread over time, or even to say for certain that it is spread over time at all. He achieves the same effect in his depictions of the process of poetic composition, distinguishing the process into parts so distinct that there no longer appears to be one single process. Being in nature, receiving inspiration and composing poetry thereby become events that may happen in a moment simultaneously. This absorbing sense of the present is, as ever, counterbalanced by the possibility that Thomson is depicting the more conventional movement from one part of the process to the next through time.

> TO me be Nature's Volume broad-display'd;
> And to peruse its all-instructing Page,
> Or, haply catching Inspiration thence,
> Some easy Passage, raptur'd, to translate,
> My sole Delight; as thro' the falling Glooms
> Pensive I stray, or with the rising Dawn
> On Fancy's Eagle-wing excursive soar.
> (Su.192–8)

Wordsworth was later to catch up Thomson's use of the word 'catching' to describe his own interaction with nature, and he would emphasise the impossibility of delineating neatly this process of inspiration. Great forms in nature are like great minds, he would write, and both

> can send abroad
> Kindred mutations; for themselves create
> A like existence; and whene'er it dawns
> Created for them, catch it; – or are caught
> By its inevitable mastery[.]
> (*TP*, XIV.93–7)

In each of these passages Thomson and Wordsworth portray the poet's participation in nature as one of reciprocity. Wordsworth makes 'catching' and 'sending' apparently simultaneous; Thomson has 'catching' and 'falling', and has the catch actually precede the fall. They are not logically related in the sentence – one refers to catching inspiration, the other to falling glooms – but their proximity in the lines means that our normal expectation of causality and linearity, which would place 'catching' after 'falling', is turned on its head. Furthermore, the acts of reading (the 'Page' of nature), writing ('translating') and being in nature are all depicted as simultaneous. It is true that as we move through the passage we read the 'perusing', then the 'catching inspiration', then the translating, in a linear succession, as if we are following a nice neat process. But according to the 'Or' in the third line, the 'catching inspiration' is an alternative existing alongside the reading in this ideal hypothetical present. Then the two subsequent acts of catching and translating are conflated into one single, immediate action of 'catching . . . to translate'. And then the perusing, the catching and the translating are all absorbed by the phrase 'My sole Delight', which suggests the contradictory possibilities that they are all part of one connected process, and that they are simultaneous in time. On top of this, all these actions are made simultaneous with the poet's being in external nature, '*as* thro' the falling Glooms . . . I stray'. Thomson is deliberately melting these actions, that we normally conceive of as distinct parts of a connected, linear sequence (the process of seeing nature, thinking and then writing about it), into one all-absorbing present, while still preserving the possibility that they are distinct and unconnected in time with that 'Or'.

Another account of the process-or-moment of poetry creates a similar effect:

> And, as I steal along the sunny Wall,
> Where Autumn basks, with Fruit empurpled deep,

> My pleasing Theme continual prompts my Thought:
> Presents the downy Peach; the shining Plumb,
> With a fine blueish Mist of Animals
> Clouded[.]
> (Au.673–8)

Jonathan Kramnick has given a masterful reading of the three-dimensional spatial quality of Thomson's images, including this one in which the 'blueish mist of animals' shades and shapes the view of the plum behind it. Extension in space is visible in Thomson's scenes even at the microscopic level: 'Thomson's eye moves along the surface of crowded space, so even air teams [sic] with bugs, dust, and droplets.'[32] Space is 'crowded' with different levels, conceived in three dimensions yet perceived as a single 'clouded' image. In the same way, this passage both distinguishes moments in time and refuses to distinguish them. There are even multiple possible levels of reality interacting here – imagined experience with supposedly 'real', present experience – although the precise nature of that interaction is obscure. Reuben A. Brower noted that it is 'a very odd thing' for a 'theme' to 'present' a(n imagined?) peach;[33] in response, Cohen explained that the theme is not that of Thomson's poem, but of the Book of Nature, which presents a (real) peach.[34] When we reach the catalogue of fruits, it is no longer clear that it is real nature, and the real season of autumn, presenting to the poet these fruits, or whether it is the mind presenting them to itself, and/or the poem 'Autumn' presenting them on the page. There is no distinction between the fruits as external inspiration for Thomson's poetry, and as that poetry itself; they appear to him in nature, and they appear in the poem, simultaneously. This is something that a nature poet might take for granted, but by drawing attention to the dual existence of the fruit as 'theme' and real fruit, Thomson is making a point of his deliberate drawing of the two into one temporal present. It is similar to the effect at the opening of 'Spring', when 'Come' refers both to the season of spring and the poem 'Spring'. Of line 9 in that opening passage, 'Which thy own Season paints', Shaun Irlam writes: 'The bold ambiguity regarding which is the grammatical subject and which is the object of the verb "paints" unsettles and problematizes the locus of priority that commands the poem from the outset.'[35] The 'priority' of experience before the written record of that experience is no longer assured.

By retaining the possibility of a linear process of poetic composition Thomson is able to temper the potential ethical problem with his depiction of poetic composition as spontaneous. Removing process from composition leaves no time for labour or effort, qualities that ought to be valued by a poet writing in the Miltonic–georgic tradition. Both the dangers and attractions of this conception of poetic composition are explored in the depiction of the notoriously lazy Thomson in *The Castle of Indolence* (lines supposedly penned by Lyttelton, although retained in the poem by Thomson):

> A Bard here dwelt, more fat than Bard beseems;
> Who void of Envy, Guile, and Lust of Gain,
> On Virtue still, and Nature's pleasing Themes,
> Pour'd forth his unpremeditated Strain,
> The World forsaking with a calm Disdain:
> Here laugh'd he careless in his easy Seat,
> Here quaff'd encircled with the joyous Train;
> Oft moralizing sage; his Ditty sweet
> He loathed much to write, ne cared to repeat.
> (I.LXVIII, 604–12)[36]

This is a portrait of a poet who has no inclination to 'write' or 'repeat' his 'unpremeditated Strain', because to 'write' or 'repeat' it would be to extend the moment of composition into a process involving effort over time. But *The Seasons* refuses to draw the same sharp distinction between industry and indolence around which *The Castle of Indolence* is constructed. In *The Seasons* Thomson implies that even as he pours 'forth his unpremeditated strain', in that very moment the same strain is being recorded, instantaneously and effortlessly 'translated' into writing, and his depictions of his creative process refer to the undisciplined vagrancy of thought, to his 'straying' and 'wandering'. But both his revisions and his self-portraits of the poet also hint at more effortful processes of composition as his theme 'prompts' him to continue a narrative or to develop an idea (his theme is 'urgent' in the MS version of the fruits passage, and 'urges' rather than 'prompts' him in 1730). As an anonymous critic noted in 1827, although *The Seasons* of all poems seems 'that it owes nothing to labour, hardly even to thought', the heavily revised manuscript of 'Winter'

> evinces the extraordinary labour that has been employed upon it. . . . A bright thought may, indeed, be struck out in a moment of inspiration; but many moments may be required to clothe it in words, and hours of labour may have been expended in refining, pruning, and polishing.[37]

Conflating the subject and form of his poetry, his 'theme' with his 'thought', allows Thomson to reflect, as he describes his own movement in nature, upon the movement of his verse. We find that it is at once a smooth progress and a halting, recursive wandering:

> THUS up the Mount, in airy Vision rapt,
> I stray, regardless whither; till the Sound
> Of a near Fall of Water every Sense
> Wakes from the Charm of Thought: swift-shrinking back,
> I check my Steps, and view the broken Scene.
> (Su.585–9)

Here we have what appears to be a straightforward continuation of a narrative, which describes the poet's walk and then his 'check'. It is in fact, at the same time, a kind of interlude in the process that is the poem's being written. The 'Sense', which wakes, and the 'Thought', which is woken from, may refer to the succeeding and preceding paragraphs respectively: the succeeding one is a prospect poem about the sights, sounds and sensations of the waterfall, and the preceding is a passage about imagined spirits (including, after 1738, the lament for Stanley). So these five lines are as if outside the poem, looking in, noting how the poet moves from 'Thought' to 'Sense', even as they fulfil the more conventional requirements of narrative action. The poet is narrating his movement between paragraphs in the form of another paragraph; it is as if the poet pauses in the process of writing and considers what he has written and is about to write, but this pause is itself caught in poetry, a present moment on the brink between, in which he possesses both 'Thought' and 'Sense'.

Are these five lines about movement, or stillness? The reader's movement through the poem is similarly two-fold. On the one hand, these lines, together with the preceding and succeeding paragraphs, depend for part of their meaning on a linear reading of all three paragraphs. On the other, these five lines serve to hold those other two passages apart. They are distinct in space (physically held apart by these lines), distinct in time (in the narrative of his walk) and even distinct in levels of reality (one is the stuff of sleep, the other of 'waking'). These five lines also make perfect sense on their own; their context invests them with added meaning, but also detracts. The preceding lines on Stanley inflect Thomson's 'straying' in these lines with psychological significance, but can the reflection on a dead friend really be what the phrase 'charm of Thought' refers to? The succeeding lines, however, seem to confirm the narrative linearity of the poem, following on 'smooth[ly]' from these five lines:

> SMOOTH to the shelving Brink a copious Flood
> Rolls fair, and placid; where collected all,
> In one impetuous Torrent, down the Steep
> It thundering shoots . . .
>   it rushes broad
>   . . . it sends aloft
> A hoary Mist . . .
> Now flashes o'er the scatter'd Fragments, now
> Aslant the hollow'd Channel rapid darts
> . . .
> It gains a safer Bed, and steals, at last,
> Along the Mazes of the quiet Vale.
> (589–606)

These lines describing the waterfall express the power that caused the narrator to shrink back, and at first the arrangement of the description into 'scatter'd Fragments' seems to cohere with the 'broken Scene' described in the preceding lines. But just as it is easy to see how the former lines lead into these, it is relatively easy to understand both the spatial and temporal organisation of this scene. Its components exist simultaneously, but there are also two linear processes being described here: the progression of the water (of, say, a single drop of water as it flows through the river), and the progression of the narrator's eyes as he follows its line. The horizon of the prospect view enjoyed by a human observer then determines the apparent closure of the scene: the water's journey seems to end ('at last') when it reaches the farthest point the narrator can see in the vale. So far, so straightforward.

The difficulty comes after this description of the waterfall. Up until 1738, these lines were followed by an explicit continuation of this miniature prospect poem:

> WITH the rough Prospect tir'd, I turn my Eyes
> Where, in long *Visto*, the soft-murmuring Main
> Darts a green Lustre, trembling, thro' the Trees;
> Or to yon Silver-streaming Threads of Light,
> A showery Beauty beaming thro' the Boughs.
> ([1727] 467–71)

Thomson then cut this reference to the 'prospect' and 'visto', perhaps to avoid the imprecision of that 'Or' and its reminder that everything we read is hypothetical, or perhaps he realised that the subsequent lines contained description too spatially and temporally extended to describe the view of a human poet in a specific place at a specific time. How could this man by the waterfall perceive two mutually exclusive states of affairs that are, besides, hidden from him in the wood: 'all the tuneful Race, / Smit by the afflictive noon, disordered droop, / Deep in the Thicket; or, from Bower to Bower / Responsive, force an interrupted Strain' (611–15)? Thomson then reminds us again that all is hypothetical as he starts the next paragraph, 'BESIDE the dewy Border let me sit', and in the 1730 edition the context of the prospect view is renewed again:

> AND what a various prospect lies around!
> Of hills, and vales, and woods, and lawns, and spires
> And towns betwixt, and gilded streams; till all
> The stretching landskip into smoak decays.
> ([1730] 530–3)

In the 1744 edition these lines are moved nearly a thousand lines later in 'Summer' (1438–41). This means that instead of developing the prospect that he sees from 'the dewy Border', the narrator seems to launch into a new prospect poem, distinct from the ones viewed from the 'Mount' or the 'Border' both spatially and ontologically: 'Now come, bold *Fancy*, spread a daring Flight, / And view the Wonders of the *torrid Zone*' (631–2). One effect of Thomson's various revisions to this passage is to omit two explicit references to the 'prospect' framework of the scene that had been established in the lines describing his ascent up the mount. What had been a reasonably sustained prospect poem in the 1730 edition is splintered, by 1744, into a collection of disjointed paragraphs, and the elements of the prospect view itself distributed, 'scatter'd', across the length of 'Summer'.

Those five lines on Thomson's ascent up the mount, and their arrangement in the context of the preceding and succeeding paragraphs, encourage us to read this section of 'Summer' as one seamlessly flowing whole, but also to read them as emphatically separate units, which therefore may be simultaneous in time, or may be utterly removed from one another in time. Like Thomson's here, our movement is somehow at once a straightforward journey 'up the Mount' (or through the poem), and a 'stray[ing], regardless whither'. Here, in fact, Thomson anticipates the change that Horrocks has located a few years after *The Seasons*, in the mid-century: the Romantic 'figure of the wanderer or traveler . . . develop[ing] out of a re-imagining of the prospect overview'. Wanderers appear in *The Seasons* not only as 'ghostly opposites' to the prospect-viewer, as Horrocks contends; Thomson's prospect-viewer is already wandering himself.[38] Since its publication, readers have disagreed over whether progress or wandering is the structural principle that shapes both *The Seasons* and the experience of reading it. This critical disagreement is the subject of the next chapter.

Notes

1. Some of my discussion of the Damon and Musidora episode appeared in an earlier form as 'Versions of Damon and Musidora: The Realization of Thomson's Story in Revisions and Illustrations', *Studies in the Literary Imagination* 46.1 (2013): 47–70.
2. Jonathan Bate, 'Living with the Weather', *Studies in Romanticism* 35 (1996): 431–47 (438–9).
3. Sandro Jung, 'Image-making in James Thomson's *The Seasons*', SEL 53 (2013): 583–99 (592).
4. Ibid., 588. For a similar account of Thomson's punctuation of movement with images of petrification, see Katarina Stenke, '"The well-dissembled Mourner": Lightning's (Dis)course in the Still Lives of Thomson's "Celadon and Amelia"', *Studies in the Literary Imagination* 46.1 (2013): 19–46.
5. Stenke, 'Parts and Wholes in Long Non-narrative Poems', 126.
6. John Scott, *Critical Essays on Some of the Poems, of Several English Poets* (London: James Phillips, 1785), 342.
7. Denys Van Renen, '"A Hollow Moan": The Contours of the Non-human World in James Thomson's *The Seasons*", in *Animals and Humans: Sensibility and Representation, 1650–1820*, ed. Katherine Quinsey (Oxford: Oxford UP, 2017): 75–98 (91).
8. David Fairer, *English Poetry of the Eighteenth Century, 1700–1789* (London and New York: Routledge, 2003), 139.
9. Morson, *Narrative and Freedom*, 117–18.
10. Jung, 'Image-making', 589.
11. Goodman, *Georgic Modernity*, 64.
12. Ibid., 3, 9.
13. Cohen, *Unfolding*, 22–3.
14. Pat Rogers, *The Augustan Vision* (London: Weidenfeld & Nicolson, 1974), 124. For a cogent reading of the role of 'Autumn' as the conclusion to a narrative of the poem's growth, see Kwinten Van De Walle, 'From Inter- to Intratextuality: "Autumn" as the Conclusion to *The Seasons*' in Jung and Van De Walle, *Genres*, 43–58.
15. James Sambrook, 'Introduction', TS, lxv-vi.
16. James Sambrook, *James Thomson, 1700–1748: A Life* (Oxford: Clarendon Press, 1991), 91.
17. Cohen, *Art of Discrimination*, 72.
18. Cohen, *Unfolding*, 106–7.

19. William Wordsworth, 'Essay, Supplementary to the Preface', in *Wordsworth's Literary Criticism*, ed. W. J. B. Owen (London: Routledge & Kegan Paul, 1974): 68–98 (204).
20. William Hazlitt, 'On Thomson and Cowper', in *Lectures on the English Poets*, 244–60 (249)
21. Cohen, *The Art of Discrimination*, 324.
22. Sandro Jung, 'Painterly "Readings" of *The Seasons*, 1766–1829', *Word & Image: A Journal of Verbal/Visual Enquiry* 26 (2009): 68–82 (69).
23. The Clarendon Press edition has the line numbers for the 1730 version of this passage out by one (it has ll. 982–6 for 981–5 and so on); I have retained the original numbering found in the 1730 quarto *Seasons* (London: Andrew Millar).
24. Sebastian Mitchell, 'James Thomson's Picture Collection and British History Paintings', *Journal of the History of Collections* 23 (2011): 127–51 (138).
25. *The Seasons. By Mr Thomson* (London: Andrew Millar, 1730).
26. Cohen gives a list of twenty English editions of *The Seasons* between 1736 and 1782 in which Kent's illustrations appeared (*Art of Discrimination*, 265).
27. Jung interprets the new image as depicting Musidora looking at Damon, thus 'establishing a direct connection' with him and deviating from the textual version of the story. ('Print Culture and Visual Interpretation in Eighteenth-Century German Editions of Thomson's *Seasons*', *Comparative and Critical Studies* 9 (2012): 37–59 (41).)
28. See Somervell, 'Versions of Damon and Musidora', Figures 1a and 1b.
29. Jung, 'Image-making', 586.
30. Hannah Sullivan, *The Work of Revision* (Cambridge, MA: Harvard UP, 2013), 25.
31. The economic logic behind the illustrations is demonstrated and analysed by Kwinten Van De Walle in 'Editorialising Practices, Competitive Marketability, and James Thomson's "The Seasons"', *Journal for Eighteenth-Century Studies* 38 (2015): 257–76.
32. Jonathan Kramnick, 'An Aesthetics and Ecology of Presence', *European Romantic Review* 26 (2015): 315–27 (320).
33. Reuben A. Brower, 'Form and Defect of Form in Eighteenth-Century Poetry: A Memorandum', *College English* 29.7 (1968): 535–41 (538).
34. Cohen, *Unfolding*, 204.
35. Shaun Irlam, *Elations: The Poetics of Enthusiasm in Eighteenth-Century Britain* (Stanford: Stanford UP, 1999), 159.
36. Thomson, *Liberty*, 195.
37. Anon., 'Thomson – The Poet', *New-York Mirror, and Ladies' Literary Gazette* 5 (22 September 1827): 85.
38. Horrocks, '"Circling Eye" and "Houseless Stranger"', 665, 670.

Chapter 6

Unforced Method: Reading *The Seasons*

In his 1781 'Life of Thomson', Samuel Johnson remarked:

> The great defect of the *Seasons* is want of method; but for this I know not that there was any remedy. Of many appearances subsisting all at once, no rule can be given why one should be mentioned before another; yet the memory wants the help of order, and the curiosity is not excited by suspense or expectation.[1]

Here Johnson makes several of the points that Joseph Frank was to make nearly two hundred years later: not only that a text can depict things that exist simultaneously, but that in doing so its parts lose the 'rule' of narrative time that gives meaning to the chronological order in which the poet has arranged them. Johnson states this more explicitly in his commentary on Pope's 'Windsor-Forest': 'the scenes, which [descriptive poems] must exhibit successively, are all subsisting at the same time, [so that] the order in which they are shown must by necessity be arbitrary, and more is not to be expected from the last part than from the first.'[2]

In his 1807 lecture on Thomson, Percival Stockdale quoted Johnson's above assessment and remarked that it 'is absolute nonsense'.[3] In 'Summer', Stockdale argued,

> The Poet surveys, paints, and enforces ... a summer's morning; noon; evening; and night; as they succeed one another, in the course of nature; (for surely the *many appearances*, in *any* season, do not *subsist all at once*.) – If *this* is not method, I know not what *is*.

Even the interpolated tales, he claims, do not disrupt the flow of the poem: 'The most admired poems have their episodes, which by no means destroy, or confuse, the order of the principal fable.'[4] As for the lack of suspense or expectation, Stockdale retorted, the mind reading *The Seasons* 'proceeds with a delightful expectation; for it expects to meet with most excellent poetry; and it is never disappointed; with poetry which flows, in a natural, and easy succession of sentiments, and imagery'.[5]

Thomson's first biographer, Robert Shiels, had made a similar comment to Johnson in his 1753 life of the poet, observing that within each book of *The Seasons*, 'There appears no particular design; the parts are not subservient to one another; nor is there any dependance [sic] or connection throughout; but this perhaps is a fault almost inseparable from a subject in itself so diversified'. Shiels concludes that 'each season may rather be called an assemblage of poetical ideas, than a poem, as it seems written without a plan'.[6] Yet despite claiming that there is no 'dependance or connection' between the parts, Shiels somehow also agrees with Stockdale that the parts of the poem 'flow naturally'.[7]

In his 1777 *Strictures, Critical and Sentimental, on Thomson's Seasons*, John More did perceive connection between the parts of *The Seasons*, but it was these connections that, for More, prevented wholeness, as they made 'what critics have called, in the canting and technical jargon of their art, *unity of subject*', impossible.[8] Here More agrees with Shiels that 'In this respect [of the variety of his subject], no Poet ever trod on more slippery ground, or had a more difficult point to manage, than Thomson'.[9] More suggests that this is because 'Distinct as the seasons of the year may seem to a superficial observer, the weather, the objects, and the sentiments which discriminate them most, yet run into one another'.[10] That is, Thomson is prevented from holding a single subject or even season clearly in view before being drawn on to another, not (or not only) across space, but through the time of 'the seasons of the year' and the length of time within each of those seasons. For More, when he points out that the 'shadowing Roses' at the start of 'Spring' 'are not certainly quite so early in our island', Thomson has been tempted beyond the present moment in time by the associative train of his thought.[11] More reads this as a strength: 'His thoughts, which rarely expand around him, bear onward as it were in a straight line, in so much that all his collateral descriptions, like the branches of a tree, either spring spontaneously, or are grafted with inimitable grace, on whatever constitutes the leading burden of his song.'[12] The tree, which surely does 'expand around' itself, is an oddly spatial image for More to choose, but he seems to be invoking its characteristic of organic (or cultivated) growth rather than its fully grown structure. In order to embrace this onward movement, More advocates reading *The Seasons* 'from end to end, and inspect[ing] the agreeable workings of your own feelings, as you proceed'.[13]

The variety in these responses to the poem, from Johnson's impression that Thomson's images are 'subsisting all at once' to More's that 'His thoughts . . . rarely expand around him', testifies to the temporal ambiguity of the poem's natural descriptions. These responses also demonstrate that the question of whether the movement of the eye is through time or across space has implications for the question of how the poem is read, and vice versa. If the movement is through time, the implication is that the reader's own eye must encounter the poetry in chronological sequence in order to comprehend the flowing of time and causal connections that are the poetry's subject. But if the movement is across space, then the necessity to read in the order in which the lines are laid out diminishes; we can comprehend the different images as they are laid out in space regardless of the order in which we encounter them. As Johnson puts it, 'the order in which they are shown must by necessity be arbitrary'. In the opening passage of 'Spring', for example, if all the objects described are simultaneous rather than progressive stages in the process of spring's coming, there is no reason why we need to look at the mountains shedding their snows before we turn to the birds on the marsh. How we understand the relationships between natural objects described in the poem affects how we understand the relationship between parts of the poem. And how we read the poem – as 'an assemblage' of separate images or 'from end to end' – affects how we perceive its portrayal of natural causation.

In this chapter I contend that this question – whether the eye depicted in *The Seasons* moves across time or space – is a crucial one distinguishing two schools of Thomson criticism. We see it here differentiating very early responses to the poem, but the distinction has persisted to the present day. Most readers, like Shiels, give concessions to both sides of the question, acknowledging that the poem appears oddly disjointed, yet somehow still manages to 'flow'. But as we saw with critics of Milton in Chapter 3, readers have frequently given their preference to one approach or the other, as they advocate (or defend) either the linear or what Stefanie Lethbridge calls the 'anthological' method of reading.[14] The former resembles the linear reading advocated by so many readers of *Paradise Lost*, but differs in that the emphasis is given not to narrative order but to organic processes of growth and elaboration. The latter has much in common with what I called, in Chapter 3, the 'commonplacing' reading of Milton, but there is a subtle difference in that the extracted parts of *The Seasons* are rarely juxtaposed or complemented with other parts drawn from elsewhere, and rather invite reading in isolation. As Lethbridge has demonstrated, eighteenth-century long poems and especially non-narrative poems like *The Seasons* were often read 'in isolated fragments'.[15]

As with reading approaches to *Paradise Lost*, there are implications too for both authorial and readerly control. Readers of *The Seasons*, like Milton's readers, often describe the linear reading as a kind of submission to the power of either poem or poet, whereas the reader exercises their own power in extracting parts to read in isolation. What makes *The Seasons* such a successful non-narrative poem is not its 'want of method', but its 'unforced method': Thomson's arrangement of parts in such a way that readers are allowed a choice in whether they are swept along by hints of continuity, shade softening into shade, or whether like Keats they wander around the region of the poem, picking and choosing at their whim. As Stenke has observed, Thomson often invites the reader to imagine his poem as a maze; this is a spatial form through which ongoing movement can be guided with prompts or dead ends, but a reader or poet can decide to take a sudden new direction.[16] The result, as with *Paradise Lost*, is necessarily paradoxical, but rather than try to decide between these two perspectives and two methods we ought rather to ask how Thomson wrote a poem that could cause Jonathan Swift to remark in 1732 that *The Seasons* 'are all Descriptions, and nothing is doing',[17] and Heather Keenleyside to retort, nearly three hundred years later, that 'in *The Seasons* everything "is doing"'.[18]

The Tapestry

In 1973 Wallace Jackson argued that the eighteenth century saw the emergence of affective 'immediacy' as 'the paramount effect of the work of art' as opposed to instruction and education;[19] James Noggle has more recently modified this claim, arguing that 'in the eighteenth century . . . two temporal poles – intense immediacy and the long process – govern the discourse of taste together, neither negating nor fully harmonizing with each other'.[20] In his analysis of Virgil's long poems at the end of the seventeenth century, Joseph Addison is able to accommodate both extremes by developing a theory of a particular genre of long poem as a spatial form. In his 1697 'Essay on the Georgics', Addison describes one of Thomson's main models for *The Seasons*:

> And if there be so much Art in the choice of fit Precepts, there is much more requir'd in the Treating of 'em; that they may fall in after each other by a Natural unforc'd Method, and shew themselves in the best and most advantageous Light. They shou'd all be so finely wrought together into the same Piece, that no course Seam may discover where they joyn; as in a Curious Brede of Needle-Work, one Colour falls away by such just degrees, and another rises so insensibly, that we see the variety, without being able to distinguish the total vanishing of the one from the first appearance of the other.[21]

The *Georgics*, according to Addison, consists of small units (its 'Precepts') that are arranged into one 'same Piece', in which those smaller units exist in simultaneity. No unit is 'forc'd' in by that which precedes it; this lack of force in the method that determines which unit falls in after another suggests a delicate fragility to the structure, even the possibility that they could be arranged in alternative configurations, and certainly the impossibility of the reader's guessing exactly what will come next. William Youngren, analysing this analysis of Addison's, takes issue with the implied passivity of the artwork:

> Despite the talk of rising and falling, vanishing and appearing, Addison's analogy makes it clear that he is thinking of the Georgic as something that can be viewed all at once. Having taken in the whole, we are then free, just as with a painting or a tapestry, to let the eye move delightedly from one part of the poem to another. There is no suggestion that the poem itself moves through time, thereby determining or shaping the mental states or actions of the responding reader.[22]

This is slightly unfair. Youngren goes on to argue that in his later years Addison helped to develop a theory of 'the effect of literature on the mind as a process that takes place through time as the reader reads, a process to some extent determined and shaped by the temporal sequence of words that constitute the poem', but such a theory is clearly already nascent in this passage.[23] Addison acknowledges that there is a temporal dimension to the experience of reading, and one that occurs in a particular successive order that is guided, if not controlled, by the artwork itself: the parts 'fall in after each other', one 'falls away', another 'rises'. Addison implies, as Youngren rightly notes, that the whole can be 'viewed all at once', but he also talks of 'the total vanishing of the one [part] from the first appearance of the other'. Literal spatial forms like tapestries, paintings and landscapes can still direct the viewer's eye with prompts and hints. The eye is not forced but invited to encounter the parts in the particular order that the artist has designed.

Johnson complained of *The Seasons*' 'want of method', but 'unforc'd Method' gives a better sense of Thomson's organisational skills. Even when the movement he describes is clearly across space, Thomson does often give himself a guide, if not a rule, by which to control that movement. Johnson's own admission that Thomson 'thinks in a peculiar train' suggests as much.[24] In the last chapter we saw his miniature prospect poem following a waterfall down to a river. A little earlier in 'Summer' he follows the line of a brook:

> AROUND th' adjoining Brook, that purls along
> The vocal Grove, now fretting o'er a Rock,
> Now scarcely moving thro' a reedy Pool,
> Now starting to a sudden Stream, and now
> Gently diffus'd into a limpid Plain;
> A various Groupe the Herds and Flocks compose,
> Rural Confusion! On the grassy Bank
> Some ruminating lie; while others stand
> Half in the Flood, and often bending sip
> The circling Surface.
> (Su.480–537)

The movement across space is clear, but this might also be a movement through time, following the water of the river as it travels. Zoë Kinsley writes (of the general character of *The Seasons*, though she may well have had this particular passage in mind) that Thomson

> achieves both temporal succession *and* spatial arrangement. The river flowing through a landscape, the light of the sun's rays passing over a valley, the wind blowing the clouds across the sky: all of these are active movements through space and time that provide a definite sequence by which the objects of the landscape are encountered and can be described while retaining a sense of their physical place in that scene.[25]

I thoroughly agree with Kinsley that, in these lines and elsewhere, Thomson successfully communicates both temporal succession and spatial arrangement, but not with her suggestion that the movement through space as much as that through time provides the 'definite sequence by which the objects of the landscape are encountered'. If the movement were only through space, that sequence would lose its necessity, because these objects would have no causal 'dependance' (as Shiels put it) on each other. Part of a scene, a prospect, but not part of a process, each image would possess and retain its own internal integrity.

The georgic repetition of 'now' in the above 'Summer' passage might encourage us to read in this way, as it suggests that all parts of the scene exist in one now: the rock, the pool, the stream and the limpid plain all exist simultaneously in time. The different parts of the river are equivalent to the cows and sheep, some of whom lie 'while' others stand. The river remains at one place 'fretting o'er a Rock' even as, from another point in space, it appears 'Now scarcely moving'. The 'nows' invite us to hold the different parts of this passage in our minds at once (to imagine a kind of static landscape painting), and hence receive the impression of spatial variety. The order in which we encounter the parts no longer matters. On the other hand, each 'now' refers to a new time in the process of the eye moving across the larger scene, and this has the effect of distinguishing each part of the scene into a new moment in time, its own 'now'. If we read in this way, our mind's eye does not imagine (in the literal sense of 'image') an expansive scene with a river that is doing all of these things at once. As we read, we picture each part of the river's progress separately and successively, as though we followed the course of one droplet of water. We can read each image as part of a flowing, continuous progression.

Whether the 'present' time is understood to be one, two or ten lines long, its relation to past and future time is ambiguous. In this passage each 'now' is both distinct from and integrated into its surroundings, and it is impossible to say what relation it has to the next or preceding 'now': is it simultaneous with it, moving or 'softening' into it, or perhaps even totally separate from and unrelated to it, existing at another time? After all, if we do not read these lines as describing a continuous process, we could understand each image as not necessarily simultaneous with every other but as a totally distinct moment in time. This water we see 'starting' perhaps wasn't that water we saw 'moving' through the pool a few seconds ago when we read the previous line – perhaps this water went through the pool minutes, hours, days, or many seasons ago or perhaps it hasn't been through yet at all.

Apprehending that the different images may be either simultaneous with or discrete from one another in time permits us to extract them from their place in the whole, a practice that would feel more like an affront to the poem's intention if the parts were apprehended as belonging to a continuously flowing process. This is true too at the larger scales of verse paragraphs and entire seasons. Disjointed from the parts before and after by the suggestion that they may not represent moments in a continuum, the parts lose their 'dependance' upon one another and upon their place in the whole. Each part is, to echo Boethius, 'governing itself'.

We find this kind of reading registered in the anthologising habits of many readers over the centuries since the poem's publication. Though to extract is potentially to disregard or forget about the larger whole, this hermeneutic method assumes and implies a particular conception of the whole. It apprehends the whole as a collection of parts 'subsisting all at once' as opposed to arranged in a progressive unfolding structure. Many readers have felt empowered by the 'still' quality of the poem, the idea of all its parts as simultaneous, not just to view the whole synchronically but to move between the sections at will, and often to extract passages altogether, since as Shiels points out no part seems 'subservient' to another. Lethbridge has demonstrated the extent to which *The Seasons* was anthologised in the eighteenth century; many readers' first, only or most regular engagements with the poem would have been through anthologies.[26] In Jung's words, eighteenth-century readers understood *The Seasons* itself 'as an anthology, a collection of flowers, from which they could select'.[27] In modern criticism, the extreme version of this kind of reading is Oscar Kenshur's, who argues that *The Seasons* is constructed as a collection of fragments because Thomson values differentiation as the prerequisite of order; 'disorder ... occurs when distinctions are blurred or effaced.'[28] This would seem at odds with Johnson's conception of the parts of the poem being temporally simultaneous, but simultaneity as well as temporal distance enables independence, as it rejects the connectiveness of continuous movement or causal relation. This fragmenting approach to reading the poem is only the next step after Shiels's assumption that 'The Four Seasons [should be] considered separately, each Season as a distinct poem', as would have seemed natural to readers who remembered the printing of 'Winter', 'Summer' and 'Spring' in the 1720s – and not in the order in which they appeared together in 1730.[29]

Every event described in *The Seasons* cannot, of course, be simultaneous with every other. For all Thomson's equation of particular seasons with particular places, it cannot be winter at the same time as summer in the British Isles. The moment at which Amelia is alive cannot be simultaneous with the moment at which she is dead. But by questioning the relation between even moments that cannot be simultaneous, Thomson questions their participation in a single unfolding of a single year. Each event takes place in a particular point in the year, but at what point and in what year? By disrupting the flow, Thomson fragments his poem and those fragments cannot be placed with confidence in a continuous iteration of the cycle. Which *now* is 'first' and which is 'last' is impossible to say. It then becomes natural to treat the poem as a collection of moments that do not unfold successively, and so the poem, if not every event depicted within it, comes to appear spatially extended rather than temporally.

This is true not only at the enormous scale of each book of *The Seasons*, but at the scale of individual images or even lines. Boswell tells an amusing anecdote about when Johnson and Shiels (whom Johnson employed as an amanuensis to work on the *Dictionary*) were discussing *The Seasons* together. Shiels, Thomson's first biographer, was an enthusiastic fan of the poet and composed an abominable eulogy on him ('Musidorus') after Thomson's death. No doubt aware of this, and wishing to prove his point that Thomson's 'fault is such a cloud of words sometimes, that the sense can hardly peep through', Johnson reported to Boswell that 'I took down Thomson, and read aloud a large portion of him, and then asked, – Is not this fine? Shiels having expressed the highest admiration. Well, Sir (said I,) I have omitted every other line.'[30] Facetious as he was, Johnson was making an important point about how the *Seasons* invites itself to be read. And perhaps Shiels was in turn making an important point when he didn't (or didn't care to) notice Johnson's joke. Taking a cue from Johnson, R. D. Havens observed in 1922 that 'The truth seems to be that when off his guard Thomson relapsed into writing not metrical paragraphs but separate lines'.[31] In fact Thomson may not have been 'off his guard' at all, but was composing 'self-generating' lines that would recreate for his reader his own apprehension of time.[32] There are 'effects' in the poetry that, as Spacks argues, 'depend on units about a hundred lines long'; there are also effects that depend upon our refusal to read in this way.[33]

A methodological issue with the anthological hermeneutic is that Thomson's poetry is rarely only a movement across space; it always at least reserves for itself the possibility that it describes a movement through time, even if this is only the time it takes for the eye to pass over a large still scene. The impression the poetry gives, even at points of disjunction, that all may be a single continuous unfolding makes it difficult to decide where we draw the line and define a 'part'. Each

'Shade' is always softening into the next 'Shade', 'run[ning] into . . . another', as More phrases it. Even across the boundaries separating each book of the poem it is possible to detect continuity that invites us to read the whole continuously. This is the problem facing readings like Kenshur's, which centre upon the poem's fragmentation into parts, but don't address the very real problem of identifying where one part ends and another begins, or indeed the size of a part. The effect of Thomson's method of blurring yet still implying temporal boundaries is that we can isolate even tiny units as distinct moments or scenes within one moment, but we can also identify continuity at every level. Whenever I try to extract a portion of the poem, I feel the tug of the following lines, as these might be the necessary next 'Shades' in what is in fact one continuous process over time.

The quintessential reading of the poem in this continuous way, in the tradition of More, is Cohen's *The Unfolding of the Seasons*. Cohen carries out and advocates a linear reading, but even this monumental defence of the poem as an unfolding process has to include qualifications. *The Unfolding* is unclear on the extent to which its linear reading is cumulative: 'The poem represents . . . a serial way of looking at experience unified lexically and imagistically within completed fragments.'[34] A 'season is "whole"', Cohen explains, 'in the sense that it is composed of a cluster of completed fragments joined by various devices of transition and internally joined by imagery, repetition, thematic and stylistic interplay'.[35] Who would disagree? But if each fragment is 'complete' in itself, what does the 'serial way of looking' add to our experience? Why do we have to encounter these fragments in any specific order? *The Unfolding* proceeds by reading the poem in parts, and although it moves through them in order it cannot always demonstrate how each part is an extension or elaboration of what precedes, as the 'unfolding' image implies. Nevertheless, Cohen's project testifies to the fact that Thomson's poem invites this kind of continuous reading as well as the fragmented kind, and *The Unfolding* demonstrates the value of such a reading.

'The eighteenth-century long poem', writes Richard Terry, is 'constantly involved in puzzling over its amphibian status as both a congeries of parts and a constructed integrity'.[36] When we try to trace a continuous movement in the poem between passages, difficulty arises because Thomson sustains a paradoxical balance. In his transitions he does deliberately retain a sense of continuity; there is almost always some embryonic hint that we can identify in the preceding lines to explain the movement of the poem. Yet as in his depictions of the poetic process, Thomson also deliberately eschews the ordinary logic of linear process, confounding our expectations of progressive movement upwards, outwards or onwards, and replacing these with sudden turns or returns. Thomson constructs a movement that invites a linear reading and invites us to identify the organic growth and evolution of the poetry, but simultaneously requires us to forget or leave behind what we have read in order to embrace the poetry we confront in the new present.

At Last, The Rain

After his description of the biblical Deluge in 'Spring', and how 'THE Seasons since have, with severer Sway, / Oppress'd a broken World' (317–18), Thomson goes on naturally enough to describe that broken world, in the form of humanity's newly inharmonious relationship with nonhuman nature. Whereas in the Golden Age humans disported with wild beasts, now they contend with the wolf and tiger (342–6). Whereas before they fed on herbs and fruits, now they kill their faithful sheep and oxen for food (349–70). But Thomson cuts off his vegetarian argument:

> 'tis enough,
> In this late Age, adventurous, to have touch'd
> Light on the Numbers of the *Samian* Sage.
> High HEAVEN forbids the bold presumptuous Strain,
> Whose wisest Will has fix'd us in a State
> That must not yet to pure Perfection rise.
> Besides, who knows, how *rais'd* to higher Life,
> From Stage to Stage, the *Vital Scale ascends*?
> (371–8)

Thomson has undermined the power of his previous lines. Yet he lets them remain in the poem, to be just 'touch'd', and felt in the moment at which they are read, before they are piously dismissed. Thomson's readers are allowed to be moved by the arguments of 'the feeling Heart', then permitted to forget those arguments, so that they are not obliged to implement them in their lives (370). How much of the preceding poetry are we supposed to retain in our memories, and how much let fall away, as we read on in the passage which follows this injunction to forget?

> NOW when the first foul Torrent of the Brooks,
> Swell'd with the vernal Rains, is ebb'd away;
> And, whitening, down their mossy-tinctur'd Stream
> Descends the billowy Foam: now is the Time,

> While yet the dark-brown Water aids the Guile,
> To tempt the Trout.
> (379–84)

This is one of the oddest tonal and temporal disjunctions in the poem.[37] It seems to have forgotten the theme of animal rights, or rather to have taken to heart the argument that humans are not yet ready to be humane. But then there is a return:

> The well-dissembled Fly,
> The Rod fine-tapering with elastic Spring,
> Snatch'd from the hoary Steed the floating Line,
> And all thy slender watry Stores prepare.
> But let not on thy Hook the tortur'd Worm,
> Convulsive, twist in agonizing Folds;
> Which, by rapacious Hunger swallow'd deep,
> Gives, as you tear it from the bleeding Breast
> Of the weak, helpless, uncomplaining Wretch,
> Harsh Pain and Horror to the tender Hand.
> (384–93)

The admonishment of use of live bait recalls Thomson's injunctions against cruelty in lines 347–70, but forgets the dismissal of this argument in lines 371–8. Reading the fishing scene requires simultaneous remembrance and forgetfulness – it was anthologised in several poetry collections in the eighteenth century, as well as excerpted in treatises on fishing. (Later in 'Spring', Thomson will use fish again to give the most explicit expression of his poetry's self-forgetfulness. After a description of sea-monsters he dismisses, and yet of course leaves in the poem, his preceding lines: 'But this the Theme / I sing, enraptur'd, to the BRITISH FAIR, / Forbids, and leads me to the Mountain-brow' [830–2].)

Though its relation to the reflection on animal rights is ambiguous, this fishing passage may (also or instead) be looking further back (in the poem, though not so far back in history), referring by 'vernal Rains' not to the Deluge but to the rainfall described in lines 172–c. 191 before Thomson got distracted by the Golden Age and the Flood. However, by virtue of their recurrence in every iteration of the spring season, the idea of 'vernal Rains' is just as accessible and familiar to those who are reading these lines out of their larger context. The rainfall that Thomson does describe earlier in 'Spring' is itself the culmination of a long passage describing the 'pleasing Expectation' (162) of nature.

> At last,
> The Clouds consign their Treasures to the Fields;
> And, softly shaking on the dimpled Pool
> Prelusive Drops, let all their Moisture flow
> In large Effusion, o'er the freshened World.
> (Sp.171–5)

As well as following the immediately preceding lines, this rainfall could also be read as a delayed answer to the initial invocation at the opening of 'Spring' to 'COME . . . come, / And from the Bosom of yon dropping Cloud . . . on our Plains descend' (1–4). To read the rainfall in this context, as following on from the opening, within its own cumulatively unfolding passage of 'Expectation', and leading to the fishing scene, is indeed 'pleasing', as it gives a sense of anticipation and fulfilment. On the other hand, as we saw in Chapter 4, it is not only possible but perhaps equally or even more pleasing to read those first lines of 'Spring' as self-contained and fulfilling themselves in the present. Those lines stood sufficient without the later 'answer', and the later description of nature's expectation, and this later release of the rain can stand sufficient too. Even these five lines on the rain, located between expectation and resulting satisfaction, seem to be deliberately self-contained. 'At last' looks back to the process leading up to this moment but also separates this moment off from the rest. These lines are part of a larger whole, as is any moment within a georgic cycle, but Thomson also 'shuts the Scene' (Sp.35), and even each fragment within a scene, like his husbandmen. Afterwards, 'The stealing Shower is scarce to patter heard' (176).

Just a few lines after describing how 'At last, / the Clouds consign their Treasures to the Fields', Thomson repeats a depiction of the scene (so that it wasn't 'last', really), in a couple of lines, 'THUS all day long the full-distended Clouds / Indulge their genial Stores' (186–7), which lead to the depiction of the rainbow. In his *Critical Essays* of 1785, the poet-critic John Scott (another friend of Johnson's) criticised Thomson for 'such frequent reiteration of the same ideas in different expressions. The writer may experience no disgust from this abundance, but the reader must; for he has conceived the thought, and wishes not to dwell upon it, but to quit it for another.'[38] (Later, Stockdale would reply to critics who accused Thomson of dwelling too long: Thomson 'never dwells too long for *me*'. He would also pick up More's image of the poem as a tree: 'if he *is*, sometimes redundant . . . it is the excess of a blooming, and luxuriant tree; an excess that you would prune with regret.')[39] Scott is responding to a tension inherent in Thomson's method: Thomson invites us to dwell at length on one moment, but he also gives rise to Scott's wish, 'to quit [the present scene] for another'. What justifies this instance of repetition about the clouds, for Scott, is that this second iteration stands sufficient on its own: 'This passage has great merit.'[40] It is both a repetition of the earlier lines, and a new scene altogether. 'Thus' might refer to the specific rain that Thomson has just described, or it might refer to any rain, in any spring. Later in 'Spring', rain will come again: 'the teeming Clouds / Descend in gladsome Plenty' (888–9). It is as if the 'earlier' rain, and Thomson's description(s) of it, are happening again, or never occurred or are yet to occur, all at once.

Unifying Method

The fact that *The Seasons* constantly threatens to break into isolated fragments – in its depiction of natural causation, its arrangement of its supposedly narrative tales, its textual history and the structure of its parts – speaks to the structural vulnerability of the long non-narrative poem. It also speaks to the long poem's capacity to articulate, even in the reading experience it creates, non-linear conceptions of time. But that alarming (even while also potentially empowering) vulnerability to fragmentation has led critics to seek themes or ethical principles that can unify the poem into a more stable whole. Terry has proposed that *The Seasons*

> forces its readers to enact the mental process of theodicy . . . the need the reader feels to piece together some unifying meaning, to build up coherence from the poem's miscellany of discrete parts, entails a textual hermeneutics exactly counterpart with the religious reasoning of theodicy.[41]

Terry implicitly assumes a linear reading, which seems related to his impression that the poem 'forces' its readers. He admits that this harmonising vision is only achieved at the end of the poem, and that the experience in the present of reading 'is one of plurality and disorder', but still this is quite an optimistic interpretation, based on a privileging of the ending's claims to coherence: that, by the end of a linear reading experience, we have an idea not only of a whole but of a harmoniously unified whole.[42] Lethbridge has similarly 'assert[ed] the poem's coherence in its cultural functionality' rather than any specific theme or statement, although she identifies a secular function. She argues that Thomson's mixture of natural philosophy and classical and modern poetry was meant 'to contribute to the development of moral practice through aesthetic means': 'While the ideas he uses are contradictory, the effect he tries to achieve remains coherent, he wants to encourage virtuous conduct . . . particularly the exercise of compassion and benevolence.'[43] Rather than learning to harmonise disparate parts (either of nature or the poem), or receiving an education in virtuous living, I suggest that the reader's experience as created by *The Seasons* is the one of the man described in 'Autumn', who enjoys the natural world because he both apprehends the seasons in motion, 'attends . . . thro' the revolving Year' (1305–6), and focuses on the present too, 'sees [nature] in her every Shape' (1307), and 'Takes what she liberal gives, nor thinks of more' (1309). Such a perspective is able to celebrate the long recurrent processes of growth and decay that create every moment, including those causes that remain unknown and unseen; and also to appreciate the divinity immanent and immediate in every moment.

Neither of the hermeneutic methods that I have outlined provides 'unity' per se. On this Shiels and More agree – for the former each season was an 'assemblage of poetical ideas', for the latter 'unity of subject' was impossible in the poem – even with their contrasting apprehensions of the poem's temporality and structure. Both spatial and temporal movement are dimensions in which Thomson registers variety, and apprehending the poem as a wide space (like Shiels) or as an extended timeline (like More) is only a different way of apprehending its 'subject in itself so diversified'. What we do have is a unity of method, the 'unforced method' I have been describing, on the parts both of the poet and of the reader. In taking this method as a unifying force I am following John Barrell and Harriet Guest, who have pointed out the difference between 'method', which was commented upon frequently by eighteenth-century critics, and 'consistency' (by which they mean thematic, tonal or moral consistency), seeking which, or demonstrating the lack of which, preoccupied readers in the twentieth century.[44] For eighteenth-century readers, Barrell and Guest argue, long poems were permitted 'to contradict themselves'.[45] Barrell argues elsewhere that *The Seasons* does not possess a 'unifying vision' in the twentieth-century sense.[46] Instead, as Dennis Desroches writes, if Thomson's poem moves from theme to theme 'it nevertheless remains remarkably single-minded in the rhetorical strategy it uses to present these themes'.[47] The unforced method of *The Seasons* is an apprehension of the world (and the poem) as extended and various both in time and space, and the persistent fusion of these two dimensions into one vision.

Chapter 4 began with Thomson's depiction of his own poem as a 'Train': 'A simple Train, / Yet so delightful mix'd... Shade, unperceiv'd, so softening into Shade; / And all so forming an harmonious Whole' ('Hymn', 21–5). I will end this section on *The Seasons* with Thomson's depiction of it as a spatial form, a 'Dome':

> Shall little haughty Ignorance pronounce
> His Works unwise, of which the smallest Part
> Exceeds the narrow Vision of her Mind?
> As if upon a full-proportion'd Dome,
> On swelling Columns heav'd, the Pride of Art!
> A Critic-Fly, whose feeble Ray scarce spreads
> An Inch around, with blind Presumption bold,
> Should dare to tax the Structure of the Whole.
> And lives the Man, whose universal Eye
> Has swept at once th' unbounded Scheme of Things[?]
> (Su.321–30)

The references to 'Works', 'Art' and of course the 'Critic-Fly' make it impossible for the reader not to see this passage about God's creation as also about *The Seasons*. Thomson suggests that a truly synchronic view 'of the Whole', including the whole of a very long poem, is beyond humans' capacity. Yet in the 'Hymn' Thomson himself characterises 'the harmonious Whole' by characterising the relation between the parts, 'Shade . . . softening into Shade'. His point here that humans cannot 'tax the Structure of the Whole' hints as much at the inconsistency or elusiveness of that structure as at its scale; at any point in that structure we cannot know for sure whether we are at one point in a moving 'Train' or at one point on a stationary 'Dome'. *The Seasons* is both at once.

Notes

1. Johnson, 'Thomson', in *The Lives of the Poets*, xxiii, 1276–94 (1293).
2. Johnson, 'Pope', in *The Lives of the Poets*, xxiii, 1032–270 (1195).
3. Percival Stockdale, 'Lecture XII. Thomson', in *Lectures on the Truly Eminent English Poets* (London: Longman, Hurst, Rees, Orme, and W. Clarke,1807): II.74–144 (110–11).
4. Ibid., 111.
5. Ibid., 114.

6. Robert Shiels, *The Lives of the Poets of Great Britain and Ireland*, 5 vols (London: R. Griffiths, 1753), v, 202.
7. Ibid.
8. More, *Strictures*, 33.
9. Ibid., 33.
10. Ibid., 33–4.
11. Ibid., 34.
12. Ibid., 40.
13. Ibid., 122.
14. Stefanie Lethbridge, 'Anthological Reading Habits in the Eighteenth Century: The Case of Thomson's *Seasons*', in *Anthologies of British Poetry: Critical Perspectives from Literary and Cultural Studies*, ed. Barbara Korte et al. (Amsterdam: Rodopi, 2000), 89–104.
15. Ibid., 96.
16. Katarina Stenke, '"Devolving through the Maze of Eloquence": James Thomson's *The Seasons* and the Eighteenth-Century Verse Labyrinth', *Journal for Eighteenth-Century Studies* 39.1 (2016): 5–23.
17. Jonathan Swift, letter to Charles Wogan (2 August 1732), in *Correspondence of Jonathan Swift*, ed. Harold Williams, 5 vols (Oxford: Oxford UP, 1965), iv, 53. Quoted in James Sambrook, 'Introduction', *TS*, xxix.
18. Heather Keenleyside, 'Personification for the People: On James Thomson's *The Seasons*', *ELH* 76 (2009): 447–72 (451).
19. Wallace Jackson, *Immediacy: The Development of a Critical Concept from Addison to Coleridge* (Amsterdam: Rodopi, 1973), 69.
20. James Noggle, *The Temporality of Taste in Eighteenth-Century British Writing* (Oxford: Oxford UP, 2012), 1.
21. Joseph Addison, 'Essay on the Georgics', in John Dryden, *Poems, 1697*, ed. Vinton A. Dearing et al. (Berkeley: University of California Press, 1987), 146.
22. William Youngren, 'Addison and the Birth of Eighteenth-Century Aesthetics', *Modern Philology* 79 (1982): 267–83, 272.
23. Youngren, 'Addison', 274. Youngren distinguishes this from the 'static clarity of moral presentation' valued by Restoration critics (272).
24. Johnson, 'Thomson', in *The Lives of the Poets*, xxiii, 1276–94 (1291).
25. Zoë Kinsley, 'Landscapes "Dynamically in Motion": Revisiting Issues of Structure and Agency in Thomson's *The Seasons*', *Papers on Language and Literature* 41 (2005): 3–25 (9).
26. Lethbridge, 'Anthological Reading Habits'.
27. Sandro Jung, 'Print Culture, High-cultural Consumption, and Thomson's *The Seasons*, 1780–1797', *Eighteenth-Century Studies* 44 (2011): 495–514 (498).
28. Oscar Kenshur, *Open Form and the Shape of Ideas: Literary Structures as Representations of Philosophical Concepts* (Lewisburg: Bucknell UP, 1986), 82. Even Kenshur, however, in a nod to the alternative hermeneutic,

claims that these fragments, having been differentiated, are then 'reintegrated into a harmonious whole' (86).
29. Shiels, *Lives of the Poets*, 202.
30. James Boswell, *Life of Johnson*, ed. R. W. Chapman (Oxford: Oxford UP, 1970), 743.
31. R. D. Havens, *The Influence of Milton on English Poetry* (Cambridge, MA: Harvard UP, 1922), 146.
32. Sitter, *Literary Loneliness*, 177.
33. Spacks, *The Varied God*, 19.
34. Cohen, *Unfolding*, 84.
35. Ibid., 105.
36. Richard Terry, 'Transitions and Digressions in the Eighteenth-Century Long Poem', *SEL* 32 (1992): 495–510 (49).
37. I discuss the weird temporal shifts leading up to this scene in 'The Golden Age and Iron Times', in Jung and Van De Walle ed. *Genres*.
38. Scott, *Critical essays on some of the poems, of several English poets*, 305.
39. Stockdale, 'Lecture XII', 97–8.
40. Ibid., 305–6.
41. Terry, 'Through Nature shedding influence malign', 265.
42. Ibid., 266–7.
43. Stefanie Lethbridge, *James Thomson's Defence of Poetry* (Tübingen: Max Niemeyer Verlag GmbH, 2003), 26, 64, 170.
44. John Barrell and Harriet Guest, 'On the Use of Contradiction: Economics and Morality in the Eighteenth-Century Long Poem', in *The New Eighteenth Century*, ed. Felicity Nussbaum and Laura Brown (New York: Methuen, 1987), 121–43 (122).
45. Ibid., 135.
46. Barrell, *English Literature in History*, 73.
47. Dennis Desroches, 'The Rhetoric of Disclosure in James Thomson's *The Seasons*; or, On Kant's Gentlemanly Misanthropy', *Eighteenth Century* 49 (2008): 1–24 (13).

Part III

Wordsworth

Chapter 7

Years Flowed In Between: Chronos and Kairos in *The Prelude*

The inspiring spirit who, for Milton, 'Dove-like satst brooding on the vast Abyss / And mad'st it pregnant' (*PL*, I.21–2), for Wordsworth will not sit still long enough to hatch him a 'great argument' (*PL*, I.24):

> his mind, best pleas'd
> While she, as duteous as the Mother Dove,
> Sits brooding, lives not always to that end,
> But, like the innocent Bird, hath goadings on
> That drive her, as in trouble, through the groves[.]
> (I.139–43)

There is a similar moment in Wordsworth's 'Stanzas written in my Pocket-copy of Thomson's Castle of Indolence'. Wordsworth depicts himself as a Thomsonian figure enjoying the present, the time of which is imagined as a space in which to linger: 'Here on his hours he hung as on a book; / On his own time here would he float away.' But his wish to relish the present is confounded by his vocation, in terms that recall the Miltonic dove driven through the groves (and similarly refer to the poet in the third person): 'But Verse was what he had been wedded to; / And his own mind did, like a tempest strong, / Come to him thus, and drove the weary Man along.'[1]

The driving question of Wordsworth's long poem *The Prelude* is 'was it for this?' It is a question with numerous literary sources including Virgil's *Georgics*, Milton's *Samson Agonistes* and Thomson's *Seasons*, but it is also the question that, in the above examples, drives his difference from Milton and Thomson. It is a question about causation: did, and how did, my experiences shape the person I am today? Did, and how did, the past cause the present? Milton and Thomson, as we have seen, are able to sustain a balance between the necessity of ongoing time and the independence of each moment; I aimed to strike an equivalent balance in my analysis of their long poems. But Wordsworth's autobiographical imperative, his need to 'trace / Our Being's earthly progress' (II.233–4), tips the balance in *The Prelude*. I do not wish to deny the importance of the concept of the single epiphanic moment for Wordsworth, but due to existing critical emphasis on this kind of time in his poetry, and due to what I see as the temporality that ultimately triumphs in *The Prelude*, in this section of the book I will take a more partisan position. Moments at which Wordsworth seems to transcend the chronological shape of time, when examined, lead us back to and are reintegrated into the processes of chronological time, often in order to make sense of their very distinctiveness. They reveal the importance of the 'many years [that] / Have since flowed in between' and the danger of attempting to bypass or ignore those years (II.336–7). I want to argue for not only the necessity but the profundity, beauty and power in Wordsworth's poetry of the temporality of chronos, rather than kairos.

Chronos and Kairos

Wordsworth's theory of 'spots of time, / That with distinct pre-eminence retain / A renovating virtue' (XII.208–10), and his use of the spot of time as a structural principle to shape his long poem *The Prelude*, suggests a preference for the temporality of kairos over chronos. Chronos is chronological, sequential time that is measured quantitatively and proceeds evenly. Kairos is a moment of particular opportunity or significance as measured qualitatively: the *right* time. The shape of chronos is a steady, consistent, extended timeline, while the shape of kairos is a sudden peak that disrupts that timeline. A moment of kairos might appear to stand apart entirely from the flux of time, denying its causal relationship with both past and future. This is Georges Poulet's influential theory of the Romantic experience of time, which, he wrote,

> is not provoked by an apparent or real recurrence of the past in the present, but, on the contrary, by a total exclusion of the past from the present, by a perfect absorption in the present. The present moment, then, is so intensely experienced that it seems as if its transience gives way to everlastingness, as if time stands still and becomes eternity.[2]

This absorption in the present is the kind of temporality expressed at the beginning of *The Prelude*, when the 'weight of many a weary day' is 'shaken off' (I.20–2), and Wordsworth, aspiring to Thomsonian instantaneous composition, makes a 'present joy the matter of a Song' (I.47). It is the temporality that Wordsworth celebrates in 'Home at Grasmere', in lines that describe simultaneously a spot of land and a spot of time:

> Something that makes this individual Spot,
> This small abiding-place of many men,
> A termination, and a last retreat,
> A Centre, come from whereso'er you will,
> A Whole without dependence or defect,
> Made for itself and happy in itself,
> Perfect Contentment, Unity entire.
> ([MS. B]164–70)[3]

On the other hand, instead of excluding past and future, a moment of kairos might appear to condense many times into one supreme moment. When Wordsworth entered London for the first time, for example, he felt the power of a 'weight of ages', and all of the city's history 'came and went' within him 'in a moment' (VIII.552–8). This version of kairos is what Jonathan Sachs and Andrew Piper have called 'Wordsworth's synoptic mindfulness', his articulation of 'compression, the containment of speed in the simultaneity of the all at once'.[4] This sounds like the nunc stans, or at least like Hobbes's nunc stans in which all times are compressed to a single point; it is unlike the Boethian-Miltonic nunc stans, of course, which functioned by extension rather than compression, and which was rendered spatially as a prospect rather than a spot. Whether understood as the exclusion or the compression of past and future, the kairos model of time confounds the succession and linearity of chronos.

The general consensus among critics of Wordsworth is that he values kairos over chronos. Christopher R. Miller goes so far as to claim that Wordsworth rejects chronos temporality altogether, and that in its 'recursive narrative turns . . . its flux between memory and present utterance, its moments of atemporal reverie', *The Prelude* 'everywhere implies that there is no such thing as objective time or chronology'.[5] Others acknowledge that chronos is a necessity for Wordsworth, because he writes in part to register his own linear development over time, but that it is the less profound and less poetic temporality, admirably resisted by the kairos of the virtuosic spots of time. For Wordsworth, according to Helen Regueiro, to cast an experience 'back into the alienating process of temporality' (by which she means moving, chronological time) is a necessary evil, necessary because experiences must be 'validate[d] in the world of time'.⁶ For John Beer, chronos is associated with authority, convention and a lack of risk, whereas Wordsworth privileges the 'moment of judgment, the moment of decision, the sudden illumination, the sudden despair, the Apocalypse itself – all are examples of *kairos*, united by the fact that in some sense they stand apart from the time process in which they participate'.⁷ James P. Davis writes similarly that Wordsworth 'celebrates' 'subjective time', his 'private mode of experiencing time that contrasts with the empirical, public and traditional conception of time as measured by clocks and calendars'.⁸ Jeffrey Baker identifies an explicit hierarchy of types of time in Wordsworth's poetry, with the two external, objective forms of time, 'clock-time' and 'nature's' or 'Newtonian' time, at the bottom, and at the top 'inner' or subjective time.⁹ This 'inner time', which is 'liberating and creative . . . obliterates not merely the two inferior schemes, but itself also, bringing the mind to a visionary moment, an eternal present where "we see into the life of things"'.¹⁰ In these readings we see the influence of Kermode's 1966 *The Sense of an Ending*, which posits chronos as the dull time of reality, empty of meaning. For Kermode, the bare act of telling a story, of organising events into narrative, transforms chronos into kairos (defined by the presence, rather than the exclusion, of past and future): 'that which was conceived of as simply successive becomes charged with past and future: what was *chronos* becomes *kairos*.'¹¹

But if Wordsworth's moment of kairos, his spot of time, is a peak, an 'eminence', or an elevation, it is one that opens out into a prospect, both spatial and temporal. Remembering a spot of time, he writes, 'enables us to mount, / When high, more high, and lifts us up when fallen' (XII.217–18). I argue in this chapter that Wordsworth's spots of time are not properly spots at all but are extended prospects, which, as we have seen in the poetry of Milton and Thomson, is a poetic that fuses the temporality of stasis – which can apprehend the eternity and independence of a single moment – with the temporality of chronology – which can apprehend the causal relationships that pertain between events. It is clear that none of the spots of time are strictly instantaneous (even Wordsworth's entrance to London is framed as the culmination of a journey). When examined closely, they do not reveal a single point in time that is clearly identifiable as the significant 'Centre' that is 'whole without dependence', 'made for itself', and therefore extractable from time. They are radically decentred, offering up many times that claim to contribute to the significance of the 'spot'. Seeking the origin of his own poetic power, Wordsworth finds that any seemingly single time is in fact 'Gleaming through colouring of other times' (VIII.507). Perceiving 'the ties / That bind the perishable hours of life / Each to the other' not only explains how a particular hour came to be as it is, but also what it means, for the past and for the future (VII.461–3). A spot of time, Susan J. Wolfson writes in a conflicted summary, 'suggests autonomy rather than relation, a figure whose boundaries are drawn mysteriously inward to form a piece of lyric concentration and whose very difference from a linear plot is the basis of its definition', yet the notion of the spot of time 'has the virtue of supplying seemingly anomalous events with terms of relation that emerge over the course of "time." Like the heap of garments the boy sees distinctly through the gloom, these "moments" contain latent stores of information.'[12] Peter Larkin has described the way, following every spot of time, a 'post-climactic sphere must be consolidated, even by inviting meditation on loss, old age, or on death, the pure past. Such an after-dimension is part of the constitution of any heightened occasion in Wordsworth's poetry.'[13] This after-dimension can take the form of memory – the value of a spot of time is only evident in the 'renovating virtue' it provides for Wordsworth's later years. But there is often a 'post-climactic sphere' within the remembered experience itself, as well as a pre-climactic sphere. Wordsworth locates a special moment, a kairotic spot of time, but then cannot help but trace it forwards and backwards through chronological time. He has to ask: what happened afterwards? Not just years later, but immediately afterwards? No time that is related in *The Prelude* is 'Made for itself', but must define and justify its significance through its relation, in terms both of difference and continuity, to the larger narrative: 'Was it for this?' My reading of the spots of time, therefore, reverses the process that Monique R. Morgan reads into them: 'Each of *The Prelude*'s episodes begins with a very basic narrative but is essentially a subjective lyric experience, and initial plot movement gives way to a suspension of time.'[14] It is rather the seeming suspension that gives way to movement and narrative. In these moments that are seemingly the ultimate expression of kairos, chronos is always exercising its gravitational pull.

The Prelude dramatises the failure of the long poem to be lyrical. Or, put another way, it testifies to the failure of lyric to do the work that Wordsworth wants poetry to do (the notion of a 'lyrical ballad' is another such testimony). Seeking to understand how seemingly isolated moments fit into longer processes, Wordsworth draws on the narrative epic tradition but also on the eighteenth-century traditions of non-narrative long blank verse poems: the prospect poem, the philosophical poem, the georgic. His story of personal growth is not so different from Thomson's descriptions of natural growth: both are framed as a series of picturesque scenes that seem to 'stand apart', in Beer's phrase, but which also invite us to locate them in causal relationships with past and future times. Here I take four case study 'spots of time' – Wordsworth's climbs in the Alps and Snowdon, his encounter with the scene of a murderer's gibbet and his childhood ice skating – and examine how they open out into literal as well as figurative prospects. Such prospects, as in Milton's nunc stans and Thomson's landscapes, are ways of representing a simultaneous present that, because it is spread across space instead of being condensed to a single point, is able to accommodate different possible temporal and causal relationships between its features. So Wordsworth can imagine that the several components that make up a spot of time are simultaneous, spontaneous, self-determining experiences; or that they are the connected parts of a continuous process, shaped by the moment before and shaping the moment after.

At the end of *The Prelude*, Wordsworth recalls how at the beginning of his project he imagined both his life and his poem as a prospect view:

> Anon I rose
> As if on wings, and saw beneath me stretched
> Vast prospect of the world which I had been
> And was; and hence this Song, which like a lark
> I have protracted . . .
> . . .
> Yet centring all in love, and in the end
> All gratulant, if rightly understood.
> (XIV.379–87)

These lines clearly allude to Milton's prospects, particularly to Eve's dream and the prospect in *Paradise Regain'd*, but likely also Thomson's prospect of an African landscape in 'Summer', in which 'Plains immense / Lie stretch'd below . . . And vast Savannahs' (690–3). The 'stretched' nature of the prospect translates directly into the 'protracted' nature of the song, the extension of the view mapping onto the structure of a long poem, space turning into time. The prospect is not shapeless, but its 'centre' and 'end' are moral principles rather than spatial or temporal coordinates. The reference to 'love' as the 'centre' might seem like a platitude, but 'love' is an important factor in Wordsworth's construction of a temporality that reintegrates the spontaneous moment of kairos into the successive time of chronos. If kairos is subjective time, chronos is intersubjective. Whether marked by natural or artificial means, the seasonal cycle or the chiming of a college bell, it is the time experienced by communities of people across both space and time. We see in the spots of time that the return to chronos is not a failure to sustain the solipsism of kairos, but a triumphant, epiphanic reintegration into community.

Although 'natural time' and 'clock-time' are often distinguished and contrasted, they are both forms of chronos in that they mark time's passing.[15] The basis for each is cyclical (the turning of the planet, the cycle of the seasons, the circle of the dial), but against repetition they also register difference. Singular events are allowed to leave their marks. 'The seasons came', Wordsworth recalls in *The Prelude*,

> And every season wheresoe'er I moved
> Unfolded transitory qualities,
> Which, but for this most watchful power of love,
> Had been neglected; left a register
> Of permanent relations else unknown.
> (II.288–93)

For Thomson, historical events are subsumed into a cycle that leaves little room for concepts of 'before' and 'after': even death is something that can happen or not happen in any given year. But by the end of the eighteenth century, natural time was no longer only, or even predominantly, cyclical. It was also linear and, importantly, cumulative. Theories of evolution were coalescing. Rapid developments in geological stratigraphy revealed and promoted an earth history that took the form of amassed layers. The Earth and seasons kept turning, connecting the humans and nonhumans who experience these cycles across generations, but each turn left a little trace behind, and made the present a little different from the past: 'accidents and changes . . . To chronicle the time'.[16]

Even humanmade clocks and calendars, so often maligned as representatives of empty capitalist time, both incorporated traces of the past and signalled their dependence on natural time and the material nonhuman world. The French Revolutionary calendar was a new invention, but it incorporated traditional rural iconography. Attempts to standardise time globally in this period constructed (in theory if not in practice) a planetary community joined by clocks, but also highlighted regional differences in time – not only those created by the Earth's longitudes but those created by local clocks' notorious inaccuracy.[17] This flexibility and imprecision is the other face of homogeneous time, which Benedict Anderson, taking the term from Walter Benjamin, famously argued to be the newly dominant temporality of the late eighteenth century. In homogeneous time, 'simultaneity is, as it were, transverse, cross-time', connecting a person in Wales with a person in revolutionary France with a person in North America in the shared time of, say, 13 July 1798.[18]

The great poem of homogeneous time is Cowper's *The Task* (1785), in which the poet in his English rural retreat is confronted, in newspapers, 'with ev'ry day's report / Of wrong and outrage with which earth is fill'd' (II.6–7).[19] Cowper recognises the ethical importance of a global community sharing the present, but also the horror that simultaneity only emphasises difference, because a shared present cannot overcome vast difference in experience. As Mary A. Favret has shown, Cowper was all too aware that war was mediated, commodified and delayed before he had limited access to it, in the form of newspapers.[20] The horror lies in the realisation that hundreds of deaths were taking place at the exact moment, not when he was reading about those deaths, but when he was tending his cucumbers perhaps, or reclining on the sofa. The form of his long poem – using epic length to describe trivial pursuits – replicates this shock of temporal disproportion, as things of such different scale and import can take up the same amount of time. As Lamb put it, 'Cowper delays you as much, walking over a Bowling Green, as [Milton] does, travelling over steep Alpine heights, where the labour enters into and makes a part of the pleasure.'[21]

Wordsworth's interest in the idea of homogeneous time-shared-across-space is more optimistic than Cowper's; homogeneous time connects him to Coleridge in Malta or to his brother John at sea.[22] And for Wordsworth, the experience of a shared present that connected him with his historical contemporaries was not opposed to but intimately associated with the experience of ongoing time that connected him with other people in other times, including but not limited to past and future versions of himself. The time that is registered by both natural and humanmade clocks and calendars is the time that both separates and connects Wordsworth with past and future, and it is an experience of time that he shares with present, past and future communities.

The Alps and Snowdon

Both Milton and Thomson used the prospect poem as a framework for thinking about causation: a character or narrator's contemplation of the relation between elements in space maps onto contemplation about the relation between moments and events in time. Thomson's lines in 'Summer' in which he describes his ascent up a 'Mount' to view a 'broken Scene', which I analysed in Chapter 5, seems particularly to have influenced Wordsworth and Coleridge. They both use the ascent-to-a-prospect trope in order to reflect upon the difference between isolation – that of a moment in time and of themselves – and the protracted social life.

Book 6 of *The Prelude* questions the distinction Lamb makes between crossing the Alps and crossing a bowling green. Crossing the Alps is neither a single identifiable point nor a heroically long labour, but a sociable pastime. Wordsworth famously laments that he did not notice that he had crossed the Alps, but the poem does quietly notice it. The time most likely to mark the crossing was, in fact, the communal 'noon-tide meal' (566) that Wordsworth and Jones share with a party of muleteers; it is after lunch that they start the descent. The daily ritual obscures the epiphanic moment that Wordsworth thought he wanted, and the lunch is not remembered as particularly sublime. Kate Rigby has argued that 'what the speaker values most about this alpine region is not only, or even primarily, its sublime landscape . . . but rather the mode of human dwelling that he believed ("romantically", to be sure) was to be found in its pastoral vales'.[23] But it is worth asking whether there is an implicit alchemical connection between that mundane experience and the profound one that follows.[24] Does that lunch open the way, with the help of a Swiss peasant, to the visionary 'giddy prospect' (633) of 'woods decaying, never to be decayed, / The stationary blasts of waterfalls' (625–6)? These are the natural signs that register movement, growth and decay but that persist over such lengths of planetary time that they are 'fellow-travellers' (622) with all who cross the Simplon Pass.

When he crosses the Alps, Wordsworth discovers that moving through time in expectation of a point, a single moment of climax, will result in missing the experience itself, which is extended through time. Climbing Snowdon, on the other hand, for all his 'eager thoughts' of reaching the top and seeing the sunrise (XIV.31), Wordsworth takes the time to register the duration of the journey itself, instead of ignoring the journey in expectation of the destination. He even takes note of the 'small adventure' of the shepherd's dog finding a hedgehog (25). This brief scene is then 'over' but not 'forgotten' (27), preserved in the poetry as a marker of the time passing on the journey. 'Thus might we wear a midnight hour away' (32). He is rewarded, not by the light of the sun that he had expected, but by the more beautiful light of the moon, that creeps up on him unawares in a way that is both gradual and sudden:

> When at my feet the ground appeared to brighten,
> And with a step or two seemed brighter still;
> Nor was time given to ask or learn the cause;
> For instantly a light upon the turf
> Fell like a flash; and lo!
> (XIV.35–9)

The light falls 'instantly ... like a flash', and Wordsworth says explicitly that there was not 'time' to trace it to its cause. As a result, the moonlight appears causeless, self-generating. This is the temporality of kairos, in which epiphany comes in a moment and must be grasped at. But Wordsworth, although he does not in that moment ask 'the cause', also contextualises that 'instant' of the flash within a longer process of brightening. It may only be 'a step or two', and in the poetry a line or two, but that short amount of time shows that the flash was the culmination both of their effortful climb uphill and of the moon's own rise. Mark Hewson has written that 'The thought that Wordsworth's poetry seeks to produce ... depends on time as duration', noting that many of Wordsworth's poems emphasise their nature as 'prolonged'.[25] But Hewson locates the experience of heightened consciousness of duration outside the ordinary flow of time, arguing that it is resistant to movement and 'essentially different from the cognition of transience and mortality'.[26] Similarly Miller, reading the expression of duration in Wordsworth's spots of time that occur at evening, calls the effect 'a dilation of time'.[27] I propose instead that such moments, at which we and Wordsworth are strongly conscious of the duration of his experience, are rather moments of enhanced alertness to the time that is always ongoing; and that the duration in which Wordsworth is interested is not the outstretching of a single moment in time, but a genuine passage of time that registers change as well as continuity. Across the spots of time light can appear to brighten, then seem brighter still, and finally flash out. If Thomson had written this scene, it would have been unclear whether he described the moonlight's gradual appearance from one moment to the next, or a single moment in time in which we can trace the spread of moonlight across the ground. In Wordsworth's hands, the process over time cannot be obscured; these lines do entail a movement across space, but we are also shown 'turf' being illuminated that was dark the moment before.

Wordsworth's prospect view from Snowdon includes 'fixed' (58) waterfalls, recalling his own journey in the Alps and Thomson's up the 'Mount'. The passage also recalls Satan's assessment of cosmic hierarchy from the top of Mt Niphates, when Wordsworth considers the relationship between the 'inferior stars' and the 'sovereign elevation' of the moon (52–4). All of these prospect poems are reflections on the speaker's own relative power, his capacity to comprehend that which he sees (in both senses of encompassing and understanding) in tension with his smallness and his submission to greater forces. Furthermore, the temporal simultaneity of components in a prospect view obscures the causal relationships between those components – one thing might have caused another, but when, how and in what order, is impossible to know – thereby making possible any number of potential causal relationships. The mode of the prospect poem, then, is ideal for Wordsworth's contemplation of the 'interchangeable supremacy' (84) shared between the mind and the external world. But the prospect poem also makes space and time for Wordsworth's subsequent reflections on his own 'progress', as the prospect of landscape turns imperceptibly into a prospect of his life, with the various routes and connections that can be traced between its moments:

> Oh! who is he that hath his whole life long
> Preserved, enlarged, this freedom in himself
> . . .
> In one perpetual progress smooth and bright? –
> A humbler destiny have we retraced,
> And told of lapse and hesitating choice,
> And backward wanderings along thorny ways
> (XIV.130–8)

In addition to their own internal duration, the spots of time emphasise the time that extends beyond their seeming boundaries. '[T]he real power of Wordsworth's moments', writes Baker, is 'the immense energy within them, their power to make the reader's imagination work backward and forward in an instant.'[28] In a spot of time, 'The reader's mind . . . not only works back and forth between the time of writing and the time of the incident, but between both of these and the past which was perceived at the time of the incident and which was a necessary part of the experience'.[29] In a spot of time we confront a 'weight of ages' (VIII.552), but although we may think of past and future 'in an instant', the past is emphatically not brought into simultaneity with the present. Wordsworth emphasises the processes that have occurred over the time between past and present. In this way, the weight of ages that Baker addresses possesses duration; in turn the duration that Hewson and Miller address extends across not just a moment, but ages.

The social dimension of Wordsworth's experience on Snowdon is not immediately obvious (although he does specify that he climbed with a friend, the shepherd, and the dog), because the transition from love of nature to 'spiritual' or 'intellectual Love' (188, 207), to love for Dorothy and Coleridge, is protracted over several hundred lines. A comparable process is condensed and therefore more legible in Coleridge's own 'Fears in Solitude', a poem the opening and closing of which owe much to *The Seasons*. At the end of this poem Coleridge directly adapts Thomson's ascent 'up the Mount' in 'Summer', and the similarities with Wordsworth's account of the Snowdon ascent are obvious too:

> On the green sheep-track, up the heathy hill,
> Homeward I wind my way; and lo! recalled
> From bodings that have well nigh wearied me,
> I find myself upon the brow, and pause
> Startled! And after lonely sojourning
> In such a quiet and surrounded nook,
> This burst of prospect, here the shadowy main,
> Dim tinted, there the mighty majesty
> Of that huge amphitheatre of rich
> And elmy fields, seems like society –
> Conversing with the mind, and giving it
> A livelier impulse and a dance of thought!
> And now, beloved Stowey! I behold
> Thy church-tower, and, methinks, the four huge elms
> Clustering, which mark the mansion of my friend;
> And close behind them, hidden from my view,
> Is my own lowly cottage, where my babe
> And my babe's mother dwell in peace!
>   . . . all my heart
> Is softened, and made worthy to indulge
> Love, and the thoughts that yearn for human kind.[30]

Like the flash of moonlight on the slopes of Snowdon, the momentary 'burst of prospect' that startles Coleridge takes its significance from its place in a longer process, and particularly from its 'after-dimension' in which the figurative 'society' achieved with nonhuman phenomena shades into love and yearning for human society.

The Gibbet

In the spot of time that he labels as such in Book 12, Wordsworth recalls a time when as a child he stumbled across the scene of a murderer's execution. But this 'spot' is not so firmly or stably located at a particular time as it first appears. The encounter with a mouldered gibbet actually took place in the Quantocks in the late 1790s, not in Wordsworth's childhood in Cumbria.[31] The account itself reflects thematically this instability of origin. The chains and bones are gone, but the spot remains as both a communal memorial to the murder, due to the murderer's name being carved into the turf, and as a kind of communal calendar. From 'year to year, / By superstition of the neighbourhood, / The grass is cleared away' (242–4): this is a spot where local people mark each year's passing with the ritual of clearing the grass. In the space of a few lines, then, a weight of ages pours in upon us: the 'former times' when the murderer was hanged (235); 'soon after that fell deed was wrought' when the name was carved (239), which Wordsworth then emphasises was in 'times long past' (242); the continuity of communal memory 'from year to year' since (242); and 'this hour', years after the experience, when the letters are still legible (244). Condensed though they are to a few lines, the significance of these various invoked times is their extension through and connection over many years.

Wordsworth is then compelled to describe the times following this encounter. The encounter with the letters takes place in a 'bottom' (235), a basin in the moor, but Wordsworth then 'reascend[s] the bare common' (248) and takes in a miniature prospect view:

> A naked pool that lay beneath the hills,
> The beacon on the summit, and, more near,
> A girl, who bore a pitcher on her head,
> And seemed with difficult steps to force her way
> Against the blowing wind. It was, in truth,
> An ordinary sight; but I should need
> Colours and words that are unknown to man,
> To paint the visionary dreariness
> Which, while I looked all round for my lost guide,
> Invested moorland waste, and naked pool,
> The beacon crowning the lone eminence,
> The female and her garments vexed and tossed
> By the strong wind.
> (249–61)

Finally we are brought further forward, into the more recent past, 'When, in the blessed hours / Of early love, the loved One at my side, / I roamed, in daily presence of this scene' (261–3) and 'Youth's golden gleam', 'these remembrances', return to his mind (266–8). Larkin argues that there is a fundamental semantic 'gap' between the various components in this scene, and that 'The way these "spots of time" maintain that gap by not collapsing the between is the more haunting'.[32] There is no logical connection between the encounter with the letters in the turf and the encounter with the pool, beacon and girl, except that one takes place after the other. In this way, Larkin claims, the spots of time 'provoke memory towards its own weak exception to linear time: not simply against durational flow but as speculating a more composite lattice of feeling de-pressurizing the impetus of that onrush'.[33] But that 'between' that Wordsworth refuses to collapse *is* 'durational flow', is the period of time 'between' each encounter. The 'lattice of feeling' that connects the girl to the letters is not an 'exception to linear time' but an overlay upon it, a pattern that depends on the particular order of events and the small amount of time between them. Two things have happened in 'between': fear has turned to dreariness, and Wordsworth has ascended from the 'bottom' to the 'common'. The 'vision' in 'visionary dreariness' is the result of the latter movement as well as the former alteration: his power to 'invest' what he sees with his own feeling, rather than his feeling being shaped by what he sees, is represented by the literal ascent-to-a-prospect view. What connects the three components of the prospect view, the pool, the beacon and the girl, is only their spatial contiguity and temporal simultaneity, which allows Wordsworth to comprehend them within one 'sight' and 'invest' them with a unifying emotional significance for himself. And Wordsworth's ability to comprehend and combine the disjointed components of one spatially extended scene signifies his potential capacity to comprehend and combine the temporally distributed components of a narrative. This is a passage in which we are invited to wonder what connects things that are sequential or simultaneous in time, to question whether these connections are arbitrary or imaginary, but to conclude that moral and emotional continuity exists alongside, or rather through, temporal and spatial continuity. Although the connections are faltering and faint, we must read the girl in the light of the letters and the letters in the light of the gibbet, and all in the light of the 'blessed hours' years later when Wordsworth revisits the scene in the company of Dorothy. Wordsworth's mental work in seeking those connections is his own participation in the same process of commemoration enacted by the locals who clear the grass: all work to sustain the continuous history of the spot. The ability to trace the causal timeline forward and back is a demonstration of the mind's power. It is this power that Wordsworth fears he lacks when, following the recollection of this spot of time, he laments that

> the hiding-places of Man's power
> Open; I would approach them, but they close.
> I see by glimpses now; when age comes on,
> May scarcely see at all[.]
> (279–82)

Ice Skating

The spots of time open out into wider prospects, both spatially and temporally, and in doing so find shared ground. The continuous story into which the spots are reintegrated is one that stretches not just beyond Wordsworth's childhood, but beyond his lifetime. It encompasses long lengths of time that are local and global, human and nonhuman. My claim that forms of community are enabled by a return to the time of chronos might seem sentimental, conservative, perhaps even Victorian. It does slightly evoke Leslie Stephen's 1876 description of Wordsworth's attitude to mountains:

> The mountains are not with him a symbol of anti-social feelings. On the contrary, they are in their proper place as the background of the simple domestic affections. He loves his native hills, not in the Byronic fashion, as a savage wilderness, but as the appropriate framework in which a healthy social order can permanently maintain itself.[34]

For Stephen, this is high praise. Evan Gottlieb offers a similar reading of Wordsworth's well-known self-professed transition from love of nature to love of mankind, but approaching from an ecocritical perspective is cynical about the results: 'whatever geology might be discovering about the earth's unpredictable productivity, its ultimate stability could still be counted on as a basis of human life and, by extension, morality.'[35] Whereas Charlotte Smith's poetry, Gottlieb argues, suggests that 'human and planetary temporalities cannot be unproblematically aligned', Wordsworth has faith that 'human history and natural history are gently "bound each to each"'.[36] It is true that Wordsworth expresses faith in the continuity of both nonhuman nature and human society, and aims to blur rather than draw the distinction between these. But Wordsworth's epiphanies of geologic or planetary time are bound up with the return to human community, not because the natural world is a 'framework' for 'a healthy social order', or because it is subordinated to its function for humans; but because planetary time is a temporality shared by humans and nonhumans across space and time. People of different generations and nationalities have witnessed the same 'blasts of waterfalls' in the Alps and from Snowdon, and those waterfalls have witnessed them. Emphasis on the interchange does mean that the facts that waterfalls and mountains both predate and will potentially outlast humans, and that neither nonhuman nature nor human society is eternal, slip out of sight; but catching a glimpse of the points at which human and planetary temporalities do align is necessary in order to understand both humans and nonhumans as 'fellow-travellers', ethically as well as temporally connected.

The ice-skating scene in Book 1 of *The Prelude* dramatises the reintegration of the isolated individual into the community that is enabled by the reintegration of the isolated moment into the ongoing movement of time. This and the other spots of time in Book 1, Edward E. Bostetter observes, 'are all linked together by the word "motion"; they are illustrative of the way in which the child became conscious of the world outside him as a living, moving force, during each of the four seasons of the turning year':[37]

> Not seldom from the uproar I retired
> Into a silent bay, – or sportively
> Glanced sideway, leaving the tumultuous throng,
> To cut across the reflex of a star
> That fled, and, flying still before me, gleamed
> Upon the glassy plain: and oftentimes,
> When we had given our bodies to the wind,
> And all the shadowy banks on either side
> Came sweeping through the darkness, spinning still
> The rapid line of motion, then at once
> Have I, reclining back upon my heels,
> Stopped short; yet still the solitary cliffs
> Wheeled by me – even as if the earth had rolled
> With visible motion her diurnal round!
> Behind me did they stretch in solemn train,
> Feebler and feebler, and I stood and watched
> Till all was tranquil as a dreamless sleep.
> (447–63)

For Morgan, Wordsworth's departure from the 'tumultuous throng' to chase the star is 'the poem's abandonment of actions and characters to pursue the poet's subjective relationship to what is permanent and transcendent'.[38] This is the classic account of Wordsworth's approach to time, history and community, identified by John Krapp as a masculine Romanticism in which William, the male poet, 'has a poetic power over the narrative of a material history ... turning inward when the outward is no longer fulfilling', in contrast to Dorothy's poetry, which refigures 'community as the site of social hope within time'.[39] I would qualify Morgan's reading, and suggest that this scene resembles more closely the temporal perspective that Krapp ascribes to Dorothy: this spot of time does dramatise a search for the permanent and transcendent, but it does not find this in 'abandonment' of narrative and community. This is another moment of exhilaration and apparent empowerment that is really a lack of control, when the body is given over to the wind. Wordsworth's separation from the 'throng' is followed by a reintegration into that community ('When we had given . . .'), which foreshadows a return to the world of time. In Morgan's reading the 'visible motion' of the 'diurnal round' represents the height of subjectivity: 'When Wordsworth stops and is still, the entire world seems to revolve around him.'[40] Certainly, at the height of his attempted virtuosity, the disjunction between the subjective and the objective shape of time is at its most striking and dizzying. But the epiphany is the recognition not of kairos, but of chronos. It might seem odd to label the diurnal round of the planet – its visibility, furthermore, imagined rather than real – as chronos, but the image alerts Wordsworth to the moving, successive, continuous time that exists outside and prior to his mind. His attempt to 'stop short' motion, and with it time, only emphasises by contrast the turning of the planet: a measure of time that, although it usually goes unnoticed, is shared by everyone at every point in history. But the two gradually realign in Wordsworth's perception ('Till all was tranquil').

'[I]s that moment' asks David Ferry of the skating scene, 'a perception into the dimension of time, the very action of time itself; or is it something else, an insight into the eternal, a dimension of "time" other than the one we know? It is both, time and the eternal at their point of conjunction.'[41] It is not clear whether Ferry is suggesting that Wordsworth's paused perspective or the swirling round of planetary time offers this 'insight into the eternal'. Both are in fact representations of different kinds of time, kairos and chronos, both of which are visible to Milton's God in eternity. The profundity of Wordsworth's vision comes out of the combination of both of these temporal perspectives, the subjective and the objective, each revealing the strangeness and power of the other. The skating scene contests Baker's claim that clock-time and nature's time are the least exciting or meaningful in Wordsworth's hierarchy of temporalities. The moment at which 'we [and Wordsworth] see into the life of things' is not that when 'inner time obliterates' outer time, but when the two are perceived alongside one another before finally the heightened moment is reintegrated into the moving world of time, and Wordsworth's subjective experience of kairos fuses with the intersubjective experience of chronos. This reintegration into chronos may resemble the 'dreamless sleep' of death, to which it inevitably leads, but it is also in this reintegration that Wordsworth achieves a 'more distinct humanity' (III.276). He draws himself back into time and back into the community of his fellow skaters. It is only as part of the community that Wordsworth can achieve both humanity and a distinction that is more meaningful than that which is achieved by removal from community, in the same way that it is only as part of a linear narrative that a spot of time can be both meaningful and outstanding.

The skating scene is followed, as Morgan acknowledges, by a reflection on this spot's place in the larger story: 'can I think / A vulgar hope was yours when ye employed / Such ministry[?]' (I.466–8). This is then followed by an explicit evocation of the seasons, as if to reaffirm the spot's place in the moving world of time. Wordsworth ponders:

> Not uselessly employed,
> Might I pursue this theme through every change
> Of exercise and play, to which the year
> Did summon us in his delightful round.
> (475–8)

The delightful round of seasons is punctuated by 'change' but also marked by continuity. The time that flows between is what creates the alarming gaps between experiences in Wordsworth's life, the gaps that make him seem to himself to be two consciousnesses. But the time that flows between, when Wordsworth can register it – a shared lunch hour on top of the Alps, the final steps into the moonlight on Snowdon, years marked by locals clearing the grass at the scene of the gibbet, an ascent from the 'bottom' to the 'common', the diurnal round of days and seasons – is also what closes the gap between the spot of time and its after-dimension, and turns the whole into one coherent narrative. The time that flows between is also what connects, even as it separates, Wordsworth with his contemporaries, with his past and future selves, and, as will be the subject of the next chapter, with past poets.

Notes

1. William Wordsworth, 'Within our happy Castle there dwelt one' [Stanzas written in my Pocket-Copy of Thomson's Castle of Indolence], in *Poems, in Two Volumes, and Other Poems*, ed. Jared Curtis (Ithaca, Cornell UP, 1983), in *The Cornell Wordsworth*, vii, 581-82 (ll. 5-6, 34-36).
2. Georges Poulet, 'Timelessness and Romanticism', *Journal of the History of Ideas* 15 (1954): 3–22 (6–7).
3. William Wordsworth, *Home at Grasmere*, ed. Beth Darlington (Ithaca: Cornell UP, 1977), in *The Cornell Wordsworth*, vi, 46–8.
4. Jonathan Sachs and Andrew Piper, 'Technique and the Time of Reading', *PMLA* 133.5 (2018): 1259–67 (1262).
5. Christopher R. Miller, *The Invention of Evening* (Cambridge: Cambridge UP, 2006), 99.
6. Helen Regueiro, *The Limits of Imagination* (Ithaca: Cornell UP, 1976), 45.
7. Beer, *Wordsworth in Time*, 31.
8. James P. Davis, *An Experimental Reading of Wordsworth's* Prelude: *The Poetics of Bimodial Consciousness* (Lewiston: Edwin Mellen Press, 1995), 127.
9. Jeffrey Baker, *Time and Mind in Wordsworth's Poetry* (Detroit: Wayne State UP, 1980), 16–17.
10. Ibid., p. 17.
11. Frank Kermode, *The Sense of an Ending: Studies in the Theory of Fiction with a New Epilogue* (Oxford: Oxford UP, 2000), 46.
12. Susan J. Wolfson, 'The Illusion of Mastery: Wordsworth's Revisions of "The Drowned Man of Esthwaite", 1799, 1805, 1850', *PMLA* 99 (1984): 917–35 (926–7).
13. Peter Larkin, *Wordsworth and Coleridge: Promising Losses* (New York: Palgrave Macmillan, 2012), 13.
14. Monique R. Morgan, *Narrative Means, Lyric Ends: Temporality in the Nineteenth-Century British Long Poem* (Columbus: Ohio State UP, 2009), 9.
15. The recent book *Romanticism and Time: Literary Temporalities*, ed. Sophie Laniel-Musitelli and Céline Sabiron (Cambridge: Open Book Publishers, 2021), contains several chapters on the distinction between the inhumanity of clock-time and alternative, preferable forms of time-keeping.
16. William Wordsworth, 'The Brothers', in *Lyrical Ballads, and Other Poems, 1797–1800*, ed. James Butler and Karen Green (Ithaca: Cornell UP, 1992), in *The Cornell Wordsworth*, iv, 147–8 (ll. 144–60).

17. See Stevenson, *Reading the Times*, 2–11.
18. Benedict Anderson, *Imagined Communities: Reflections on the Origin and Spread of Nationalism* (London: Verso, 1983, repr. 1991), 24.
19. Cowper, *The Poems of William Cowper*, 139.
20. Mary A. Favret, *War at a Distance: Romanticism and the Making of Modern Wartime* (Princeton: Princeton UP, 2009).
21. Lamb and Lamb, *Letters*, iii, 23.
22. Christopher R. Miller discusses the importance of homogeneous time in Wordsworth's poem 'John's Grove' (*Invention of Evening*, 93–4).
23. Kate Rigby, *Reclaiming Romanticism: Towards an Ecopoetics of Decolonization* (London and New York: Bloomsbury, 2020), 14.
24. On the ambiguity of Wordsworth's reaction immediately following their discovery that they had crossed the Alps, before they continue their walk, see Robert A. Brinkley, 'The Incident in the Simplon Pass: A Note on Wordsworth's Revisions', *The Wordsworth Circle* 12.2 (1981): 122–25.
25. Mark Hewson, 'The Scene of Meditation in Wordsworth', *The Modern Language Review* 106 (2011): 954–67 (961).
26. Ibid., 960.
27. Miller, *Invention of Evening*, 101.
28. Baker, *Time and Mind*, 145.
29. Ibid., 159.
30. Samuel Taylor Coleridge, *The Major Works*, ed. H. J. Jackson (Oxford: Oxford UP, 1985, repr. 2008), 98.
31. Alan Bewell, 'Wordsworth's Primal Scene: Retrospective Tales of Idiots, Wild Children, and Savages', *ELH* 50.2 (1983): 321–46.
32. Peter Larkin, 'Wordsworth's Maculate Exception: Achieving the "Spots of Time"', *Wordsworth Circle* 41.1 (2010): 30–5 (33).
33. Ibid.
34. Leslie Stephen, 'Wordsworth's Ethics' (1876), in *William Wordsworth (Bloom's Classic Critical Views)*, ed. Harold Bloom (New York: Infobase, 2009): 247–68 (257).
35. Evan Gottlieb, 'Anthropocene Temporalities and British Romantic Poetry', in *Romanticism and Time*: 25–47 (29).
36. Ibid., 35, 32.
37. Edward E. Bostetter, *The Romantic Ventriloquists* (Seattle: University of Washington Press, 1963), 16.
38. Morgan, *Narrative Means*, 87.
39. John Krapp, 'Female Romanticism at the End of History', *Texas Studies in Literature and Language* 46.1 (2004): 73–91 (76–7).
40. Morgan, *Narrative Means*, 88.
41. David Ferry, *The Limits of Mortality* (Middletown, CT: Wesleyan UP, 1959), 177.

Chapter 8

Hung O'er the Deep: Wordsworth's Allusions and Revisions

When Keats, in his annotations to *Paradise Lost*, described Milton as 'more than delphic', he alluded in part to Milton's sense of the historical distance between himself and the events described in his poem (see Chapter 2). In Book 3 of *The Prelude*, Wordsworth associates Milton with Cassandra, another prophet whose accounts of the future were misunderstood. It is a strange passage in which the attempt to impose new shape upon time, and draw things that should be separated by time into one simultaneous present, is shown not only to be impossible, but perhaps undesirable, even immoral. Wordsworth describes getting drunk as a student in Milton's old Cambridge rooms:

> Yea, our blind Poet, who, in his later day,
> Stood almost single, uttering odious truth,
> Darkness before and danger's voice behind;
> Soul awful – if the earth hath ever lodged
> An awful Soul, I seemed to see him here
> Familiarly, and in his Scholar's dress
> Bounding before me, yet a Stripling Youth,
> A Boy, no better, with his rosy cheeks
> Angelical, keen eye, courageous look,
> And conscious step of purity and pride.
>   Among the Band of my Compeers was One
> Whom Chance had stationed in the very Room
> Honoured by Milton's Name. O temperate Bard!
> Be it confest that, for the first time, seated
> Within thy innocent Lodge and Oratory,
> One of a festive Circle, I poured out
> Libations, to thy memory drank, till pride
> And gratitude grew dizzy in a brain

> Never excited by the fumes of wine
> Before that hour, or since. Then, forth I ran,
> From that assembly through a length of streets
> Ran, Ostrich-like, to reach our Chapel door
> In not a desperate or opprobrious time,
> Albeit long after the importunate bell
> Had stopped, with wearisome Cassandra voice
> No longer haunting the dark winter night.
> Call back, O Friend! a moment to thy mind
> The place itself and fashion of the Rites.
> With careless ostentation shouldering up
> My Surplice, through the inferior throng I clove
> Of the plain Burghers, who in audience stood
> On the last skirts of their permitted ground
> Under the pealing Organ. Empty thoughts!
> I am ashamed of them: and that great Bard
> And Thou, O Friend! who in thy ample mind
> Hast placed me high above my best deserts,
> Ye will forgive the weakness of that hour,
> In some of its unworthy vanities
> Brother to many more.
> (III.286–324)

The student Wordsworth described here makes two mistakes, both involving an attempt to overleap the proper chronological spread of time. He claims that the past is present, in the form of Milton 'before' him spatially rather than temporally. He also claims that the future is present: his empty thoughts are his vanity, pride and superiority, his 'familiar' identification with Milton as a great poet before time has allowed him to earn and prove that status. This reorganisation of the ordinary shape and spread of time appears first as power but is revealed to be 'weakness', an intoxicated delusion.

The depiction of the youthful Milton, himself conscious of his pride when he is 'no better', hints at Wordsworth's subsequent error. Wordsworth here appears as Milton did at the start of Book 4 of *Paradise Lost*, using his knowledge of Milton's own future to read greatness into what was a mere boy (Milton's compatriots at Cambridge mocked his self-assurance). Echoing Milton's more-than-delphic voice calling back to Adam and Eve, Wordsworth's thoughts at Cambridge and his own poetry now are Cassandra voices, or rather more-than-Cassandra-voices, trying and failing to speak across a century and a half to the young Milton. Lucy Newlyn has argued that the predominant tendency in the Romantic reception of Milton has been to mythologise him, 'to subordinate humanity to divinity'.[1]

Certainly Lamb's laments at the manuscript of 'Lycidas', which I discussed in Chapter 3, suggest this kind of mythologising. But it is worth noting the Romantic counter-current that emphasises Milton's existence as a historical figure, the fact that time had to reveal the validity of Milton's hopes and ambitions, and that his poetry was the product of time and labour. Coleridge wrote to Thomas Poole in 1800:

> Future greatness! Is it not an awful thing, my dearest Poole? What if you had known Milton at the age of thirty, and believed all you now know of him? – ... Would it not be an assurance to you that your admiration of the Paradise Lost was no superstition, no shadow of flesh and bloodless abstraction, but that the *Man* was even so, that the greatness was incarnate and personal?[2]

The 'greatness' may be present before its proof, but only perceptible to those who know the future in the past. Hazlitt expressed a similar sentiment, but acknowledged its impossibility, in his essay on 'Whether genius is conscious of its powers?':

> 'What a pity,' said some one, 'that Milton had not the pleasure of reading Paradise Lost!' He could not read it, as we do, with the weight of impression that a hundred years of admiration have added to it ... with the sense of the number of editions it has passed through with still increasing reputation, with the tone of solidity, time-proof, which it has received from the breath of cold, envious maligners, with the sound which the voice of Fame has lent to every line of it! ... no one can anticipate the suffrage of posterity. Every man, in judging of himself, is his own contemporary.[3]

For Hazlitt, not only was it the passage of time that allowed Milton to fulfil his destiny of being a great poet, but it was the passage of time across the eighteenth century that turned *Paradise Lost* into a great poem.

Wordsworth knew of the spread of time that divided him from Milton. His most famous lines on his predecessor express exactly that sorrow: 'Milton! thou should'st be living at this hour.'[4] The Cassandra voice of the college chapel bell, however, provides a hint of consolation. The Cassandra voice of the bell is particularly significant here because it represents two seemingly opposed conceptions of time: the repetitive, supposedly oppressive clock-time that it chimes, and the prophetic vision that transcends that clock-time. The introduction of the bell at this point reminds Wordsworth, who had been revelling in his own transcendence of the temporal separation between himself and Milton, that time and history are carrying on with the same unbending discipline as that of the college wardens. But to compare the voice of the bell to Cassandra is to reinvest that dull tread of time itself with portentous meaning. Time moves on in spite of Wordsworth's attempts at closing the temporal gap between himself and the past, and yet that movement itself has meaning that, like Cassandra's prophecies, may be as yet unknown (perhaps deferred beyond *The Prelude*, only to be revealed in the perpetually deferred future of *The Recluse*). The institutional clock-time represented by the bell has another meaning here, too: while the pastness of the bell's ringing within the memory itself is emphasised in 'long after' and 'No longer', this is a bell that rings with irritating consistency for every Cambridge student. A tradition that spans centuries is invoked to join Milton, Wordsworth and Coleridge in their shared experience, when Coleridge is asked to 'Call back . . . a moment to thy mind / The place itself and fashion of the Rites'.

The flowing time that separates Wordsworth from Milton is also the time that gives that relationship meaning; it is the time in which Milton achieved his ambitions, in which Wordsworth will achieve his, and in which Milton's works took on the multiple meanings that they had for Wordsworth and his contemporaries. As I did with Milton's similes in Chapter 2 and Thomson's revisions in Chapter 5, in this chapter I will examine Wordsworth's allusions in order to understand how Wordsworth is able to bring multiple times (in this case from the past of literary history) into the present and yet retain a sense of the chronological extension and order of those times; how he is able to do justice to the years that have flowed between even in the very moment of allusion.[5] In doing so I aim to highlight the temporal and historical quality of allusion itself. I turn at the end of this chapter to Wordsworth's own revisions, and argue that these also function as allusions to an earlier poet and therefore to the literary past.

Allusion

Robin Jarvis argues that Wordsworth's Miltonic allusions lead us to so many complex and contradictory meanings that their content becomes less important than their nature *as* allusion: 'a text [*The Prelude*] which pulls in so many directions at once . . . seems to allude more than anything . . . to its own capacity to allude.'[6] I suggest that the continuities and discontinuities in meaning evoked by Wordsworth's allusions are important not only, perhaps not even primarily, in their content, but in what they express about the relationship between different texts as the representatives of different times.

Sharon M. Setzer's approach to reading Wordsworth's allusions reconciles the two opposing schools which see either the poetry of Milton as the single dominant source text, or the 'concept of the labyrinth' of multiple sources as 'a new interpretive center, an essentialist foreconceit to which everything that matters in Wordsworth's poetry must be referred';[7] I agree with Setzer's conclusion that Milton's poetry does not provide a stable source of meaning for Wordsworth, but nor is his very real influence lost in a Daedalian, undecipherable mess of source material to which we can lazily give up our search for meaning. It is necessary at least to try to follow Wordsworth's allusions to their sources, even when the route is convoluted, in order to understand the poetry; 'to do more to come to terms with those moments when the Miltonic subtext contributes to the multiplicity of that something else'.[8] Setzer notes that 'the lines of influence leading from Milton to Wordsworth and Coleridge are complicated by numerous eighteenth-century Miltonic imitations', and offers David Mallet as an example of a poet whose 'transformations' of Milton 'established a precedent' for Wordsworth in his use of the same Miltonic material.[9] Taking up Setzer's suggestions for how to read Wordsworth's allusions, I would argue that Thomson is the primary mediating figure in the model that she outlines. I would however disagree with her suggestion that 'while the maze of influence reaches out to include figures such as Mallet and De Quincey, their voices ultimately constitute digressions from Wordsworth's ongoing conversation with Milton'.[10] Thomson's voice, at least, if it does not overpower that of Milton, is central to the conversation and to our understanding of Wordsworth's relationship with Milton.

The 'lineage of literary history as we would understand it today', writes John Strachan, is 'the line from Milton, Thomson and Cowper through to Wordsworth.'[11] However, due to Wordsworth's notorious critique of eighteenth-century 'poetic diction' in his 'Preface to the Lyrical Ballads',[12] and his 'Essay, Supplementary to the Preface' in which he criticises Thomson's 'vicious style' and 'false ornaments',[13] his indebtedness to Thomson has been systematically underestimated by critics. This is in spite of the clear evidence that Thomson's poetry was important to Wordsworth: he read *The Seasons* aloud on his way to school as a child,[14] he read the 1730 edition between 1809 and 1811,[15] he carried into the 1820s an idea to write 'a short life of [Thomson], prefixed to a Volume' of his poetry,[16] and of course he alluded to Thomson's poetry throughout his writing career. Edwin Stein counts thirty-five echoes of Thomson's poetry in Wordsworth's (but he considers only two-thirds of Wordsworth's complete poetical works, and I believe the true number of Wordsworth's allusions to Thomson to be far higher); this is far less than the 550 echoes of Milton that Stein counts, but more than of Pope, Virgil, Cowper or Chaucer, and the same number as of Coleridge.[17] As this last comparison demonstrates, the recent and valuable emphasis in Wordsworth criticism on the importance of his contemporary networks, and his collaborations with members of his circle such as Coleridge and Dorothy Wordsworth, should not lead us to neglect the importance to Wordsworth of his predecessors. They are just as present in his poetry, although they are present as representatives of the past.

Where Thomson's influence receives more than a passing mention in Wordsworth criticism, and analysis of the relationship between him and Wordsworth goes beyond assertion of the latter's simple superiority over his predecessor,[18] this analysis is still often vague. Thus two of the most sensitive (though still quite brief) studies of their relationship, by Stein and Adam Potkay, refer to a 'naturalizing mood'[19] and 'picturesque artistry'[20] respectively as Thomson's main legacy. A 'more interesting legacy' has been identified by Goodman in *Georgic Modernity and British Romanticism*.[21] Goodman's argument that Thomson and Wordsworth share an interest in mediation, both in the sensual apprehension of the external world and in the apprehension of history, is key to understanding Wordsworth's relationship to Thomson. My contention, building upon Goodman's argument, is that Wordsworth puts the mediatory language of Thomson to work in his poetry, through allusion, in order to articulate temporal mediation; and furthermore, that this temporal mediation is expressive not of the power of the subjective mind to overcome the extension of chronological time, but of the power of the subjective mind to perceive that very extension, and the processes that occur within it.

Thomson is and was generally thought of as a poet of immediacy, who reveals to us the world as it really is: 'Thomson, in his Seasons . . . dared to use nothing but a pencil and pallet, and his own eyes, in delineating nature.'[22] But Wordsworth's allusions to *The Seasons* suggest that he read Thomson at least as much as a poet of mediation: it is the Thomsonian 'Eye', seemingly providing direct access to the world, that can be an obstructive prism between world and mind. Wordsworth is attracted to those images in *The Seasons* in which the external world is distorted by the senses and the mind, and in which the mind is in turn affected by the distortions of nature. In Book 8 of *The Prelude*, in Wordsworth's panegyric on shepherds, we have a succession of Thomsonian allusions: 'awful Solitudes' (222) is taken from 'Summer', where 'great *Nature* dwells / In awful Solitude' (702–3) (Akenside had turned this into the plural 'awful Solitudes' in the revised version of *The Pleasures of [the] Imagination*, published 1770);[23] 'And when the Spring / looks out' (229–30) recalls Thomson's 'Look'd out the joyous SPRING, look'd out and smil'd' (Wi.16); 'His staff portending like a Hunter's Spear' (246) takes us back to 'Advancing full on the protended Spear' (Au.462). Then we reach a moment of climactic (remembered) vision:

> By mists bewildered, suddenly mine eyes
> Have glanced upon him distant a few steps,
> In size a Giant, stalking through thick fog,
> His sheep like Greenland bears; or, as he stepped
> Beyond the boundary line of some hill-shadow,
> His form hath flashed upon me, glorified
> By the deep radiance of the setting sun[.]
> (VIII.264–70)

We have here a passage, and a memory, that could claim the label of one of Wordsworth's 'spots of time': moments from childhood, realised now in short passages of verse, in which young Wordsworth felt a heightened communion with nature that was both beautiful and frightening. They are the moments when, in Harold Bloom's words, we most feel the poetry's 'strong sense of being alone with the universe, with no myth or figure to mediate between ego and phenomena'.[24] But though Wordsworth dismisses other literary sources, claiming his shepherd to be 'Far more of an imaginative form / Than the gay Corin of the groves' (284–5), there has been another figure stalking the poetry since the first allusive moment when we were told, ingenuously, of 'him who treads / Companionless your awful solitudes!' (221–2). That figure is Thomson; as well as the above allusions, Wordsworth's supposedly 'Companionless' stalking shepherd himself descends from 'Autumn':

>   wilder'd, o'er the Waste
> The Shepherd stalks gigantic. Till at last
> Wreath'd dun around, in deeper Circles still
> Successive closing, sits the general Fog[.]
> (726–9)

The shepherd, Wordsworth's vision of whom is mediated by the fog, is an 'imaginative form' of Thomson himself, whose presence is both invoked and obscured by Wordsworth's lines. What Wordsworth claims to be a moment of 'severest solitude' turns out to be filtered through another poet's language, from a past beyond that of Wordsworth's youth (260).

Similarly, in Book 2 Wordsworth recalls how as a child he sat

> Alone upon some jutting eminence,
> At the first gleam of dawn-light, when the Vale,
> Yet slumbering, lay in utter solitude.
> How shall I seek the origin? where find
> Faith in the marvellous things which then I felt?
> Oft in these moments such a holy calm
> Would overspread my soul, that bodily eyes
> Were utterly forgotten, and what I saw
> Appeared like something in myself, a dream,
> A prospect in the mind.
> (344–53)

Wordsworth's desire for an end point (his life's crowning achievement, the writing of *The Recluse*) is matched by a desire for an 'origin': 'The Writer must introduce the truth with such accompaniment as shall imply that he has mounted to the sources of things.'[25] But a true origin or end point, which would be a moment of kairos, eludes him. The question 'How shall I seek the origin?' seems to be severing this moment, itself a 'jutting eminence' of time, from its place in the larger causal timeline, but may instead be lamenting the infinitude, or at least enormity, of past time, which makes the search futile. 'Who knows', he asked a few lines earlier, echoing both Milton's Satan (*PL*, V.856–8) and his Adam (VIII.250–1), 'the individual hour in which / His habits were first sown, even as a seed?' (II.206–7).

But the question 'How shall I seek the origin?' also has a disingenuous function, as does the image of young Wordsworth '*Alone* upon some jutting eminence' (my emphasis). There is one source for this memory, at least, that can be traced, though it may not be the ultimate origin. That source is Thomson's 'Summer', from which Wordsworth has taken his 'jutting eminence'. As an origin it is gestured towards in the quotation of 'jutting eminence', then elided in the declaration of solitude; the relationship of this passage to Thomson's is as convoluted and ambivalent as that between Wordsworth's dominating 'mind' and his 'forgotten', although clearly important as a source, 'bodily eyes'. Some seventy years before Wordsworth wrote this passage, Thomson had depicted a shipwrecked man, as

>   Day after Day,
> Sad on the jutting Eminence he sits,
> And views the Main that ever toils below;
> Still fondly forming in the farthest Verge,
> Where the round Ether mixes with the Wave,
> Ships, dim-discover'd, dropping from the Clouds.
> At Evening, to the setting Sun he turns
> A mournful Eye, and down his dying Heart
> Sinks helpless[.]
> (941–9)

This passage of *The Seasons* is clearly invoked in *The Prelude*, but what meaning does it bring to our reading of Wordsworth's episode, other than its unsettling of his claims to solitude and originality? It brings additional times – those of Thomson's writing in 1727, as well as the fictional 'Day after Day' of the story told – which bring with them not only additional, but troubling meanings. Thomson's passage is one in which the seen world of nature combines with the mind's creative powers to form dream-images (ships) and appear sympathetic to human feelings. On the one hand, when Wordsworth thinks of Thomson, when the older poet is present enough in his mind to produce direct quotation, Wordsworth is thinking of this communion with nature that Thomson epitomised for the eighteenth and early nineteenth centuries. Wordsworth is suppressing the melancholy aspect of Thomson's passage, which is about the delusive potential of the 'ennobling interchange' between human and non-human (*TP*, XIII.374). Thomson describes the dangers and deceptions of solipsism, and countering the potential power of the man's mind is his lack of control over his mind, and nature's capacity to deceive human perception. We know that Wordsworth was alert to this aspect of Thomson's passage, since he echoes it in Book 3 in the simile of 'a lone shepherd on a promontory, / Who, lacking occupation, looks far forth / Into the boundless sea, and rather makes / Than finds what he beholds' (516–19). To some extent, Wordsworth is so impressed by the glory and mystery of the immanence between nature and mind that Thomson encapsulates here, that even in this moment of hopelessness Wordsworth finds hope in the sheer power of the mind to act upon nature in this way; he then develops in his own poetry this interpretation of Thomson's passage, turning it into something 'marvellous'. But the darkness of Thomson's passage cannot be forgotten once the reader follows this allusion to its source, and it remains intact in Thomson's poetry despite the transformation that Wordsworth enacts upon it. Wordsworth's quotation of 'jutting eminence', therefore, is also an encoded meaning, as the ghosts of Thomson's false forms haunt Wordsworth's question, 'where [shall I] find / Faith . . .?' Thomson represents the wonder and immediacy of the mind's communion with nature, as well as the worrying implications of this communion: that the powerful interplay between our minds and nature might act sometimes to obscure truth. This gives rise, in Wordsworth's poetry, to a statement that, placed in the wider context of Thomson's poetry, appears disturbing as well as marvellous: 'What I saw / Appeared like something in myself, a dream.'

What these fluctuations between possible meanings tell us is that Wordsworth's instincts to define a spot of time in his past as its own self-sufficient origin are struggling with his sense of the importance and influence of other times, and other sources outside himself. These further receding pasts are necessary to understanding how the present time came to be as it is, but they also bring with them meanings that may contradict the interpretation that he would seem to give, and that we would instinctively make, of the present (or past present).

The kind of natural, sensual mediation that we see in the stalking shepherd and jutting eminence passages – fog, mist, haze – is repeatedly associated with Thomson in *The Prelude*.[26] But even more important to Wordsworth's poetry is the mediation of time, the 'many years [that] / Have since flowed in between'. For exploration of this kind of mediation, Thomson's *Seasons* provides fewer ready prototypes. As I argued earlier, Thomson's concern is to scramble, not highlight, the chronological order of things. Yet Thomson is used by Wordsworth to explore temporal mediation too. This is possible because he represents a past time in which he created images that linger in Wordsworth's mind and find echoes in Wordsworth's own experience, but that also remain dangerously free of Wordsworth's control. Furthermore, Thomson represents a point in the length of time that has separated Wordsworth from Milton.

Time separates Wordsworth from his past self, but also reveals the significance and meaning of that past. So too does the time that separates him from Milton provide him with the tools to interpret Milton, and to turn Milton's poetry to his own purposes. His reading of Milton is repeatedly modified by his reading of Thomson. This was not unusual at the time of Wordsworth's composition; one can consider a work like the libretto to Haydn's *Die Schöpfung* (1798), ostensibly based on Book 7 of *Paradise Lost* but owing at least as much to *The Seasons*' natural description, to perceive Thomson's penetrating influence on contemporary readings of Milton.[27] In *The Prelude*, this mediation is put to meaningful use, highlighting as it does both the continuity of 'the great Family that still survives', and the differences between the members of that family (XII.62); Milton, Thomson and Wordsworth are shown to be related, but not identical.

At one particular 'spot of time' in *The Prelude*, we see at the level of narrative memory's mediation of experience, and at the level of allusion, Thomson's mediation of Milton. Wordsworth remembers how, as a young boy, he witnessed the dragging of Esthwaite to recover the body of a drowned man:

>   some looked
> In passive expectation from the shore,
> While from a boat others hung o'er the deep,
> Sounding with grappling irons and long poles.
> (V.446–9)

As the man's body is raised, 'a spectre shape / Of terror' (452–3), the boy's natural response is modified for his 'inner eye had seen / Such sights before' in books (455–6). His mind exerts its strength, resisting being 'Possessed' by the scene (455), but that strength is an ambivalent one, possibly preventing the child's natural and proper emotional response. Furthermore, he draws this strength from an external source: his vision at the time is shaped by the memories of reading, as these memories 'hallowed the sad spectacle ... like the works / Of Grecian Art, and purest Poesy' (458–61). Even Wordsworth's ability in the present to express this memory in poetry has been shaped by books he has read. As the dead man is raised, so too is the 'spirit' of Thomson (458). 'Hung o'er the deep' is a direct quotation from both 'Spring', 'High from the Summit of a craggy Cliff, / Hung o'er the Deep, such as amazing frowns / On utmost *Kilda*'s Shore' (755–7), and 'Autumn', 'Hung o'er the Deep, / That ever works beneath his sounding Base' (796–7). That the 'Autumn' passage should have stuck in Wordsworth's mind is unsurprising: it beseeches humanity's '*Genius*' to 'trace the Secrets of the dark Abyss' (777–8). The 'Spring' passage, meanwhile, describes a father eagle pushing his young from the nest to fly for themselves. A Freudian or perhaps Bloomian reading of Wordsworth's attraction to this episode suggests itself. More important than the content of this episode in 'Spring' from which Wordsworth quotes, though, is that these are lines that refer back to another line by Milton, which describes the border between Earth and Heaven (and between time and eternity): 'The rest was craggy cliff, that overhung' (*PL*, IV.547). Thomson's poetry is acting, like time itself, as a medium in both senses of the word, simultaneously facilitating and impeding access. Wordsworth has taken Thomson's reworking of this line for his own poem rather than the original, but the Miltonic line, and therefore the history of Miltonic reception by poets in the years between Milton and Wordsworth, are real presences in Wordsworth's poem too. Thus, the raising of the drowned man from the dark lake ought to be read, in part, as a figure for what is going on in Wordsworth's poetry at the level of intertextuality. All these lines of poetry form layers, lurking somewhere beneath the surface of Wordsworth's own lines, which melt into one another and melt too into the experience itself, so that seeing, being, reading and writing become almost inseparable.[28] Almost because by tracing the history of the phrase 'Hung o'er the deep' back through time we can still identify some of the different layers, and perceive how they are related by an evolution in meaning that does not fully efface any of its component stages.

Many of the spots of time are characterised by the image of 'hanging'. There is the account (to which I shall return in the next chapter), just before the drowned man episode, of the Boy of Winander: 'in that silence while he hung / Listening' (V.383–4). Later the Boy is buried in a churchyard that 'hangs / Upon a slope' (394–5). Wordsworth recalls the times 'when I have hung / Above the Raven's nest ... I hung alone' (I.330–6). There is the boat-stealing episode when Wordsworth reflects that 'o'er my thoughts / There hung a darkness' (I.393–4). When attempting to describe figuratively this uncertainty and 'darkness' in his communions with the external world, and in his memories of those childhood communions, Wordsworth uses the same imagery of hanging and boats:

> As one who hangs down-bending from the side
> Of a slow-moving boat ...
>   solacing himself
> With such discoveries as his eye can make,
> Beneath him, in the bottom of the deep[.]
> (IV.256–60)

'Hung' and its variants, 'hangs' and 'hanging', are words that seem to exert the poet's power over the passing of time and narrative, slowing them down, allowing the poem to pause and 'sound the deep' – to acknowledge the depth of mystery in the poet's communion both with nature and the past, and simultaneously to try to demystify it. 'Hung' is a word that, Andrzej Warminski has written, 'unhinges the economy of loss and restoration'.[29] A moment of hanging appears to be one of suspended time, resistant to the natural flow of time. It can represent either of the two definitions of kairos: a moment removed from the passage of time, or a moment that condenses all times within it simultaneously. Either way, it apparently overcomes the objective shape of linear, successive, chronological time. And yet to hang is only an illusory overcoming of the force of gravity. The persistence of that force is what gives meaning to the resistance of it, and creates the kinetic energy that gives the one hanging a dual sense of power and powerlessness. And Wordsworth's moments of hanging are not really overcomings of chronos, nor are they really moments of solitude.

Given that the image of hanging in *The Prelude* has been examined so extensively (most so by Paul de Man in his 1967 lecture on 'Time and History in Wordsworth'), it is surprising that no one has recognised its Thomsonian pedigree.[30] Wordsworth wrote at some length on the word 'hangs' in his 'Preface to Poems' of 1815, but he wrote of its use by Virgil, Shakespeare and Milton, particularly Milton's 'As when farr off at Sea a Fleet descri'd / Hangs in the Clouds' (*PL*, II.636–7). 'Here', Wordsworth extols of Milton's usage, 'is the full strength of the imagination in the word, *hangs* . . . taking advantage of its appearance to the senses, the Poet dares to represent [the fleet] as *hanging in the clouds*.'[31] We are reminded of Thomson's ships 'dropping from the Clouds' in his 'jutting eminence' passage – a passage, like Milton's, in which the 'appearance of the senses' dictates the literary presentation of those ships. In August 1811, in a letter to Sir George Beaumont, Wordsworth remembered the strength of this image and in his expression of it, Milton's passage and Thomson's are blended together:

> It was about the hour of sunset, and the sea was perfectly calm; and in a quarter where its surface was indistinguishable from the western sky, hazy, and luminous with the setting Sun, appeared a tall sloop-rigged vessel, magnified by the atmosphere through which it was viewed, and seeming rather to hang in the air than to float upon the waters. Milton compares the appearance of Satan to a *fleet* descried far off at sea; the visionary grandeur and beautiful form of this *single* vessel, could words have conveyed to the mind the picture which Nature presented to the eye, would have suited his purpose as well as the largest company of vessels[.][32]

The magnifying effect of the mist from his 'shepherd stalking' passage, and the setting sun and hazy horizon from the 'jutting eminence' passage, serve to filter Wordsworth's interpretation of his own vision that was already involved with Milton's writing. That Thomson must have been in Wordsworth's mind as he wrote this letter is undeniable: he had quoted six lines from *The Castle of Indolence* earlier in the same paragraph. As Wordsworth struggles for words to convey what he saw, he turns not only to Milton's but to Thomson's words, and Thomson's thoughts, who was most able of all poets to translate into poetry 'the picture which Nature presented to the eye', even when the picture that Nature presented was not that of rational reality. Whether the poetry of his predecessors is assisting Wordsworth in finding 'words to convey' his own original vision, or whether it is acting as a prism, which predetermines and even distorts the 'appearance of the senses', is impossible to tell. The latter is a definite possibility, as Wordsworth described in the drowned man episode the power of past reading to shape his perception at the moment of experience, not just at the moment of articulation.

Wordsworth does not mention Thomson in his eulogy on the word 'hangs' in the 'Preface', but when he remembered the men dragging the lake and envisioned them 'hanging' from their boats, it was to Thomson, not Milton directly, that he turned. The past time separating Wordsworth from Milton cannot be overcome, but is registered in the ghostly presence of Thomson and his poetry. Within a brief word or phrase is condensed many years of history, and with them multiple meanings; but when we begin to trace those meanings, we find that they cannot be understood as single points in literary history, nor as one single point in the present in which Wordsworth writes. They are 'with the generations of mankind / Spread over time, past, present, and to come, / Age after age, till Time shall be no more' (XIV.109–11). Only by seeing them 'Spread' in this way can we perceive the process of mediation that has brought about Wordsworth's poetry in the present, and that makes sense of his poetry in the present.

Revision

The Prelude participates in literary history not only in its status within the Miltonic tradition of long blank verse poems and its numerous allusions to earlier texts, but in its own textual history. Any part of *The Prelude* that we read is also part of another narrative, that of Wordsworth's revisions to the poem. What began as the 150-line-long

'Was it for this' fragment, written in 1798, became the two-part poem of 1798–9, then the thirteen-book poem known as the 1805 *Prelude*, and it remained in a state of regular revision until the poet's death in 1850 (although the last major revisions had been made by 1839). The creation of what we know as *The Prelude* extends even beyond Wordsworth's death when we take into account the contributions of his posthumous editors.

Wordsworth's revisions, more than those of most poets, have been invested with meaning in and of themselves, not just as contingent factors in the production of ultimate meaning. Zachary Leader writes that 'when [Wordsworth] revises a poem he does so not out of indifference to – or to repudiate – the intentions of a former self, but to assert his identity with that self. Because that self is still felt as, or needs to be felt as, *this* self, revision is no violation.'[33] On the other hand, Stephen M. Parrish judges that 'the early Wordsworth was a better poet than the late Wordsworth, for the plain reason that he was closer to the sources of his inspiration, and less inhibited by the various orthodoxies (poetical, religious, and political) that he succumbed to in his later years'.[34] I am interested less in whether the revisions record a process of growth or decline than in the fact of this record at all, and how Wordsworth's revisions draw attention to their status as revisionary; how Wordsworth makes it difficult to perceive each version as a self-sufficient entity independent of its place in a longer process. Larkin, after observing the need in Wordsworth's poetry for an 'after-dimension' to any described experience, goes on to add that the same impulse 'calls for a working out in terms of the relations between discrete and chronologically disparate texts'.[35] Larkin is discussing the relation between earlier and later poems by Wordsworth, but his comment applies equally to Wordsworth's 'working out' of the relations between different texts by different authors, as we have seen. And Wordsworth's interest in the 'postclimactic' – the resumption of the time of chronos within which the moment of kairos fits – also finds its realisation in his treatment of the relation between 'discrete and chronologically disparate' versions of the same poem.

Sometimes the revisions function to add this 'after-dimension' at the level of content. The most famous case, of Wordsworth's (in)famous revisions to the Boy of Winander episode, is discussed in the next chapter. The 'spot of time' involving the murderer's gibbet, which I discussed in the last chapter, also obtained the after-dimension in which the older Wordsworth revisits the scene in subsequent revisions, after the spot's first appearance in the 1799 fragment. The Wordsworth who contemplates the Boy of Winander's grave and who returns to the scene of the gibbet is a projection of Wordsworth as he revises his poem, as he reflects on the scene (both the landscape and the lines of poetry) and reinterprets the significance of what he remembers in the light of its continuing effect in later years. The revision is itself, then, an after-dimension at the level of form. Wolfson writes that Wordsworth's revisions have the effect of 'dispersing authority across time and unseating any one moment as the limit of meaning'.[36] The revisions question the self-sufficiency of 'any one moment': not just the moment of experience but the moment of composition. As in the case of Wordsworth's return to the scene of the gibbet, the interpretation of that later time may seem out of kilter with what the spot seemed to represent at the time: a spot signifying fear followed by dreariness has become a spot signifying tranquillity. The 'loss or gain / Inevitable' are simultaneous; if there is a loss, there is also in Stephen Gill's words 'a live engagement with the past that reactivates it into conjunction with the present'.[37] Although they add complexity, the 'after-dimensions' also represent an approach closer to complete understanding, as the meaning of any one moment comes from its place in a larger, longer whole that unfolds over time, and the more times on the timeline that come into view, the closer to complete our understanding of that whole. We are not to forget the horror of the spot as it was initially experienced, but only to better perceive what this horror meant for the longer narrative, which seems in this instance to be positive.

Because Wordsworth's conception of history is additive, we must not forget the poetry as it appeared before the act of revision. Wordsworth's revisions often retain traces of and subtly allude to, rather than fully displace, their origins in past versions of the poem. An example is the revision that Wordsworth carried out upon the Arab dream scene in Book 5, when he translates what had been a friend's vision, related to him, into a dream of his own. In its content the Arab dream articulates Wordsworth's desire for a moment of kairos – the climax is 'now at hand', a moment in which the Arab must seize his opportunity and fulfil his seemingly impossible destiny of preserving the stone and shell (98) – and its subsequent absorption (both reassuring and anti-climactic) into a longer narrative. The dreamer does not see him burying the objects, as he claims he will; we and the dreamer see him instead resume his journey, 'hurrying o'er the illimitable waste' (137). The journey seems futile, 'With the fleet waters of a drowning World / In chase of him', but the dreamer never doubts that it is worthwhile, even if it might end in failure (138–9). There is, however, no sign that it will end: the Arab is left presumably forever 'wandering upon this quest!' (150). He and Wordsworth both move through time 'feeling still / That, whatsoever point they gain, they yet / Have something to pursue' (II.321–3). The Arab is not the hero of a moment, but a representative of perseverance.[38]

Wordsworth's revision to this episode reflects, or reiterates, the apprehension of ongoing and durational time that it represents in its content:

>   One day, when, in the hearing of a Friend,
> I had given utterance to thoughts like these,
> He answered with a smile, that, in plain truth
> 'Twas going far to seek disquietude;
> But, on the front of his reproof, confess'd
> That he, at sundry seasons, had himself
> Yielded to kindred hauntings. And forthwith
> Added, that, once
>   . . . these same thoughts
> Came to him
> ([1805] V.49–61)

>   One day, when from my lips a like complaint
> Had fallen in presence of a studious friend,
> He with a smile made answer that in truth
> 'Twas going far to seek disquietude,
> But, on the front of his reproof, confessed
> That he himself had oftentimes given way
> To kindred hauntings. Whereupon I told
> That once
>   . . . these same thoughts
> Beset me[.]
> ([1850] V.50–62)

Instead of Wordsworth's self being severed in two, as in the revision to the Boy of Winander episode, here what had been the experience of another becomes Wordsworth's own. Instead of adding another level of temporal distance and reflection as in the gibbet spot, Wordsworth seems to be drawing closer to the source by making the dream his own. But in fact, the impulse is the same: to multiply both the levels of time and the levels of community that give context and meaning to the experience. As a dream, like a spot of time the sequence seems self-contained, brought to an abrupt close by waking. But Wordsworth contextualises the dream within the longer narrative not only of his reading on the beach, but of his conversation with a friend. Now the experience can be 'kindred' not just between two friends, but between Wordsworth, his friend and Wordsworth's selves across time, when 'these same thoughts / Came to him' (which is already implied in the 'kindred hauntings') becomes 'these same thoughts / Beset me [at another time]'. The 'One day' that opens this episode, which in the original version had been the time of his friend relating his dream, is not omitted in the revision. This additional time of conversation is, in the 1850 version, seemingly redundant: six-and-a-half lines lead up only to Wordsworth recounting his own dream as he might have done without this introduction. Yet Wordsworth has retained this shadow of the earlier version. In retaining the 'haunting' presence of his earlier version in the presence of his friend, his friend's own 'kindred hauntings' that were expressed in the 1805 version haunt the 1850 version without finding explicit expression.

The effect is similar to Wordsworth's revision of the Vaudracour and Julia tale in Book 9 of *The Prelude*; instead of cutting the tale completely, he retains an odd reference to it, so that the later version strangely registers the earlier:

> Oh! happy time of youthful Lovers! (thus
> My Story may begin) O balmy time
> . . .
> So might – and with that prelude did begin
> The Record; and in faithful Verse was given
> The doleful sequel.
> . . .
> Yet deem not my pains lost:
> For Vaudracour and Julia (so were named
> The ill-fated pair) in that plain Tale will draw
> Tears from the hearts of others when their own
> Shall beat no more. Thou, also, there may'st read,
> At leisure, how the enamoured Youth was driven . . .
> ([1850] IX.553–69)

By retaining the trace of the story in this later version, rather than omitting it entirely, Wordsworth is referring his reader, if they understand his meaning here, to other texts: overtly to his 1820 *Poems* where 'Thou . . . there mayst read' the story as it had been published separately, but also to the earlier version of *The Prelude*, by quoting and referring to 'The Record' and 'faithful Verse' that followed 'that prelude' in the earlier version.

Although Wordsworth presumably never intended for the 1805 or earlier versions of *The Prelude* to be seen (and perhaps not the

1850 version either), his revisions so often seem to relish their status as revisionary that they appear to direct readers to earlier versions, and to register the process and logic that joins them within one continuous process of writing and revising. By apprehending both the 1805 and 1850 versions at once, and apprehending them as parts of a continuous, developing process, 'New creation is generated from earlier; our understanding and enjoyment of both are enhanced by perceiving the relationship'.³⁹ Revising to create a new version of *The Prelude*, then, is a repetition of Wordsworth's endeavour within the poem, in both his allusions and his accounts of 'spots of time': to shape the present out of the materials of the past, and to understand the past in the context of 'years [that] / Have since flowed in between'.

Notes

1. Lucy Newlyn, Paradise Lost *and the Romantic Reader*, 62.
2. Samuel Taylor Coleridge, *The Collected Letters of Samuel Taylor Coleridge*, ed. Earl Leslie Griggs (Oxford: Clarendon Press, 1956, repr. 1966), i, 584.
3. William Hazlitt, *Table Talk: Opinions on Books, Men, and Things*, 2 vols (New York: Wiley & Putnam, 1845), i, 37–8.
4. William Wordsworth, 'London, 1802', in *Poems, in Two Volumes, and Other Poems*, ed. Jared Curtis (Ithaca, Cornell UP, 1983), 165.
5. Some of my discussion of Wordsworth's allusions appeared in an earlier form as 'Mediating Vision: Wordsworth's Allusions to Thomson's *Seasons* in The Prelude', *Romanticism* 22.1 (2016): 48–60.
6. Robin Jarvis, *Wordsworth, Milton and the theory of poetic relations* (London: Palgrave Macmillan, 1991), 134.
7. Sharon M. Setzer, 'Excursions in the Wilderness: Wordsworth's Visionary Kingdoms and the Typography of Miltonic Revision', *Studies in Romanticism* 30 (1991): 367–89 (367).
8. Ibid., 368.
9. Ibid., 373–4.
10. Ibid., 374.
11. John Strachan, '"That is true fame": A Few Words about Thomson's Romantic Period Popularity', in *James Thomson: Essays for the Tercentenary*, ed. Richard Terry (Liverpool: Liverpool UP, 2000): 247–70 (259).
12. William Wordsworth, 'Preface and Appendix to Lyrical Ballads', in *Wordsworth's Literary Criticism*, 68–98 (74).
13. William Wordsworth, 'Essay, Supplementary to the Preface', in *Wordsworth's Literary Criticism*, 192–218 (204).

14. Anon. (probably based on information from the Wordsworth's apothecary, Richard Scambler), 'Memoir of William Wordsworth, Esq.', *New Monthly Magazine* 11 (1819): 48–50 (48). Quoted in Duncan Wu, *Wordsworth's Reading, 1770–1799* (Cambridge: Cambridge UP, 1993), 136.
15. Duncan Wu, *Wordsworth's Reading, 1800–1815* (Cambridge: Cambridge University Press, 1993), 226.
16. William Wordsworth, letter to Alexander Dyce (12 January 1829), in *The Later Years, Part 2, 1829–1834*, ed. Ernest de Selincourt, 2nd edn, rev., arr. and ed. Alan G. Hill (Oxford: Oxford UP, 1979, repr. 2000), in *The Letters of William and Dorothy Wordsworth*, ed. Hill, 8 vols (Oxford: Oxford UP, 1978–93), v, 3.
17. Edwin Stein, *Wordsworth's Art of Allusion* (University Park, PA: Penn State UP, 1988), 10.
18. For assertion of this 'qualitative difference' see for instance Donald Wesling, *Wordsworth and the Adequacy of Landscape* (London: Routledge & Kegan Paul, 1970), 18.
19. Stein, *Wordsworth's Art of Allusion*, 178.
20. Adam Potkay, *Wordsworth's Ethics* (Baltimore: Johns Hopkins UP, 2012), 16.
21. Goodman, *Georgic Modernity*, 111.
22. C. H. Townsend, 'An Essay on the Theory and the Writings of Wordsworth. Part III', *Blackwood's Magazine* 26 (1829): 774–88 (781).
23. Mark Akenside, *The Poetical Works of Mark Akenside*, 2 vols (Philadelphia: B. Johnson, 1804), ii, 125, I.691.
24. Harold Bloom, *The Visionary Company* (London: Faber & Faber, 1961), 129.
25. William Wordsworth, *Essays on Epitaphs*, in *Wordsworth's Literary Criticism*, 120–69 (149).
26. See Somervell, 'Mediating Vision', for further examples.
27. See for detailed analysis of Thomson's mediation of Milton in Haydn's adaptation Neil Jenkins, 'The Libretto of Haydn's "The Creation". New Sources and a Possible Librettist', *Haydn Society Journal* 24.2 (2005): 2–84.
28. Recognition of this intertextuality adds another dimension to Wolfson's point that 'the image of the drowned man, its sad spectacle seemingly lodged in the safe house of books [. . .] is] revealed to play within the mind in an endless spectacle of reading and rereading.' ('Revision as Form: Wordsworth's Drowned Man', in *William Wordsworth's* The Prelude: *A Casebook*, ed. Stephen Gill (Oxford: Oxford UP, 2006), 73–121 (108).)
29. Andrzej Warminski, 'Missed Crossing: Wordsworth's Apocalypses', *Modern Language Notes* 99 (1984): 983–1006 (995).
30. Paul de Man, 'Time and History in Wordsworth', in *Romanticism and Contemporary Criticism*, ed. E. S. Burt, Kevin Newmark, and Andrzej

Warminski (Baltimore: Johns Hopkins UP, 1993), 74–94. De Man also proclaims the significance of 'hangs' for Wordsworth in *The Rhetoric of Romanticism*, though goes into less detail than in the lecture (New York: Columbia UP, 1989), 88–9.
31. William Wordsworth, 'Preface of 1815', in *Wordsworth's Literary Criticism*, 175–91 (180–1).
32. Wordsworth, letter to Sir George Beaumont (28 August 1811) in Christopher Wordsworth, *Memoirs of William Wordsworth*, 2 vols (London: Edward Moxon, 1851), i, 278.
33. Zachary Leader, *Revision and Romantic Authorship* (Oxford: Clarendon Press, 1996), 38.
34. Stephen M. Parrish, 'The Whig Interpretation of Literature', *Text* 4 (1988): 343–50 (346).
35. Larkin, *Wordsworth and Coleridge*, 13.
36. Wolfson, 'Revision as Form', 74.
37. Stephen Gill, *Wordsworth's Revisitings* (Oxford: Oxford UP, 2011), 37.
38. I discuss some of the environmental and geological implications of this passage in 'Wordsworth and the Deluge', *Studies in Romanticism* 58.2 (2019): 183–208.
39. Gill, *Wordsworth's Revisitings*, 10.

Chapter 9

A Feeling of the Whole: Reading *The Prelude*

Readers of *The Prelude* have, like readers of *Paradise Lost*, tended to privilege certain parts of the poem over others. There has been greater consensus over which parts should be favoured than in the case of Milton's poem, however. Who wouldn't prefer the Boy of Winander passage to the reflection on education that precedes it? Wordsworth provides his reader with a vocabulary, the term 'spots of time', for labelling these preferred parts, and a model in his own autobiographical practice for selecting them: 'I have singled out / Some moments' ([1805] VIII.174–5). And whereas readers of *Paradise Lost* have often privileged either the earlier or later books, the most frequently and intensely read parts of *The Prelude* are scattered throughout its length (the first two books, however, contain the greatest density of such parts). The result is that *The Prelude*'s popular, critical and pedagogic reception has been one of fragmentation. Its scattered spots of time are, if not extracted wholesale, identified as 'dominating' other parts and drawing the reader's attention away from the flatlands in between the peaks. But Wordsworth, I have been arguing, was trying to return narrative to the long poem. Just as the experiences related in the supposedly contained spots of time open out into wider prospects of space and time, and derive their significance from longer processes, so the spots of time as parts of the poem derive at least some of their significance from the whole, and their specific place within it. The reader of *The Prelude*, like Wordsworth himself, enjoys moments of seeming kairos, but must then recover the more subtle and effortful rewards of chronos, of the long reading experience over time, and appreciate what has 'flowed in between'.

Wordsworth famously conceived not only of *The Prelude* but of his entire corpus as a space, the parts of which exist simultaneously:

> The preparatory poem is biographical, and conducts the history of the Author's mind to the point when he was emboldened to hope that his faculties were sufficiently matured for entering upon the arduous labour which he had proposed to himself; and the two works have the same kind of relation to each other, if he may so express himself, as the Ante-chapel has to the body of a Gothic church. Continuing this allusion, he may be permitted to add, that his minor Pieces, which have been long before the Public, when they shall be properly arranged, will be found by the attentive Reader to have such connection with the main Work as may give them claim to be likened to the little Cells, Oratories, and sepulchral Recesses, ordinarily included in those Edifices.[1]

Such a spatial form, however, is visible only in retrospect, when all Wordsworth's works 'shall be properly arranged'. His description of *The Prelude* itself is temporal in two ways, both in itself and in its relation to *The Recluse*. It 'conducts the history of the Author's mind' to an end point; that is, the reader of *The Prelude* follows a biographical narrative. It also comes before *The Recluse* in time as well as space. An ante-chapel exists at the same time as its cathedral, but is encountered first. Like God's nunc stans prospect view or Addison's account of *The Georgics* as a tapestry, this is a spatial form that allows its reader, viewer or visitor to recognise the potential temporal relations that pertain between parts, and guides them to experience one part first, then another.

The 'connection' between Wordsworth's poems as he conceives it therefore resembles the connection between times in his own life, which can be viewed retrospectively as an extended spatial prospect, but must be also apprehended as parts of an ongoing process. The same is true when the part is not a single poem within a corpus, but a smaller part within a poem. *The Prelude* is both a part and itself consists of multiple parts. When it comes to reading *The Prelude*, Wordsworth invites us to see 'the parts / As parts, but with a feeling of the whole' (VII.735–6), and to see the whole not as a static entity, for all that its component parts may appear static, but as a moving and developing (but always remembering) progression. This probably sounds obvious, but the 'feeling of the whole' that early readers had was not always salutary. The whole, some critics felt, was not worthy of its better parts.

A Dissected Map

The earliest commentary on Wordsworth's writing of long poems is, of course, commentary on *The Excursion*, published in 1814.

The Excursion, like *The Prelude*, also consists of smaller stories (mostly recounting the lives of various characters, as recalled by the primary characters) linked by a framing narrative (the meetings and conversations of those primary characters). The framing narrative is not particularly progressive or teleological; the poem as a whole appears, in Coleridge's words, as an 'eddying instead of progression of thought'.[2] When Coleridge describes reading passages of minutely accurate descriptive poetry in *The Excursion*, he depicts the poem as a very particular kind of landscape:

> It must be some strong motive (as, for instance, that the description was necessary to the intelligibility of the tale) which could induce me to describe in a number of verses what a draughtsman could present to the eye with incomparably greater satisfaction by half a dozen strokes of his pencil, or the painter with as many touches of his brush. Such descriptions too often occasion in the mind of a reader, who is determined to understand his author, a feeling of labour, not very dissimilar to that, with which he would construct a diagram, line by line, for a long geometrical proposition. It seems to be like taking the pieces of a dissected map out of its box. We first look at one part, and then at another, then join and dove-tail them; and when the successive acts of attention have been completed, there is a retrogressive effort of mind to behold it as a whole.[3]

The problem with *The Excursion*, for Coleridge, is that it does not function effectively either as a spatial or a temporal form. Too much 'effort' is required by the reader both to 'complete' the 'successive acts of attention' involved in a linear reading and to 'behold it as a [simultaneous] whole'. The 'joins' between the parts are too imperfect for the poem either to flow in time or fit into one coherent picture. We end up reading 'line by line'. Coleridge contrasts this with Milton's natural description, in which 'co-presence of the whole picture flashe[s] at once upon the eye' – this is in spite of the fact that it takes time to read Milton's lines too.[4]

Part of Coleridge's objection to these non-narrative sections of *The Excursion* is their sheer length – the longer a verse of natural description, the harder it is for the reader to imagine all the elements of the scene existing 'at once'. The unwieldy length of *The Excursion*, the disunity of its parts, and the superiority of certain parts over others, are the typical complaints of its early readers. They also employ a range of spatial form images, especially landscapes, to describe both its strengths and flaws. For Hazlitt, '[t]he poem of *The Excursion* resembles that part of the country in which the scene is laid. It has the same vastness and magnificence, with the same nakedness and confusion'.⁵ Francis Jeffrey, notoriously critical of the poem, wrote that

> there are scattered up and down the book, and in the midst of its more repulsive portions, a very great number of single lines and images that sparkle like gems in the desert [sic], and startle us with an intimation of the great poetic powers that lie buried in the rubbish that has been heaped around them. . . . When we look back to them, indeed, and to the other passages which we have now extracted, we feel half inclined to rescind the severe sentence which we passed on the work at the beginning: – But when we look into the work itself, we perceive that it cannot be rescinded. . . . while we collect the fragments, it is impossible not to lament the ruins from which we are condemned to pick them.⁶

John Herman Merivale made a similar point in the *Monthly Review*: 'brilliant as are the occasional flashes of genius . . . they serve only to throw light enough on the dark, heavy, confused heaps of nothingness through which they burst.'⁷ Some critics argued that Wordsworth should have 'blended' or 'smoothed' the parts of the poem with more care, in order to create a continuously flowing experience for the reader. In the *British Critic* review: 'he should probably have smoothed off many allusions which now come so abrupt and unexpected as to startle even his more experienced readers.'⁸ In the *Augustan Review*: 'The seventh Book, which is a continuation of the subject, might have been dispensed with, by blending some parts of it with the preceding. The interest of a poem should gradually rise.' (*The Excursion* is on this point contrasted with *The Seasons*: 'It may be said that Thomson's poem of the "Seasons" is disjointed; but it embraces one year, and the vicissitudes of that year are so painted, that no want of connection appears.') For the author of this review, the internal disjointedness of *The Excursion* matched its ambivalent relationship with the rest of *The Recluse*: noting that the poem was presented as a preface to a poem not yet published, they remarked that '[t]he want of connection is therefore candidly acknowledged'.⁹ (The reviewer for the *New Monthly Magazine* was not convinced that *The Excursion* would be so distinct from its sequels: 'Mercy upon the reader, and still more upon the reviewer! for it seems this ponderous volume is only the prelude to two others of an equal size, and similar materials.')¹⁰

Their imagery suggests that the early critics of *The Excursion* didn't want the poem to behave like an unfolding narrative, so much as like an attractive landscape. The problem was that it was an ugly landscape – a dissected map, a rough desert, its parts disjointed, instead of a Capability Brown design with smooth, gradual rises. When Southey defended the poem against Jeffrey, he suggested not only that the poem was powerful but that it was a structurally sound and unified natural form: 'Jeffrey I hear has written what his admirers call a *crushing* review of the *Excursion*. He might as well seat himself upon Skiddaw and fancy that he crushed the mountain.'[11]

Some of the early commentary on *The Prelude* sounds very similar to reviews of *The Excursion*, which are nervous about the poem's status as a fragment as well as its own internal fragmentation. Thomas Babington Macauley used a strikingly similar image to those used by Jeffrey and Merivale to describe the inconsistency of the poem, describing 'the endless wildernesses of dull, flat, prosaic twaddle; and here and there fine descriptions and energetic declamations interspersed'.[12] The anonymous reviewer for the *Eclectic Review* observed in 1850 that

> we approach [*The Prelude*] with curiously-mingled emotions – mingled, because although a fragment, it is so vast, and in parts so finished, and because it may be regarded as at once an early production of his genius, and its latest legacy to the world. It seems a large fossil relic – imperfect and magnificent – newly dug up, and with the fresh earth and the old dim subsoil meeting and mingling around it.[13]

The Prelude is early and late, finished and unfinished, a vast whole that is both a part and made up of uneven parts. This reviewer found that 'In contemplating the 'Prelude' as a whole, we feel that all our formerly-expressed notions of his poetry are confirmed' including 'the clumsiness of the connecting links in the history', 'the superb and elaborate architecture of particular passages – the profundity of certain individual thoughts, and the weight and strength of particular lines'.[14]

The Eclectic Review's review, of which more soon, was one of the more effusive reviews in 1850. The generally tepid contemporary reception of the 1850 *Prelude* – for various reasons, outlined by Gill in *Wordsworth and the Victorians* – is probably one reason why its Victorian reception history has been comparatively neglected.[15] Another is critical preference for the 1805 version published by Ernest de Selincourt in 1926, as W. Michael Johnstone has argued.[16] There are several early accounts of reading *The Prelude* that deserve closer attention, however. Tim Milnes has argued, for example, that *The Prelude* was a crux of the 1870s debate between Leslie Stephen and Matthew Arnold over whether Wordsworth should be read as a philosopher or a poet.[17]

The great Victorian defender of *The Prelude*, Milnes suggests, was Walter Pater, whose 1874 essay in the *Fortnightly Review* defends the value of the poem. Yet even Pater argues that *The Prelude*'s value is in its parts, not its whole. 'Of all poets equally great', he reflects, Wordsworth 'would gain most by a skilfully made anthology. Such a selection would show, in truth, not so much what he was, or to himself or others seemed to be, as what, by the more energetic and fertile quality in his writings, he was ever tending to become.'[18] He wishes that Wordsworth had been more self-selective across his entire oeuvre:

> But although the necessity of selecting these precious morsels for oneself is an opportunity for the exercise of Wordsworth's peculiar influence, and induces a kind of just criticism and true estimate of it, yet the purely literary product would have been more excellent, had the writer himself purged away that alien element. How perfect would have been the little treasury, shut between the covers of how thin a book! Let us suppose the desired separation made, the electric thread untwined, the golden pieces, great and small, lying apart together.[19]

When he quotes his selected treasures from Wordsworth, Pater gathers lines from different poems and places them next to each other as though they form a new poem. Each line is both distinct from its fellows and placed in speaking conjunction with them: 'lying apart together'. Pater enacts, that is, a commonplacing reading not only of *The Prelude* but of the rest of the cathedral. When he revised this essay for his 1889 collection, *Appreciations*, he added a note: 'Since this essay was written, such selections have been made, with excellent taste, by Matthew Arnold and Professor Knight.'[20] His reference to Arnold's 1879 *Poems of Wordsworth* is slightly ironic. As Gill has pointed out, 'Arnold only prints excerpts [of *The Prelude*] which Wordsworth himself had made' and published in his lifetime (so that the 1850 *Prelude* 'might as well not have been published', and the collection does not 'give any sense of Wordsworth's command of large poetic structures').[21] The 'writer himself' had, in a sense, as Pater wished, 'purged away that alien element' in his own lifetime. Wordsworth was *The Prelude*'s original extractor.

Many Victorian readers saw both *The Excursion* and *The Prelude*, as well as the larger corpus of which they were sections, as uneven spatial forms whose better parts needed either to be more smoothly blended into the whole or extracted entirely. Their uses of landscape imagery to describe these poems speaks to the way that approaching a text as a spatial form enables this kind of reading, which pays little heed to the actual order of the parts. While *The Excursion* has if anything fallen rather than gained in readerly appreciation, twentieth- and twenty-first-century readers are less likely to characterise *The Prelude* as a scattering of gems in otherwise 'endless wildernesses of dull, flat, prosaic twaddle'. But readers are still drawn to the spots of time: 'When I read *The Prelude*', writes Brian Nellist, 'though I may not be certain of the significance of what I am reading, at least I know where to look in the poem ... There is agreement among critics not so much about the poem's meaning as over where its centres of gravity in every way lie.'[22] Now that readers are reluctant to dismiss entirely the parts 'in between', the distinction tends to be expressed in terms not of total severance but of dominance: particular parts of the poem are said to define and give meaning to the whole, in a similar way that we have seen readers of *Paradise Lost* ascribing superiority to certain parts of that poem. Mostly these parts are the usual suspects, the passages describing particular memories of heightened insight that are often labelled spots of time. Sometimes, as I will discuss later in this chapter, they are the books on the French Revolution. Other parts have been proposed too: Karl R. Johnson, Jr suggests that the glad preamble gives meaning to the rest of the poem: 'The successive stages seem thus to recall and measure themselves against that first anticipation.'[23] This has led to 'the anthologizing and synecdochic tendency which ... necessarily dominates critical interpretation of *The Prelude*', as David Ferris phrases the propensity that must remind us of similar leanings in readers of Thomson.[24] Of course my own method in this book, as in almost every study of any long poem, has involved extracting segments for analysis: the question is the extent to which the analysis reintegrates these extracts into a sense of the long poem as a whole and, importantly, how that whole is characterised: whether as a collection of parts existing simultaneously, available to be read in any order, or as a process, with parts that derive significance from their specific place within the longer structure.

Exercising our own power over the poem, selecting the parts that we deem most important and either extracting them or moving between them at will, disregarding the lines 'in between', does seem to replicate the activity that Wordsworth so often carries out when reading his own past life and writing his life story. The story of Wordsworth's life is not told in its proper historical chronology. For example, Wordsworth places his account of the ascent up Snowdon in Book 14 after the account of the French Revolution, although it took place between Wordsworth's visits to France in 1790 and 1792, which are recorded in Books 6 and 9.[25] Wordsworth is giving a new shape to history according to the needs of his narrative. He extracts that time from its objective place in chronos and frames it as a culmination, a moment of kairos. In the case of many of the other spots, it is impossible to map them onto a linear timeline of Wordsworth's historical childhood because we are not given enough information. However, from the reader's perspective, the scrambled chronology of the poem comes to function like chronos. The parts of the poem have been laid out for us in a particular order (or rather, a few different particular orders, taking into account the various versions of the poem that Wordsworth at least had some say in constructing), even if that order does not correlate precisely with history. A linear movement through the poem, then, simulates in the reading experience, even if it does not represent in its content, linear movement through chronological time. The 'flat' or mundane parts of the poem 'in between' the seemingly prominent parts are like the 'years [that] / Have since flowed in between' the prominent parts of Wordsworth's life. And like those years, these parts must be experienced as duration, not overleaped.

Many parts of the poem do demand particular attention, and offer particularly suggestive meanings that inform or infuse the rest of the poem. But the line of influence is not unidirectional. Either extracting them or raising them over and above the other parts of the poem can only be a first step in the interpretative process. Just as Wordsworth's most memorable and profound experiences must be reintegrated into longer narratives, so the reader of *The Prelude* must reintegrate the most memorable parts into the longer linear structure of the poem. *The Prelude* tells us not only in its content but in its form and structure to be wary of being 'taught to feel', even by the poem itself, 'perhaps too much, / The self-sufficing power of Solitude' when it comes to a moment of time (II.76–7).

Long Sustained Song

It is important that in his assessment of *The Excursion* as a dissected map, Coleridge refers specifically to its sections of landscape description. It is when poetry claims to represent something simultaneous, like a prospect view, that the 'successive acts of attention' involved in reading become a problem. When it comes to the narrative parts of *The Excursion*, the reader's awareness of the time it takes to read does not clearly conflict with the subject matter. Charles Lamb was drawn to particular narrative parts of the poem, but not keen to 'dissect' it: 'We might extract powerful instances of pathos from these tales – the story of Ellen in particular – but their force is in combination, and in the circumstances under which they are introduced.'[26] Although Lamb's reference to 'combination' hints at potential other ways, besides the linear, in which the parts of the poem might speak to one another, his addition of 'the circumstances under which they are introduced' suggests that he prefers reading this poem (unlike *Paradise Lost*) in its pre-arranged order.

In the case of *The Prelude*, Coleridge evidently did not object to the way the poem stimulates consciousness of the time taken to read or listen to it. His poem 'To William Wordsworth', composed after hearing *The Prelude* read aloud, reflects the organisation of the parts and the experience of encountering them in order:

> Eve following eve,
> Dear tranquil time, when the sweet sense of Home
> Is sweetest! moments for their own sake hailed
> And more desired, more precious for thy song,
> In silence listening, like a devout child,
> My soul lay passive, by thy various strain
> Driven as in surges now beneath the stars,
> With momentary stars of my own birth,
> Fair constellated foam, still darting off
> Into the darkness; now a tranquil sea,
> Outspread and bright, yet swelling to the moon.[27]

The movement of the poem is uneven, with 'surges' of intensity followed by periods of tranquillity. The image of the sea is a spatial form but this is a figure for Coleridge's 'soul'. The poem itself, Wordsworth's 'long sustained Song', moved forward in time until it 'finally closed', culminating in a 'last strain' on 'duty', 'action', and 'joy' (presumably the final concluding book).[28] For Coleridge, the experience of listening to *The Prelude* is not one of 'taking the pieces of a dissected map out of its box' because its parts, although 'various', are not disconnected. It is 'a linked lay of Truth, / Of Truth profound a sweet continuous lay': the second line elaborates on the first, specifying that though the poem is 'linked', and therefore consisting of distinct parts, it is 'continuous': the parts are joined, not disjointed.[29] Coleridge's depiction of his soul as 'passive' is reflective of the way linear readings have often been characterised, as in many of the examples we have seen, as a kind of submission to the power of the poem or poet, compared to more autonomous non-linear readings.

Coleridge's image of tidal surges anticipates the review in the *Eclectic Review*, which describes the 'monotony' of Wordsworth's corpus as 'that of the ocean surges, which break now on the shore to the same tune as they did the eve before the deluge'.[30] Although this reviewer claimed to observe 'the clumsiness of the connecting links' that bound together parts of *The Prelude*, they clearly did perceive that there were links and that they did connect the parts; in the same review the poem is described as 'a scroll of power and magic, unrolling slowly':

> Lingeringly does he walk down the deserted halls of the past, and converse with the pictures which he sees suspended there. The book reads like a long soliloquy. . . . Skiddaw, Cambridge, Paris, London, the Alps, are but milestones marking his progress onwards, from the measured turbulence of his youth, to the calm 'philosophic mind' brought him by the 'years' of his manhood. No object, however august, is here described solely for its intrinsic charms, or made awkwardly to outstand from the main current of the story. Were Ossa an excrescence, he would treat it as if it were a wart – were a wart a point of interest, he would dilate on it as if it were an Ossa. His strong personal feeling bends in all that is needful to his purpose, and rejects all that is extraneous.[31]

The image of a picture gallery is the kind of synchronic spatial form that invites the anthological or commonplacing reading: Wordsworth's memories are pictures, existing simultaneously, that he can wander between and linger over at will, and the implication is that the reader can wander at will between the parts of his poem that describe them. But the review maps a particular route onto this space: a linear journey 'down the halls'. The poet 'leads us' a particular way. The route is a smooth one, as the review goes on to add: 'Very lofty mountains are jagged, torn, and precipitous; loftier ones still are rounded off on their summits into the smoothest of contours. Thus Wordsworth shows himself rising gradually into the measure and the stature of supernal unity and peace.'[32] This seems like a direct rebuke to reviews that characterised Wordsworth's long poems as jagged landscapes, and particularly to the *Augustan Review* review, which complained that *The Excursion* did not 'gradually rise'. Despite the clumsy links, this reviewer observes,

> In reading the 'Prelude', we should never forget that his object is not to weave an artful and amusing story, but sternly and elaborately to trace the 'growth of a poet's mind'. This is a metaphysical more than

a biographical purpose. He leads us accordingly, not so much from incident to incident, as from thought to thought, along the salient points of his mental history.³³

The poem's route, of course, is not a straightforward 'progress' from youth to maturity (in terms of either age or 'mental' power). But there is a rough biographical shape to the poem, frequently if not always chronological in its organisation, and Wordsworth claims to want to 'trace a progress' in the poem. It is easy to see why many readers follow the opposite impulse to 'the anthologizing and synecdochic', and take instead the diachronic view, despite the magnetism of the spots of time and other more 'intense' parts of the poem. As in the *Eclectic Review* review, this diachronic reading is usually carried out in terms of identifying a single narrative movement, which the various episodes of the poem and their various meanings, as well as the passages in between, are supposed to serve. One well-known interpretation of the shape of the poem's argument is Geoffrey Hartman's thesis that the poem traces the imagination's gradual development beyond nature.³⁴ But Hartman's model, supported by some parts of the poem, is confounded by others: the imagination is not absent or only embryonic at the start of the poem, nor nature satisfactorily subordinated at the end. Stuart Peterfreund offers an unusual account of a structure based on generic progression. But Peterfreund's suggestion that *The Prelude* develops from pastoral through satire to epic, with each sublime 'epic' spot of time possessing increased duration, must be qualified by his admission that elements of all these genres are present for the whole length of the poem.³⁵ The most common reading of the poem's structure has probably been the one summarised by Davis: 'the expectation–disappointment–revaluation structure and the occasional glimpses into eternity'.³⁶ In none of these accounts, and the last least of all, do the spots of time or 'glimpses into eternity' fit comfortably. They occur and recur throughout the poem, 'scattered everywhere' (XII.224), even in the times in Wordsworth's life, and the books that represent them, when he had apparently lost access to nature and imaginative vision. This challenges the idea of a single linear progression, whether of improvement or degradation, over the time of Wordsworth's life or the time of his writing *The Prelude*. The reviewer for *Tait's Edinburgh Magazine* in 1850 perceived no single cumulative progress towards one end point: 'His is the ripple of the brook, and not the collective might of waters slowly gathering to break in one huge billow on the shore.'³⁷ Note again the implication that to create a linear progression is to demonstrate the poem or poet's power, his 'might', or his discipline, his 'sternly . . . lead[ing] us', as in the *Eclectic Review* review. The poem's power lies not so much in its impressive coherence as in its insistence on leading the reader through it in a particular order. This is clear in Herbert Lindenberger's formulation, which frames the relationship between reader and poem in even more combative terms: 'Those who try to boil down Wordsworth's philosophy – his concepts of nature and imagination, his politics and pantheism – from a study of *The Prelude* are usually defeated by the fact that what seems at first a body of doctrine is actually a record of the *process toward* doctrine.'[38]

The same process principle undermines attempts to lift particular parts of the poem out of their place in its long structure. I would follow Fairer's approach in his study of the Coleridge circle, which is to enact a critical 'move', informed by an understanding of Romantic poetry's debts to eighteenth-century georgic, 'from questions of unity to matters of integrity'.[39] It is the 'process toward', rather than the doctrine itself, that is the integral principle of *The Prelude*. Wordsworth's aim to 'trace a progress' is achieved not in the realisation of any single, particular kind of progress, but in the registration of the ongoingness of time and of the numerous and various links that connect the moments and events in that process. Perceiving time-as-chronos is to 'trace a progress', though it may well be an 'unreasoning progress'.

> [H]ow could there fail to be
> Some change, if merely hence, that years of life
> Were going on, and with them loss or gain
> Inevitable, sure alternative.
> ([1805] XI.38–41)

It still might be objected that, if there is no consistent progress beyond the progress of time itself, little is gained by integrating the spots of time or any other part of *The Prelude* back into the linear layout of the poem. How does the poem's internal structure reinforce its claim that the chronological experience of time is important? 'The architecture of the poem', according to Shears, 'is not organised on the basis of action, succession and consequence . . . but on the repetitions of language used to highlight the surmise of transcendence.'[40] The structure of the poem as a whole is more like repetition. '[T]he various moments of epiphany in *The Prelude* are not [unique]', as Shears claims.[41] Indeed it is difficult to see, in many instances, why one section of *The Prelude* must precede instead of follow another, or vice versa. The order in which the parts are arranged appears largely arbitrary. This seems to be

Morgan's implicit conclusion when she argues that the poem 'is a series of short lyrics united by an unusual narrative structure', and that 'structure has an associative logic that unites each episode to the final goal, rather than a causal logic that would directly link each episode to the next'.[42] She describes the activity of reading *The Prelude* as 'prospective reading': 'Wordsworth constantly directs his readers to process the text prospectively – to look forward to the end point as they read the poem, rather than to confer retrospective significance at the end of the reading process.'[43] While I agree with Morgan's point that the parts share with each other a relation to the poem's end, as well as, of course, with her fundamental principle that the process of reading the poem's structure is part of its meaning, her account does not sufficiently explain either the organisation or the quantity of these episodes. She only notes that the poem needs to be long in order to accumulate these 'short lyrics' and thereby prove 'Wordsworth's poetic prowess'.[44] And Morgan's 'prospective reading' is unidirectional, only really available to the 'first-time reader of *The Prelude*', who 'may know the endpoint but is unfamiliar with the individual episodes, and can thus experience a sense of novelty and wonder similar to what Wordsworth initially experienced'.[45] Morgan understates the importance of the retrospective reading, and the perspective of the reader who, like Wordsworth, looks back as well as forward. Like the reader who looks back over and analyses a single spot of time, this reader may look back over the whole poem and perceive something like 'causal logic', which combines the episodes into a specific composition.

The Prelude offers cyclical patterns of repetition, but differs from *The Seasons* in that it does distinguish between 'before' and 'after'. As the above lines claim, each repetition is not a perfect repetition but brings with it 'loss or gain', some small change that is registered as the years go 'on' as well as round. How these losses and gains are manifested in the poem's structure can be very subtle. I think it does matter, for example, that the Boy of Winander passage in Book 5 comes later in the poem than the 'Minstrel boy' passage in Book 2. The two spots invite comparison in the same way that the ascent up Snowdon invites comparison with the Simplon Pass episode, and numerous other spots invite comparison with one another through their use of shared imagery and language. Wordsworth revised the earlier spot of time to take place at 'Winander' too, instead of 'Windermere' (although both are names for the same lake), which strengthens the connection. Each spot tells of a boy (who is not Wordsworth, and yet is a cipher for him) alone at a lake, sending sounds into the darkness. At first, the main principle seems to be one simply of parallelism, and it isn't obvious that much is at stake in the order in which we read these passages. But there is a process, both of loss and gain, that has occurred in between these 'spots' – not in Wordsworth's life, necessarily, for we don't know when each occurred in history, but in the narrator's engagement with his memories.

In Book 2, the Minstrel boy is left 'Alone upon the rock' (170) and we do not learn what he felt or thought, or what happened to him afterwards. Our glimpse of him is oddly fleeting: a moment plucked from what was a much longer experience for the boy, and a longer life. Wordsworth is concerned in this spot with the effect upon his own mind in that moment, and afterwards: 'Thus were my sympathies enlarged' (175). But we have to ask if his 'sympathies' with other people were really so. The Boy of Winander episode posits a more ambivalent relationship between the boy and the poet. Wordsworth's revisions to the episode are notorious: the Boy's identity as the young Wordsworth in the original draft of 1798 is deferred behind a third person account, allowing Wordsworth to describe his own death and burial. In this way Wordsworth seems to close off the Boy of Winander's narrative in order to view it as a whole, from the perspective of a later outsider. But the Boy remains part of several longer narratives. He is a doppelgänger not only for Wordsworth himself but for the Minstrel boy. He 'stand[s] alone' like the Minstrel (370) and plays his own 'instrument' (374), but he is given the inner life that had been Wordsworth's in Book 2; he perceives 'the bosom of the steady lake' (390), just as the 'dead still water lay upon my mind' for Wordsworth in Book 2 (171), and the mountains and woods sink down into the lake in the Boy's vision just as the sky 'sank down / Into [Wordsworth's] heart' in Book 2 (173–4). This is not fruitless repetition of similar elements; the later spot is a realisation of 'sympathies' that were lacking in the earlier, a recognition that others have an equivalent consciousness and equivalent narrative of their own – even if Wordsworth can only come to this recognition by translating a past self into a 'third person'. Something has happened in the intervening Books, 3 and 4, to enable this difference of treatment. Those books not only tell of Wordsworth growing up, but enact the poet's development as he writes. He goes through the painful analysis of his self-centred behaviour at Cambridge, before turning in Book 4 to give, for the first time, real attention to others – Anne Tyson, his dog, the locals and then the soldier. Wordsworth's linear composition of the poem is, of course, a fiction, but it is one that the poem dramatises. Such an interpretation does not necessarily depend on reading these passages in order, but rather on a recognition that this is their order, and distance from one another, in the poem that Wordsworth arranged. Comparing these spots directly is a kind of commonplacing reading, but one that not only respects but depends upon the poetry that has flowed in between.

The French Revolution

A slightly different case needs to be addressed here: Books 10 and 11 (10 in 1805). Theresa M. Kelley complains of those readers who are drawn to the spots of time as receptacles for what they see as the poem's main meaning; it is for this reason, she supposes, that some prefer the two-part *Prelude*, 'where sublime outcroppings do dominate the argument'.[46] Kelley instead ascribes dominance to the books on the French Revolution, which she claims are the 'lens' through which all other parts of the poem, including the spots of time, should be read.[47] Similarly, Alan Liu claims that, in their very otherness, Books 10 and 11 define the rest of the poem, particularly the books that follow.[48] These Books do require slightly different treatment, although I suggest that rather than 'dominating' every other part of the poem, their traumatic effects can only be understood with reference to those other parts. Reading these Books through the 'lens' of other parts reveals that, rather than dominating, Books 10 and 11 are held slightly at bay by the rest of the poem.

In these books Wordsworth is less keen to trace the way his experience in France has shaped him in the present, and more inclined to celebrate its lack of influence. He describes a time that is so distinct from other times – including the time in which he writes – that it seems to bear no clear relation to them at all. It can neither be aligned vertically with a common interpretive paradigm nor assimilated into a linear narrative; instead, it appears as a time belonging to another world and another life altogether. The French Revolution was itself based on an attempt to access a perspective of eternity, not through nature, books or memory, but through its deification of reason: 'the reasoning faculty, enthroned / Where the disturbances of space and time . . . find no admission' (XI.329–33). But this attempt at eternity was a failure, and *The Prelude* presents revolutionary France as a time and place obsessed with, and defined by, its temporality. Books 10 and 11 are grounded in a particular moment of history, in which experience and its interpretation 'Gave way to overpressure from the times' (XII.51) – not past and future times, but the (then) present, disastrous times,

'And their disastrous issues' (52). Past and future have no meaning for such 'a time / In which apostasy from ancient faith / Seemed but conversion to a higher creed' (X.308–10); in which "Mid the depth / Of those enormities, even thinking minds / Forgot at seasons whence they had their being' (X.374–6), and Wordsworth himself wished to be 'parted as by a gulph / From him who had been' (XII.59–60); which even created its own new calendar and measures of time. Wordsworth's portrayal of the Revolution and Terror thus accords with Lynn Hunt's account of the period as a 'herculean effort to break with the past', causing a 'rupture' in time, distinct from the ordinary flow of continuity.[49] In *The Prelude* Wordsworth has characterised the period as emphatically singular: 'that very moment', 'this one time' (X.270, 272). From the distance of writing his poem, Wordsworth can perceive that the Revolution and Terror were products of 'a terrific reservoir of guilt / And ignorance, filled up from age to age' (X.477–8), and can frame Robespierre's 'Atheist Crew' (X.502) as descendants of Milton's devils (like Satan blind to their origins). Nevertheless, when viewed in the contexts of other times, revolutionary France is marked not just by its stark difference but by its utter incompatibility with other times when it comes to understanding: 'What a mockery this / Of history, the past and that to come! . . . Oh! laughter for the Page that would reflect / To future times the face of what now is!' (IX.168–74). When pre-revolutionary France is 'lingering yet an Image' in Wordsworth's mind, it does not inform his understanding, or inflect the meaning, of current events, but only 'mock[s] me under such a strange reverse' (X.509–10). Unlike any of the spots of time, which appear 'self-sufficing' but in fact take their significance from their place in a longer process, the early days of the French Revolution were a time that was entirely self-enclosed.

When Wordsworth exclaims, at the start of Book 9, 'Oh, how much unlike the past!' (22), he refers to the Revolution's uniqueness in history, in his life and in his poem. Just as his experience was different during his time in France, so his poetry must subtly alter in the Books that describe this time. Temporal continuities, the alertness to past and future times and their contribution to the meaning of the present moment, only re-emerge for Wordsworth when he leaves France, and the historically unique events there begin to draw to a close. At the end of Book 10 Wordsworth describes his return to the Lake District, when among the forms of nature 'That neither passed away nor changed' (X.527) memories of youth and old friends 'Came back upon me' (547). News of Robespierre's death – a singular historical event – intrudes upon this impression of temporal continuity, so that 'The day deserves / A separate Record' (513–14), but this revelation, and its promise of the end of the Terror, allows Wordsworth to reclaim the continuous identity that connects him with his past self. His return to the moving world of time is striking: Wordsworth revisits 'former days' not just in the form of childhood memory, but in the form of self-quotation (597). Book 10 ends with the same line that Wordsworth had used in Book 2: 'We beat with thundering hoofs the level sand' (X.603, II.137).

But although Wordsworth will claim that 'the degradation' of the Revolution 'was transient', this return at the end of Book 10 is not to something totally identical (XII.193–201). The self-quotation does not signify a lack of progress, stagnation or regression. The experience of riding on the beach is framed now not just by the memory of Wordsworth writing, but by the memory of Wordsworth as he walked along that beach after hearing of Robespierre's death. The revival of the past in this line has the reader perceive how much has remained the same and how much has changed, both in Wordsworth's life and in the poem itself, between Books 2 and 10. It is necessary to feel the temporal distance between the two instances of the line in order to understand the significance of their sameness. But if Books 10 and 11 are a 'lens' through which we must read both instances of the repeated line, those lines, too, form a frame through which we must view these Books. Neither part is 'dominant': the refraction of interpretation goes both ways.

Robespierre's death was, of course, a false promise, and Book 11 must return again to this outlying period. At the end of this book, however, Wordsworth can close this 'story' of a 'long-lived storm of great events' (XI.374–5), although he laments that France remains altered, 'with the wreck of loftier years bestrown' (391). The return, to the ordinary flow of time and of the poem, is signified by an address to Coleridge and acknowledgement of the 'One great society ... the noble Living and the noble Dead' (394–5). Book 12 begins by declaring the previous few books an aberration: 'Long time have human ignorance and guilt / Detained us ... Not with these began / Our song, and not with these our song must end' (1–8). He will go on to recount his ascent of Snowdon: like the hooves beating the sand, a deliberate return to an experience that predates the Revolution, so that the proper flow of time, which both connects and distances Wordsworth from his youth, is restored again in his poetry as (he hopes) it was restored in his life.

Throughout *The Prelude*, Wordsworth will return again and again to the same temptations of trying to extract a moment from the spread of time and to extract himself from the community. Nevertheless, we can trace an eddying process, both locally within particular passages and at the larger scale of the long poem, from self-absorption and temporal absorption in the present (in its purest form at the opening of Book 1) to the communal feeling and wider temporal perspective of Book 14; from kairos to chronos. The latter is not necessarily better than the former – it is a process of loss and gain. But the value of the latter, its humaneness and the access it provides to forms of community with the living and the dead, even though it requires the effort of traversing the years or lines 'in between', should be recognised. Even the most prosaic sections of *The Prelude*, like the 'most unfruitful hours' of Wordsworth's life (V.363), contribute to the 'feeling of the whole' (VII.736).

Notes

1. William Wordsworth, 'Preface to The Excursion', *The Excursion*, 38.
2. Coleridge, *Biographia Literaria*, XXII, in *The Major Works*, 398.
3. Ibid., 392.
4. Ibid., 393.
5. Hazlitt, 'Observations on Mr. W's Poem the *Excursion*' (1814), in *William Wordsworth (Bloom's Classic Critical Views)*: 211–13 (211).
6. Francis Jeffrey, 'Wordsworth's *Excursion*', *Edinburgh Review* XXIC (1814): 1–30. In *The Romantics Reviewed: Contemporary Reviews of British Romantic Writers*, ed. Donald H. Reiman (London: Routledge: 1972): Part A, Vol. ii, 438–53 (452–3).
7. John Herman Merivale, 'Wordsworth's *Excursion, a Poem*', *Monthly Review*, 2nd Series, LXXVI (1815): 123–36. In *Romantics Reviewed*: Part A, Vol. ii, 726–33 (729).
8. Anon., 'Wordsworth's Excursion', *British Critic*, 2nd Series, III (1815): 449–67. In *Romantics Reviewed*: Part A, Vol. i, 138–47 (146).
9. Anon., 'Wordsworth's Poems', *Augustan Review* I (1815): 343–56.
10. Anon., 'The Excursion', *New Monthly Magazine* II (1814): 157. In *Romantics Reviewed*: Part A, Vol. ii, 796–97 (797).
11. Robert Southey, to Walter Scott (24 December 1814) in *William Wordsworth (Bloom's Classic Critical Views)*, 221.
12. Thomas Babington Macauley, *Journal* (28 July 1850) in *William Wordsworth (Bloom's Classic Critical Views)*, 188.
13. Anon., 'Wordsworth's Growth of a Poet's Mind', *Eclectic Review* XXVIII (1850): 550–62 (551).
14. Ibid., 559.
15. Stephen Gill, *Wordsworth and the Victorians* (Oxford: Oxford UP, 1998), 29–31.

16. Theresa M. W. Michael Johnstone, 'Toward a Book History of William Wordsworth's 1850 *Prelude*', *Textual Cultures* 5.2 (2010): 63–91.
17. Tim Milnes, *William Wordsworth: The Prelude* (Basingstoke: Palgrave Macmillan, 2009), 26.
18. Walter Pater, 'Wordsworth' (1874), in *William Wordsworth (Bloom's Classic Critical Views)*: 173–88 (176).
19. Ibid., 177.
20. Ibid., 187.
21. Gill, *Wordsworth and the Victorians*, 108.
22. Brian Nellist, 'Lyric Presence in Byron from the Tales to *Don Juan*', in *Byron and the Limits of Fiction*, ed. Bernard Beatty and Vincent Newey (Liverpool: Liverpool UP, 1988), 39–77 (40).
23. Karl R. Johnson, Jr, *The Written Spirit: Thematic and Rhetorical Structure in Wordsworth's* The Prelude (Salzburg: Institut für Englische Sprache und Literatur, 1978), 17.
24. David Ferris, 'Where Three Paths Meet: History, Wordsworth, and the Simplon Pass', *Studies in Romanticism* 30 (1991): 391–438 (391).
25. Jonathan Wordsworth, notes to William Wordsworth, *The Prelude: The Four Texts*, ed. Jonathan Wordsworth (London: Penguin, 1995), 656.
26. Charles Lamb, 'Wordsworth's "Excursion"', in *Selected Prose*, ed. Adam Phillips (London: Penguin, 1985, repr. 2013), 65–80, 76.
27. Coleridge, *The Major Works*, 127.
28. Ibid., 126–7.
29. Ibid., 126.
30. Anon., *Eclectic Review*, 544.
31. Ibid., 556–57.
32. Ibid., 556.
33. Ibid., 555.
34. Geoffrey Hartman, *Wordsworth's Poetry 1787–1814* (New Haven: Yale UP, 1964).
35. Stuart Peterfreund, '*The Prelude*: Wordsworth's Metamorphic Epic', *Genre* 14 (1981): 441–72.
36. Davis, *Experimental Reading*, 136.
37. Anon., 'The Prelude', *Tait's Edinburgh Magazine* XVII (1850). Quoted in Milnes, *William Wordsworth*, 18.
38. Herbert Lindenberger, *On Wordsworth's* Prelude (Princeton: Princeton UP, 1963), 180.
39. David Fairer, *Organising Poetry: The Coleridge Circle, 1790–1798* (Oxford: Oxford UP, 2009), 29.
40. Shears, *Romantic Legacy*, 94.
41. Ibid.
42. Morgan, *Narrative Means*, 72, 19.
43. Ibid., 19.
44. Ibid., 91.
45. Ibid., 105.

46. Theresa M. Kelley, *Wordsworth's Revisionary Aesthetics* (Cambridge: Cambridge University Press, 1988), 91.
47. Ibid., 91.
48. Alan Liu, *Wordsworth: The Sense of History* (Stanford: Stanford UP, 1989), 380.
49. Lynn Hunt, *Measuring Time, Making History* (Budapest: Central European UP, 2008), 69.

Conclusion

'The topic of human constructions of temporality', writes Roland Racevskis,

> is one so fraught with ambiguities and complexities that it is above all in esthetic objects composed of language – literary texts – that one may find answers to some of the most slippery questions of intellectual history.[1]

It is via 'the unpredictable angles of approach provided by the aesthetic activity of figuration', Racevskis suggests, that many of the complexities and fundamental paradoxes of time (as it is encountered and perceived by humans) can be apprehended.[2] I hope that I have shown how productive the varied angles of approach available to the long poem can be in exploring the multiple ways in which humans can construct temporality. The capacity of the long poem, more than any other type of text, to act simultaneously as a spatial and as a temporal form – as a region in which to wander and as an unfolding process – enables it to 'figure' in its very form multiple constructions of temporality, and to recreate these in the reader's experience. Add to this the other 'angles of approach' that literary texts use to think about time – theme and content, revision, allusion – and the long poem is uniquely positioned to address the topic. The 'questions of intellectual history' about time that long poems have been used to address include questions about free will, scientific or religious understandings of nonhuman nature, and the continuity of human identity. Whether the poems I have been looking at provide 'answers' to these questions is debatable, but they do make visible the temporal paradoxes inherent in such questions.

Accordingly, I have been treating these poems both as parts of a continuum and as individual entities. Each constructs its own characteristic temporality according to the priorities of its author and the intellectual debates of its contemporary moment, but each also forms a part of a longer tradition. The long poem certainly did not disappear in the nineteenth century, in spite of Edgar Allan Poe's notorious proclamation:

> I hold that a long poem does not exist. I maintain that the phrase, 'a long poem', is simply a flat contradiction in terms.... But the day of these artistic anomalies is over. If, at any time, any very long poem were popular in reality, – which I doubt, – it is at least clear that no very long poem will ever be popular again.[3]

(Poe added that *Paradise Lost* 'is to be regarded as poetical only when, losing sight of that vital requisite in all works of art, unity, we view it merely as a series of minor poems'.)[4] There are plenty of long poems after 1850 that give the lie to Poe's prophecy.[5] The difference is that between Tennyson's *In Memoriam* (1850) and the twentieth century, long poems are overwhelmingly narrative in form, to the extent that the period sees the development of the verse novel in examples like *Aurora Leigh* (1856) and *The Ring and the Book* (1868–89). (A possible exception is Tennyson's *Idylls of the King* [1859–85], which employs the overarching narrative but internal discontinuity of romance.) After the end of the century, as Adam Roberts puts it, 'the shredder of Modernism was wheeled in and all long poems became, very deliberately, fragments shored against our ruin'.[6]

The period between 1660 and 1830 saw the greatest popularity and success of long poems perhaps in part because the long eighteenth century's generic trends for the long poem allowed for a balance between narrative momentum and lyrical immediacy, rather than tending to either extreme as in the Victorian and Modernist periods. Wordsworth's *Prelude*, appearing in 1850 but composed almost entirely several decades earlier, looks forward to the return of narrative to the long poem; but he also looks back to the non-narrative modes of georgic, philosophical poem, and prospect poem that had shaped the long poem in the previous century. He uses these modes, in fact, to reintroduce narrative. Even at its height in *The Seasons*, the non-narrative long poem contained within its prospect views and its reflections on the poet-figure a persistent core of narrative potential, always poised between the two possibilities of static space and moving time. The long poem is at its best when the narrative tends towards non-narrative and the non-narrative towards narrative. Biblical history is mapped onto God's prospect view in eternity, and an interpolated tale turns into a series of disjointed fragments; on the other side of the coin, landscape descriptions flower into processes of growth and decay, and spots of time open out into prospects of progress.

The prospect for long poems – new or old – in the twenty-first century is not very bright. Even people whose main occupation is the study of literature don't have enough time to read them. The new epoch of the Anthropocene, however, has opened up new and urgent paths of enquiry for the georgic and even for the prospect poem, although new experiments in these genres have so far been concentrated in prose and lyrical forms.[7] I hope that greater critical attention not just to the best long poems (there will still be books about *Paradise Lost*) but to the form of the long poem itself, beyond epic, will reinvigorate interest in the form for both readers and poets.

Notes

1. Roland Racevskis, *Time and Ways of Knowing under Louis XIV* (Lewisburg, PA: Bucknell UP, 2003), 14.
2. Ibid., 14–15.
3. Edgar Allan Poe, 'The Poetic Principle', in *The Poetical Works of Edgar Allan Poe* (London: Ward, Lock, & Co., 1882): 185–217 (185–7).
4. Ibid., 186.
5. See Natasha Moore, *Victorian Poetry and Modern Life: The Unpoetical Age* (Basingstoke: Palgrave Macmillan, 2015), 99–108.
6. Roberts, *Romantic and Victorian Long Poems*, 1.
7. See David Fairer, 'The World of Eco-georgic', *Studies in 18th Century Culture* 40 (2011): 201–18; Pippa Marland, 'Rewilding, Wilding, and the New Georgic', *Green Letters* 24 (2020): 421–36; and Walt Hunter, 'The No-Prospect Poem: Lyric Finality in Prynne, Awoonor, and Trethewey', *The Minnesota Review* 85 (2015): 144–52.

Bibliography

Primary Sources

Addison, Joseph. 'Essay on the Georgics'. In John Dryden, *Poems, 1697*, ed. Vinton A. Dearing, Alan Roper and Frost (Berkeley: University of California Press, 1987), in *The Works of John Dryden*, ed. William Frost and Vinton A. Dearing, 22 vols (Berkeley: University of California Press, 1956–90), v, 145–53.

Akenside, Mark. *The Poetical Works of Mark Akenside*, 2 vols (Philadelphia: B. Johnson, 1804).

Allestree, Richard. *Eighteen Sermons* (London: James Allestry, 1669).

Anon. 'Wordsworth's Poems'. *Augustan Review* I (1815), 343–56.

Anon. 'Memoir of William Wordsworth, Esq.'. *New Monthly Magazine* 11 (1819), 48–50.

Anon. 'Thomson – The Poet'. *New-York Mirror, and Ladies' Literary Gazette* 5 (22 September 1827), 85.

Anon. 'The Prelude'. *Tait's Edinburgh Magazine* XVII (1850).

Anon. 'Wordsworth's Growth of a Poet's Mind'. *Eclectic Review* XXVIII (1850), 550–62.

Aquinas, Saint Thomas. *Existence and Nature of God*, ed. and trans. Timothy McDermott (1964), in *Summa Theologiæ*, 61 vols (Cambridge: Cambridge University Press, 2006), ii.

Augustine, Saint. *Confessions*, trans. Henry Chadwick (Oxford: Oxford University Press, 1991).

Bloom, Harold, ed. *William Wordsworth (Bloom's Classic Critical Views)* (New York: Infobase, 2009).

Boethius. *The Consolation of Philosophy*, trans. P. G. Walsh (1999) (Oxford: Oxford University Press, 2008).

Boswell, James. *Life of Johnson*, ed. R. W. Chapman (Oxford: Oxford University Press, 1970).

Boyle, Robert. *The Works of the Honourable Robert Boyle*, 5 vols (London: A. Millar, 1744).

Byron, George Gordon, *Selected Letters and Journals*, ed. Leslie A. Marchand (Cambridge, MA: Belknap Press of Harvard University Press, 1982).

Coleridge, Samuel Taylor. *The Collected Letters of Samuel Taylor Coleridge*, ed. Earl Leslie Griggs (Oxford: Clarendon Press, 1956, repr. 1966).

Coleridge, Samuel Taylor. *The Major Works*, ed. H. J. Jackson (Oxford: Oxford University Press, 1985, repr. 2008).

Cowley, Abraham. *Poems* (London: Humphrey Moseley, 1656).

Cowper, William. *The Poems of William Cowper, Volume II: 1782–1785*, ed. John D. Baird and Charles Ryskamp (Oxford: Clarendon Press, 1995).

Cudworth, Ralph. *The True Intellectual System of the Universe* (London: Richard Royston, 1678).

Defoe, Daniel. *The Storm*, ed. Richard Hamblyn (London, Penguin 2005).

Denham, John. *Coopers Hill. A Poeme* (London: Tho. Walkley, 1642).

Denham, John. *Coopers Hill* (London: Humphry Moseley, 1655).

Dryden, John. *The Works of John Dryden*, ed. William Frost and Vinton A. Dearing, 22 vols (Berkeley: University of California Press, 1956–95).

Duck, Stephen. *The Thresher's Labour*, ed. E. P. Thompson and Marian Sugden (London: Merlin Press, 1989).

Dyer, John. *Poems* (London: J. Dodsley, 1770).

Hazlitt, William. *Lectures on the English Poets* (London: Pickering & Chatto, 1998), in *The Selected Writings of William Hazlitt*, ed. Duncan Wu, 9 vols (London: Pickering & Chatto, 1998), ii.

Hazlitt, William. *Table Talk: Opinions on Books, Men, and Things*, 2 vols (New York: Wiley & Putnam, 1845).

Hegel, G. W. F. *Aesthetics: Lectures on Fine Art*, II, trans. T. M. Knox (Oxford: Clarendon Press, 1975).

Herbert, George. *The Complete English Poems*, ed. John Tobin (London: Penguin, 1991, repr. 2004).

Hobbes, Thomas. *Leviathan* (London: Andrew Ccooke [sic], 1651).

Hobbes, Thomas. *The Questions concerning Liberty, Necessity, and Chance Clearly Stated and Debated between Dr. Bramhall, Bishop of Derry, and Thomas Hobbes of Malmesbury* (London: Andrew Crook, 1656).

Hutchinson, Lucy. *Order and Disorder*, ed. David Norbrook (Oxford: Blackwell, 2001).

Johnson, Samuel. *The Yale Edition of the Works of Samuel Johnson*, ed. Robert De Maria, 23 vols (New Haven, CT: Yale University Press, 1958–).

Keats, John. *The Letters of John Keats*, ed. Maurice Buxton Forman, 4th edn (Oxford: Oxford University Press, 1952).

Keats, John and John Milton. *Keats's Paradise Lost: A Digital Edition*, ed. Daniel Johnson, Beth Lau and Greg Kucich (*The Keats Library*, 2020) <http://keatslibrary.org/paradise-lost/> (accessed 5 July 2021).

Lamb, Charles and Mary Lamb. *The Letters of Charles and Mary Anne Lamb: 1809–1817*, ed. Edwin W Marrs, Jr (Ithaca and London: Cornell University Press, 1978).

Lamb, Charles and Mary Lamb. *Selected Prose*, ed. Adam Phillips (London: Penguin, 1985, repr. 2013).

Lamb, Charles and Mary Lamb. *Works of Charles and Mary Lamb*, ed. E. V. Lucas (London and New York: Macmillan, 1903–5).

Mallet, David. *The Excursion. A Poem. In Two Books* (London: J. Walthoe, 1728).

Marvell, Andrew. *The Poems and Letters of Andrew Marvell*, ed. H. M. Margoliouth, 3rd edn, 2 vols (Oxford: Clarendon Press, 1971).
Marvell, Andrew. *The Poems of Andrew Marvell*, ed. Nigel Smith (Harlow and London: Pearson, 2003).
Milton, John. *Milton's Paradise Lost. A New Edition, by Richard Bentley, D. D.* (London: Jacob Tonson, et al., 1732).
Milton, John. *Paradise Lost. A Poem, in Twelve Books. The Author John Milton. A New Edition, with Notes of Various Authors, by Thomas Newton, D. D.*, 2 vols (London: J. and R. Tonson and S. Draper, 1749).
Milton, John. *Tetrachordon, The John Milton Reading Room*, ed. Thomas H. Luxon (Dartmouth: 1997–2017) <https://www.dartmouth.edu/~milton/reading_room/tetrachordon/title/text.shtml> (accessed 5 July 2021).
Milton, John. *Paradise Lost*, ed. Barbara Lewalski (Oxford: Blackwell, 2007).
Milton, John. *The Complete Works of John Milton*, ed. Thomas N. Corns and Gordon Campbell, 11 vols (Oxford: Oxford University Press, 2008–).
More, John. *Strictures, Critical and Sentimental, on Thomson's Seasons* (London: Richardson and Urquhart, 1777).
Newton, Isaac. *The Opticks* (New York: Dover, 1979).
Newton, Isaac. *Philosophiae Naturalis Principia Mathematica*, trans. I. Bernard Cohen and Anne Whitman (Berkeley: University of California Press, 1999).
Philips, John. *Cyder. A Poem in Two Books* (London: Jacob Tonson, 1708).
Poe, Edgar Allan. *The Poetical Works of Edgar Allan Poe* (London: Ward, Lock & Co., 1882).
Reiman, Donald H., ed. *The Romantics Reviewed: Contemporary Reviews of British Romantic Writers* (London: Routledge: 1972).
Richardson, Jonathan [father and son]. *Explanatory Notes and Remarks on Paradise Lost* (London: James, John and Paul Knapton, 1734).
Scott, John, *Critical Essays on Some of the Poems, of Several English Poets* (London: James Phillips, 1785).
Shiels, Robert. *The Lives of the Poets of Great Britain and Ireland*, 5 vols (London: R. Griffiths, 1753).
Somervile, William. *The Chace, a Poem* (London: G. Hawkins, 1749).
Stockdale, Percival. *Lectures on the Truly Eminent English Poets* (London: Longman, Hurst, Rees, Orme and W. Clarke, 1807).
Swift, Jonathan. *Correspondence of Jonathan Swift*, ed. Harold Williams, 5 vols (Oxford: Oxford University Press, 1963–5).
Thomson, James. *The Seasons. By Mr Thomson* (London: Andrew Millar, 1730).
Thomson, James. *The Seasons* (London: John Sharpe, 1825).
Thomson, James. *The Seasons* (London: Longman, Brown, Green, and Longmans, 1847).
Thomson, James. *The Seasons*, ed. James Sambrook (Oxford: Clarendon Press, 1981).
Thomson, James. *Liberty, The Castle of Indolence, and Other Poems*, ed. James Sambrook (Oxford: Oxford University Press, 1986).

Townsend, C. H. 'An Essay on the Theory and the Writings of Wordsworth. Part III'. *Blackwood's Magazine* 26 (1829), 774–88.

Virgil. *The Georgics: A Poem of the Land*, trans. Kimberly Johnson (London: Penguin, 2009).

Wittreich, Joseph, ed. *The Romantics on Milton* (Cleveland: Case Western Reserve University Press, 1970).

Wordsworth, Christopher. *Memoirs of William Wordsworth*, 2 vols (London: Edward Moxon, 1851).

Wordsworth, William. *Wordsworth's Literary Criticism*, ed. W. J. B. Owen (London: Routledge & Kegan Paul, 1974).

Wordsworth, William. *The Cornell Wordsworth*, 21 vols, ed. Stephen Parrish (Ithaca: Cornell University Press, 1975–2007).

Wordsworth, William. *The Prelude: The Four Texts (1798, 1799, 1805, 1850)*, ed. Jonathan Wordsworth (London: Penguin, 1995).

Wordsworth, William and Dorothy Wordsworth, *The Letters of William and Dorothy Wordsworth*, ed. Alan G. Hill, 8 vols (Oxford: Oxford University Press, 1978–93).

Young, Edward. *Night Thoughts on Life, Death, and Immortality* (London: William Tegg & Co., 1859).

Secondary Sources

Ainsworth, David. *Milton and the Spiritual Reader: Reading and Religion in Seventeenth-Century England* (New York and London: Routledge, 2008).

Alkon, Paul K. *Defoe and Fictional Time* (Athens, GA: University of Georgia Press, 1979).

Allen, Thomas M., ed. *Time and Literature* (Cambridge: Cambridge University Press, 2018).

Anderson, Benedict. *Imagined Communities: Reflections on the Origin and Spread of Nationalism* (London: Verso, 1983, repr. 1991).

Astell, Anne W. *Job, Boethius, and Epic Truth* (Ithaca: Cornell University Press, 1994).

Auerbach, Erich. *Mimesis: The Representation of Reality in Western Literature*, trans. Willard R. Trask (Princeton: Princeton University Press, 1953, repr. 2003).

Baker, Jeffrey. *Time and Mind in Wordsworth's Poetry* (Detroit: Wayne State University Press, 1980).

Barrell, John. *The Idea of Landscape and the Sense of Place 1730–1840* (Cambridge: Cambridge University Press, 1972).

Barrell, John. *English Literature in History, 1730–80: An Equal, Wide Survey* (London: Hutchinson, 1983).

Barrell, John and Harriet Guest. 'On the Use of Contradiction: Economics and Morality in the Eighteenth-Century Long Poem'. In *The New Eighteenth*

Century, ed. Felicity Nussbaum and Laura Brown (New York; London: Methuen, 1987), 121–43.
Bate, Jonathan. 'Living with the Weather'. *Studies in Romanticism* 35 (1996), 431–47.
Beck, Lewis White. 'World Enough, and Time'. In *Probability, Time, and Space in Eighteenth-Century Literature*, ed. Paula R. Backscheider (New York: AMS Press, 1979), 113–39.
Beer, John. *Wordsworth in Time* (London: Faber & Faber, 1979).
Benet, Diana Treviño. 'The Fall of the Angels: Theology and Narrative'. *Milton Quarterly* 50.1 (2016), 1–13.
Bewell, Alan. 'Wordsworth's Primal Scene: Retrospective Tales of Idiots, Wild Children, and Savages'. *English Literary History* 50.2 (1983), 321–46.
Bianchi, Luca. '*Abiding Then*: Eternity of God and Eternity of the World from Hobbes to the *Encyclopédie*'. In *The Medieval Concept of Time*, ed. Pasquale Porro (Leiden and Boston, MA: Brill, 2001), 543–60.
Bloom, Harold. *The Visionary Company: A Reading of English Romantic History* (London: Faber & Faber, 1961).
Boesky, Amy. '*Paradise Lost* and the Multiplicity of Time' in *A Companion to Milton*, ed. Thomas N. Corns (Oxford: Blackwell, 2001), 380–92.
Bostetter, Edward E. *The Romantic Ventriloquists: Wordsworth, Coleridge, Keats, Shelley, Byron* (Seattle: University of Washington Press, 1963).
Brinkley, Robert A. 'The Incident in the Simplon Pass: A Note on Wordsworth's Revisions'. *The Wordsworth Circle* 12.2 (1981), 122–5.
Brower, Reuben A. 'Form and Defect of Form in Eighteenth-Century Poetry: A Memorandum'. *College English* 29.7 (1968), 535–41.
Bushnell, Rebecca. 'Time and Genre'. In *Time and Literature*, ed. Thomas M. Allen (Cambridge: Cambridge University Press, 2018), 44–56.
Carrithers, Gale H., and James D. Hardy. *Milton and the Hermeneutic Journey* (Baton Rouge: Louisiana State University Press, 1994).
Chaplin, Gregory. 'The Circling Hours: Revolution in *Paradise Regain'd*'. In *Milton in the Long Restoration*, ed. Blair Hoxby and Ann Baynes Coiro (Oxford: Oxford University Press, 2016), 265–83.
Cohen, Ralph. *The Art of Discrimination: Thomson's* The Seasons *and the Language of Criticism* (London: Routledge & Kegan Paul, 1964).
Cohen, Ralph. *The Unfolding of the Seasons: A Study of James Thomson's Poem* (Baltimore: Johns Hopkins University Press, 1970).
Coiro, Ann Baynes. 'The Personal Rule of Poets: Cavalier Poetry and the English Revolution'. In *The Oxford Handbook of Literature and the English Revolution*, ed. Laura Lunger Knoppers (Oxford: Oxford University Press, 2012), 206–37.
Colebrook, Claire. *Milton, Evil and Literary History* (London: Bloomsbury, 2008).
Colie, Rosalie. 'Time and Eternity: Paradox and Structure in Paradise Lost'. *Journal of the Warburg and Courtauld Institutes* 23 (1960), 127–38.

Connell, Philip. 'Newtonian physico-theology and the varieties of Whiggism in James Thomson's *The Seasons*'. *Huntington Library Quarterly* 72 (2009), 1–28.

Cook, Albert. 'The Transformation of "Point": Amplitude in Wordsworth, Whitman, and Rimbaud'. *Studies in Romanticism* 30.2 (1991), 169–88.

Cornes, Saskia. 'Milton's Manuring: *Paradise Lost*, Husbandry, and the Possibilities of Waste'. *Milton Studies* 61.1 (2019), 65–85.

Crawford, Rachel. 'English Georgic and British Nationhood'. *English Literary History* 65 (1998), 123–58.

Danielson, Dennis Richard. *Milton's Good God: A Study in Literary Theodicy* (Cambridge: Cambridge University Press, 1982).

Davie, Donald. 'Syntax and Music in "Paradise Lost"'. In *The Living Milton*, ed. Frank Kermode (London: Routledge, 1960), 70–84.

Davis, James P. *An Experimental Reading of Wordsworth's* Prelude: *The Poetics of Bimodial Consciousness* (Lewiston: Edwin Mellen Press, 1995).

De Man, Paul. *The Rhetoric of Romanticism* (New York: Columbia University Press, 1989).

De Man, Paul. *Romanticism and Contemporary Criticism: The Gauss Seminar and Other Papers*, ed. E. S. Burt, Kevin Newmark, and Andrzej Warminski (Baltimore: Johns Hopkins University Press, 1993).

Desroches, Dennis. 'The Rhetoric of Disclosure in James Thomson's *The Seasons*; or, On Kant's Gentlemanly Misanthropy'. *Eighteenth Century* 49 (2008), 1–24.

Dobrée, Bonamy. *English Literature in the Early Eighteenth Century, 1700–1740* (Oxford: Oxford University Press, 1959, repr. 1968).

Donnelly, Phillip J. *Milton's Scriptural Reasoning: Narrative and Protestant Toleration* (Cambridge: Cambridge University Press, 2009).

Driscoll, James P. *The Unfolding God of Jung and Milton* (Lexington: University Press of Kentucky, 1993).

Dye, E. H. 'Milton's "Comus" and Boethius' "Consolation"'. *Milton Quarterly* 19.1 (1985), 1–7.

Fairer, David. *English Poetry of the Eighteenth Century, 1700–1789* (London: Longman, 2003).

Fairer, David. '"The Year Runs Round": The Poetry of Work in Eighteenth-Century England'. In *Ritual, Routine, and Regime: Repetition in Early Modern British and European Cultures*, ed. Lorna Clymer (Toronto: University of Toronto Press, 2006), 153–71.

Fairer, David. *Organising Poetry: The Coleridge Circle, 1790–1798* (Oxford: Oxford University Press, 2009).

Fairer, David. 'The World of Eco-georgic'. *Studies in 18th Century Culture* 40 (2011), 201–18.

Fairer, David. 'The Pastoral-georgic Tradition'. In *William Wordsworth in Context*, ed. Andrew Bennett (Cambridge: Cambridge University Press, 2015), 111–18.

Fallon, Stephen M. 'Narrative and Theodicy in *Paradise Lost*'. *Milton Studies* 61.1 (2019), 40–64.
Favret, Mary A. *War at a Distance: Romanticism and the Making of Modern Wartime* (Princeton: Princeton University Press, 2009).
Ferris, David. 'Where Three Paths Meet: History, Wordsworth, and the Simplon Pass'. *Studies in Romanticism* 30 (1991), 391–438.
Ferry, Anne. *Milton's Epic Voice: The Narrator in* Paradise Lost (Chicago: University of Chicago Press, 1963, repr. 1983).
Ferry, David. *The Limits of Mortality: An Essay on Wordsworth's Major Poems* (Middletown, CT: Wesleyan University Press, 1959).
Fiore, Peter A. *Milton and Augustine: Patterns of Augustinian Thought in Paradise Lost* (University Park, PA: Pennsylvania State University Press, 1981).
Fish, Stanley. *Surprised by Sin: The Reader in* Paradise Lost (1967), 2nd edn (London: Macmillan, 1997).
Foster, John Wilson. 'The Measure of Paradise: Topography in Eighteenth-Century Poetry'. *Eighteenth-Century Studies* 9.2 (1975–6), 232–56.
Frank, Joseph. 'Spatial Form in Modern Literature, Part 1'. *The Sewanee Review* 53 (1945), 221–40.
French, J. Milton. 'Lamb and Milton'. *Studies in Philology* 31.1 (1934), 92–103.
Fulford, Tim. *Landscape, Liberty and Authority: Poetry, Criticism and Politics from Thomson to Wordsworth* (Cambridge: Cambridge University Press, 1996).
Genovese, Michael. 'An Organic Commerce: Sociable Selfhood in Eighteenth-Century Georgic'. *Eighteenth-Century Studies* 46 (2013), 197–221.
Gidal, Eric. 'Prospect and Form in the Eighteenth-Century Progress Poem'. *Ricerche di Storia dell'arte* 72 (2000), 21–8.
Gill, Stephen. *Wordsworth and the Victorians* (Oxford: Oxford University Press, 1998).
Gill, Stephen. *Wordsworth's Revisitings* (Oxford: Oxford University Press, 2011).
Goodman, Kevis. *Georgic Modernity and British Romanticism* (Cambridge: Cambridge University Press, 2004).
Gottlieb, Evan. 'Anthropocene Temporalities and British Romantic Poetry'. In *Romanticism and Time: Literary Temporalities*, ed. Sophie Laniel-Musitelli and Céline Sabiron (Cambridge: Open Book Publishers, 2021), 25–47.
Grant, Roger Mathew. *Beating Time & Measuring Music in the Early Modern Era* (Oxford: Oxford University Press, 2014).
Greene, Robert. 'Thomas Hobbes: The Eternal Law, the Eternal Word, and the Eternity of the Law of Nature'. *History of European Ideas* 45.5 (2019), 625–44.
Gregerson, Linda. *The Reformation of the Subject: Spenser, Milton, and the English Protestant Epic* (Cambridge: Cambridge University Press, 1995).

Gregerson, Linda. 'The Poem as Thinking Machine'. *Milton Quarterly* 52.1 (2018): 317–23.
Griffin, Dustin. *Regaining Paradise: Milton and the Eighteenth Century* (Cambridge: Cambridge University Press, 1986).
Griffin, Dustin. *Patriotism and Poetry in Eighteenth-Century Britain* (Cambridge: Cambridge University Press, 2002.
Groom, Nick. *The Seasons: An Elegy for the Passing of the Year* (London: Atlantic, 2013).
Grossman, Marshall. *'Authors to Themselves': Milton and the Revelation of History* (Cambridge: Cambridge University Press, 1987).
Hartman, Geoffrey. *Wordsworth's Poetry 1787–1814* (New Haven: Yale University Press, 1964).
Haskin, Dayton. *Milton's Burden of Interpretation* (Philadelphia: University of Pennsylvania Press, 1994).
Havens, R. D. *The Influence of Milton on English Poetry* (Cambridge, MA: Harvard University Press, 1922).
Havens, R. D. 'Primitivism and the Idea of Progress in Thomson'. *Studies in Philology* 29.1 (1932): 41–52.
Herman, Peter C., '"Whose fault, whose but his own?": *Paradise Lost*, Contributory Negligence, and the Problem of Cause'. In *The New Milton Criticism*, ed. Peter C. Herman and Elizabeth Sauer (Cambridge: Cambridge University Press, 2012), 49–67.
Herman, Peter C., and Elizabeth Sauer, ed. *The New Milton Criticism* (Cambridge: Cambridge University Press, 2012).
Herz, Judith Scherer. 'Meanwhile: (Un)making Time in Paradise Lost'. In *The New Milton Criticism*, ed. Peter C. Herman and Elizabeth Sauer (Cambridge: Cambridge University Press, 2012), 85–101.
Hewson, Mark. 'The Scene of Meditation in Wordsworth'. *The Modern Language Review* 106 (2011), 954–67.
Horrocks, Ingrid. '"Circling Eye" and "Houseless Stranger": The New Eighteenth-Century Wanderer (Thomson to Goldsmith)'. *ELH* 77.3 (2010), 665–87.
Hunt, John Dixon. *The Figure in the Landscape: Poetry, Painting, and Gardening during the Eighteenth Century* (Baltimore: Johns Hopkins University Press, 1976).
Hunt, Lynn. *Measuring Time, Making History* (Budapest: Central European University Press, 2008).
Hunter, Walt. 'The No-Prospect Poem: Lyric Finality in Prynne, Awoonor, and Trethewey'. *The Minnesota Review* 85 (2015), 144–52.
Hutchings, W. B., '"Can Pure Description Hold the Place of Sense?": Thomson's Landscape Poetry'. In *James Thomson: Essays for the Tercentenary*, ed. Richard Terry (Liverpool: Liverpool University Press, 2000), 35–66.
Irlam, Shaun. *Elations: The Poetics of Enthusiasm in Eighteenth-Century Britain* (Stanford: Stanford University Press, 1999).

Jackson, Wallace. *Immediacy: The Development of a Critical Concept from Addison to Coleridge* (Amsterdam: Rodopi, 1973).

Jarvis, Robin. *Wordsworth, Milton and the Theory of Poetic Relations* (London: Palgrave Macmillan, 1991).

Jenkins, Neil. 'The Libretto of Haydn's "The Creation". New Sources and a Possible Librettist'. *Haydn Society Journal* 24.2 (2005), 2–84.

Johnson, Karl R., Jr. *The Written Spirit: Thematic and Rhetorical Structure in Wordsworth's* The Prelude (Salzburg: Institut für Englische Sprache und Literatur, 1978).

Johnstone, W. Michael. 'Toward a Book History of William Wordsworth's 1850 *Prelude*'. *Textual Cultures* 5.2 (2010), 63–91.

Jung, Sandro. 'Epic, Ode, or Something New: The Blending of Genres in Thomson's *Spring*'. *Papers on Language and Literature* 43 (2007), 146–65.

Jung, Sandro. 'Painterly "Readings" of *The Seasons*, 1766–1829'. *Word & Image: A Journal of Verbal/Visual Enquiry* 26 (2009), 68–82.

Jung, Sandro. 'Print Culture, High-cultural Consumption, and Thomson's *The Seasons*, 1780–1797'. *Eighteenth-Century Studies* 44 (2011), 495–514.

Jung, Sandro. 'Print Culture and Visual Interpretation in Eighteenth-Century German Editions of Thomson's *Seasons*'. *Comparative and Critical Studies* 9 (2012), 37–59.

Jung, Sandro. 'Image-making in James Thomson's *The Seasons*'. *Studies in English Literature, 1500–1900* 53 (2013), 583–99.

Jung, Sandro and Kwinten Van De Walle, ed. *The Genres of Thomson's The Seasons* (Bethlehem: Lehigh University Press, 2018).

Keenleyside, Heather. 'Personification for the People: On James Thomson's *The Seasons*'. *English Literary History* 76 (2009), 447–72.

Kelley, Theresa M. *Wordsworth's Revisionary Aesthetics* (Cambridge: Cambridge University Press, 1988).

Kenshur, Oscar. *Open Form and the Shape of Ideas: Literary Structures as Representations of Philosophical Concepts* (Lewisburg, PA: Bucknell University Press, 1986).

Kermode, Frank. *The Sense of an Ending: Studies in the Theory of Fiction with a New Epilogue* (Oxford: Oxford University Press, 2000).

Kerrigan, William. *The Prophetic Milton* (Charlottesville: University Press of Virginia, 1974).

Kinsley, Zoë. 'Landscapes "Dynamically in Motion": Revisiting Issues of Structure and Agency in Thomson's *The Seasons*'. *Papers on Language and Literature* 41 (2005), 3–25.

Kramnick, Jonathan. 'An Aesthetics and Ecology of Presence'. *European Romantic Review* 26 (2015), 315–27.

Krapp, John. 'Female Romanticism at the End of History'. *Texas Studies in Literature and Language* 46.1 (2004), 73–91.

Langer, Ayelet C. '"Pardon may be found in time besought": Time Structures of the Mind in *Paradise Lost*'. *Milton Studies* 52 (2011), 169–83.

Langer, Ayelet C. '"Meanwhile": Paradisian Infinity in Milton's *Paradise Lost*'. *Journal of Literature and the History of Ideas* 19.1 (2012), 1–17.

Langer, Ayelet C. 'Milton's *Aevum*: The Time Structure of Prevenient Grace in *Paradise Lost*'. *Early Modern Literary Studies* 17 (2014).

Langer, Ayelet C. 'Milton's Aristotelian *Now*'. *Milton Studies* 57 (2016), 95–117.

Laniel-Musitelli, Sophie and Céline Sabiron, ed. *Romanticism and Time: Literary Temporalities* (Cambridge: Open Book Publishers, 2021).

Larkin, Peter. 'Wordsworth's Maculate Exception: Achieving the "Spots of Time"'. *Wordsworth Circle* 41.1 (2010), 30–5.

Larkin, Peter. *Wordsworth and Coleridge: Promising Losses* (New York: Palgrave Macmillan, 2012).

Leader, Zachary. *Revision and Romantic Authorship* (Oxford: Clarendon Press, 1996).

Leonard, John. *Faithful Labourers: A Reception History of* Paradise Lost, *1667–1970*, 2 vols (Oxford: Oxford University Press, 2013).

Lethbridge, Stefanie. 'Anthological Reading Habits in the Eighteenth Century: The Case of Thomson's *Seasons*'. In *Anthologies of British Poetry: Critical Perspectives from Literary and Cultural Studies*, ed. Barbara Korte, Ralf Schneider, and Stefanie Lethbridge (Amsterdam: Rodopi, 2000), 89–104.

Lethbridge, Stefanie. *James Thomson's Defence of Poetry: Intertextual Allusion in* The Seasons (Tübingen: Max Niemeyer Verlag GmbH, 2003).

Lieb, Michael. *Theological Milton: Deity, Discourse and Heresy in the Miltonic Canon* (Pittsburgh: Duquesne University Press, 2006).

Lindenberger, Herbert. *On Wordsworth's* Prelude (Princeton: Princeton University Press, 1963).

Liu, Alan. *Wordsworth: The Sense of History* (Stanford: Stanford University Press, 1989).

Low, Anthony. *The Georgic Revolution* (Princeton: Princeton University Press, 1985).

Lupton, Christina. *Reading and the Making of Time in the Eighteenth Century* (Baltimore: Johns Hopkins University Press, 2018).

Lupton, Christina and Carston Meiner, ed. *Literature and Contingency* (London and New York: Routledge, 2020).

Marcus, Leah S. 'Politics and Pastoral: Writing the Court on the Countryside'. In *Culture and Politics in Early Stuart England*, ed. Kevin Sharpe and Peter Lake (Basingstoke: Macmillan, 1994), 139–59.

Marland, Pippa. 'Rewilding, Wilding, and the New Georgic'. *Green Letters* 24 (2020), 421–36.

McKillop, Alan Dugald. *The Background of Thomson's Seasons* (Minneapolis: University of Minnesota Press, 1942).

McMahon, Robert. *The Two Poets of* Paradise Lost (Baton Rouge: Louisiana State University Press, 1998).

Miller, Christopher R. *The Invention of Evening: Perception and Time in Romantic Poetry* (Cambridge: Cambridge University Press, 2006).
Miller, Christopher. 'The Lyric Self in *The Seasons*'. In *The Genres of Thomson's The Seasons*, ed. Sandro Jung and Kwinten Van De Walle (Bethlehem: Lehigh University Press, 2018), 61–81.
Milnes, Tim. *William Wordsworth: The Prelude* (Basingstoke: Palgrave Macmillan, 2009).
Mitchell, Sebastian. 'James Thomson's Picture Collection and British History Paintings'. *Journal of the History of Collections* 23 (2011), 127–51.
Molesworth, Jesse. 'Introduction: The Temporal Turn in Eighteenth-Century Studies'. *The Eighteenth Century* 60.2 (2019), 129–38.
Moore, Natasha. *Victorian Poetry and Modern Life: The Unpoetical Age* (Basingstoke: Palgrave Macmillan, 2015).
Morgan, Monique R. *Narrative Means, Lyric Ends: Temporality in the Nineteenth-Century British Long Poem* (Columbus: Ohio State University Press, 2009).
Morson, Gary Saul. *Narrative and Freedom: The Shadows of Time* (New Haven: Yale University Press, 1996).
Myers, William. *Milton and Free Will: An Essay in Criticism and Philosophy* (London: Croom Helm, 1987).
Nellist, Brian. 'Lyric Presence in Byron from the Tales to *Don Juan*'. In *Byron and the Limits of Fiction*, ed. Bernard Beatty and Vincent Newey (Liverpool: Liverpool University Press, 1988), 39–77.
Netzley, Ryan. 'Reading, Recognition, Learning, and Love in *Paradise Regained*'. In *To Repair the Ruins: Reading Milton*, ed. Mary C. Fenton and Louis Schwartz (Pittsburgh: Duquesne University Press, 2012), 117–45.
Netzley, Ryan. *Lyric Apocalypse: Milton, Marvell, and the Nature of Events* (New York: Fordham University Press, 2015).
Newlyn, Lucy. Paradise Lost *and the Romantic Reader* (Oxford: Clarendon Press, 1993, repr. 2001).
Nicolson, Marjorie Hope. *Newton Demands the Muse: Newton's Opticks and the Eighteenth-Century Poets* (Princeton: Princeton University Press, 1946).
Noggle, James. *The Temporality of Taste in Eighteenth-Century British Writing* (Oxford: Oxford University Press, 2012).
Ott, Walter. *Causation and the Laws of Nature in Early Modern Philosophy* (Oxford: Oxford University Press, 2009).
Parker, Blanford. *The Triumph of Augustan Poetics: English Literary Culture from Butler to Johnson* (Cambridge: Cambridge University Press, 1998).
Parrish, Stephen M. 'The Whig Interpretation of Literature'. *Text* 4 (1988), 343–50.
Patterson, Annabel. *Nobody's Perfect: A New Whig Interpretation of History* (New Haven and London: Yale University Press, 2002).
Pellicer, Juan Christian. 'The Articulation of Genre in *The Seasons*'. In *The Genres of Thomson's The Seasons*, ed. Sandro Jung and Kwinten Van De Walle (Bethlehem: Lehigh University Press, 2018), 119–35.

Peterfreund, Stuart. '*The Prelude*: Wordsworth's Metamorphic Epic'. *Genre* 14 (1981), 441–72.

Potkay, Adam. *Wordsworth's Ethics* (Baltimore: Johns Hopkins University Press, 2012).

Poulet, Georges. 'Timelessness and Romanticism'. *Journal of the History of Ideas* 15 (1954), 3–22.

Priestman, Martin. *The Poetry of Erasmus Darwin: Enlightened Spaces, Romantic Times* (Aldershot: Ashgate, 2013).

Quint, David. *Inside Paradise Lost: Reading the Designs of Milton's Epic* (Princeton: Princeton University Press, 2014).

Quint, David. 'Milton, Waller, and the Fate of Eden'. *Modern Language Quarterly* 78.3 (2017), 421–41.

Racevskis, Roland. *Time and Ways of Knowing under Louis XIV: Molière, Sévigné, Lafayette* (Lewisburg, PA: Bucknell University Press, 2003).

Regueiro, Helen. *The Limits of Imagination: Wordsworth, Yeats, and Stevens* (Ithaca: Cornell University Press, 1976).

Reid, David. 'Thomson's Poetry of Reverie and Milton'. *Studies in English Literature, 1500–1900* 43 (2003), 667–82.

Revard, Stella. 'Vergil's *Georgics* and *Paradise Lost*: Nature and Human Nature in a Landscape'. In *Vergil at 2000: Commemorative Essays on the Poet and His Influence*, ed. John, D. Bernard (New York: AMS Press, 1986), 259–80.

Ricks, Christopher. *Milton's Grand Style* (Oxford: Oxford University Press, 1963).

Rigby, Kate, *Reclaiming Romanticism: Towards an Ecopoetics of Decolonization* (London and New York: Bloomsbury, 2020).

Roberts, Adam. *Romantic and Victorian Long Poems: A Guide* (London: Routledge, 1999).

Rogers, Pat. *The Augustan Vision* (London: Weidenfeld & Nicolson, 1974).

Sachs, Jonathan. 'Eighteenth-century Slow Time'. *The Eighteenth Century* 60.2 (2019), 185–205.

Sachs, Jonathan and Andrew Piper. 'Technique and the Time of Reading'. *PMLA* 133.5 (2018), 1259–67.

Sambrook, James. *James Thomson, 1700–1748: A Life* (Oxford: Clarendon Press, 1991).

Schuler, Stephen J. 'Eternal Duration: Milton on God's Justice in Everlasting Time'. *Milton Studies* 61.1 (2019), 163–85.

Setzer, Sharon M. 'Excursions in the Wilderness: Wordsworth's Visionary Kingdoms and the Typography of Miltonic Revision'. *Studies in Romanticism* 30 (1991), 367–89.

Shears, Jonathon. *The Romantic Legacy of Paradise Lost: Reading Against the Grain* (Aldershot: Ashgate, 2009).

Shoaf, R. A. *Milton, Poet of Duality* (New Haven: Yale University Press, 1985).

Silver, Sean. 'Contingency in Philosophy and History, 1650–1800'. *Textual Practice* 32.3 (2018), 419–36.

Sitter, John. *Literary Loneliness in Mid-Eighteenth-Century England* (Ithaca: Cornell University Press, 1982).

Sitter, John. 'Eighteenth-century Ecological Poetry and Ecotheology'. *Religion and Literature* 40.1 (2008), 11–37.

Sjödin, Alfred. 'The European Georgic and the Politics of Genre: Johan Gabriel Oxenstierna and *The Seasons* in Sweden'. In *The Genres of Thomson's The Seasons*, ed. Sandro Jung and Kwinten Van De Walle (Bethlehem: Lehigh University Press, 2018), 185–99.

Smith, Courtney Weiss. *Empiricist Devotions: Science, Religion, and Poetry in Early Eighteenth-Century England* (Charlottesville: University of Virginia Press, 2016).

Somervell, Tess. 'Versions of Damon and Musidora: The Realization of Thomson's Story in Revisions and Illustrations'. *Studies in the Literary Imagination* 46.1 (2013), 47–70.

Somervell, Tess. 'Mediating Vision: Wordsworth's Allusions to Thomson's *Seasons* in *The Prelude*'. *Romanticism* 22.1 (2016), 48–60.

Somervell, Tess. 'The Golden Age and Iron Times: Pastoral and Georgic in "Spring"'. In *The Genres of Thomson's The Seasons*, ed. Sandro Jung and Kwinten Van De Walle (Bethlehem: Lehigh University Press, 2018), 139–63.

Somervell, Tess. 'Wordsworth and the Deluge'. *Studies in Romanticism* 58.2 (2019), 183–208.

Spacks, Patricia Meyer. *The Varied God: A Critical Study of Thomson's* The Seasons (Berkeley: University of California Press, 1959).

Starke, Sue. '"The Eternal Now": Virgilian Echoes and Miltonic Premonitions in Cowley's "Davideis"'. *Christianity and Literature* 55.2 (2006), 195–219.

Stein, Edwin. *Wordsworth's Art of Allusion* (University Park, PA: Penn State University Press, 1988).

Stenke, Katarina. 'Parts and Wholes in Long Non-narrative Poems of the Eighteenth Century' (unpublished doctoral thesis, University of Cambridge, 2013).

Stenke, Katarina. '"The Well-dissembled Mourner": Lighting's (Dis)course in the Still Lives of Thomson's "Celadon and Amelia"'. *Studies in the Literary Imagination* 46.1 (2013), 19–46.

Stenke, Katarina. '"Devolving through the Maze of Eloquence": James Thomson's *The Seasons* and the Eighteenth-Century Verse Labyrinth'. *Journal for Eighteenth-Century Studies* 39.1 (2016), 5–23.

Stevenson, Randall. *Reading the Times: Temporality and History in Twentieth-Century Fiction* (Edinburgh: Edinburgh University Press, 2018).

Strachan, John. '"That is true fame": A Few Words about Thomson's Romantic Period Popularity'. In *James Thomson: Essays for the Tercentenary*, ed. Richard Terry (Liverpool: Liverpool University Press, 2000), 247–70.

Sugimura, N. K. 'The Question of "What Cause?": Storytelling Angels and Versions of Causation in *Paradise Lost*'. *Milton Studies* 54 (2013), 3–27.

Sullivan, Hannah. *The Work of Revision* (Cambridge, MA: Harvard University Press, 2013).
Tayler, Edward W. *Milton's Poetry: Its Development in Time* (Pittsburgh: Duquesne University Press, 1979).
Taylor, Jefferey H., and Leslie A. Taylor. *The Influence of Boethius'* De Consolatione Philosophiae *on John Milton's* Paradise Lost (Lewiston: Edwin Mellen, 2017).
Taylor, Luke. 'Milton and the Romance of History'. *Milton Studies* 56 (2015), 301–29.
Terry, Richard. 'Transitions and Digressions in the Eighteenth-Century Long Poem'. *Studies in English Literature, 1500–1900* 32 (1992), 495–510.
Terry, Richard. '"Through Nature shedding influence malign": Thomson's *The Seasons* as a Theodicy'. *Durham University Journal* 87 (1995), 257–68.
Teskey, Gordon. *The Poetry of John Milton* (Cambridge, MA and London: Harvard University Press, 2015).
Thomas, Walter Keith and Warren U. Ober. *A Mind for Ever Voyaging: Wordsworth at Work Portraying Newton and Science* (Edmonton: University of Alberta Press, 1989).
Van De Walle, Kwinten. 'Editorialising Practices, Competitive Marketability, and James Thomson's "The Seasons"'. *Journal for Eighteenth-Century Studies* 38 (2015), 257–76.
Van De Walle, Kwinten. 'From Inter- to Intratextuality: "Autumn" as the Conclusion to *The Seasons*'. In *The Genres of Thomson's The Seasons*, ed. Sandro Jung and Kwinten Van De Walle (Bethlehem: Lehigh University Press, 2018), 43–58.
Van Renen, Denys. '"A Hollow Moan": The Contours of the Nonhuman World in James Thomson's *The Seasons*". In *Animals and Humans: Sensibility and Representation, 1650–1820,* ed. Katherine Quinsey (Oxford: Oxford University Press, 2017), 75–98.
Warminski, Andrzej. 'Missed Crossing: Wordsworth's Apocalypses'. *Modern Language Notes* 99 (1984), 983–1006.
Watson, J. R. 'Divine Providence and the Structure of *Paradise Lost*'. *Essays in Criticism* 14 (1964), 148–55.
Welch, Anthony. 'Reconsidering Chronology in *Paradise Lost*'. *Milton Studies* 41 (2002), 1–17.
Wesling, Donald. *Wordsworth and the Adequacy of Landscape* (London: Routledge & Kegan Paul, 1970).
Whaler, James. 'The Miltonic Simile'. *PMLA* 46 (1931), 1034–74.
Wittreich, Joseph. *Why Milton Matters: A New Preface to His Writings* (New York: Palgrave Macmillan, 2006).
Wittreich, Joseph. 'Sites of Contention in *Paradise Lost*'. In *Milton's Rival Hermeneutics: 'Reason is But Choosing'*, ed. Richard J. DuRocher and Margaret Olofson Thickstun (Pittsburgh: Duquesne University Press, 2012), 101–33.

Wolfson, Susan J. 'The Illusion of Mastery: Wordsworth's Revisions of "The Drowned Man of Esthwaite," 1799, 1805, 1850'. *PMLA* 99 (1984), 917–35.

Wolfson, Susan J. 'Revision as Form: Wordsworth's Drowned Man'. In *William Wordsworth's* The Prelude: *A Casebook*, ed. Stephen Gill (Oxford: Oxford University Press, 2006), 73–121.

Wu, Duncan. *Wordsworth's Reading, 1770–1799* (Cambridge: Cambridge University Press, 1993).

Wu, Duncan. *Wordsworth's Reading, 1800–1815* (Cambridge: Cambridge University Press, 1993).

Youngren, William. 'Addison and the Birth of Eighteenth-Century Aesthetics'. *Modern Philology* 79 (1982), 267–83.

Index

Addison, Joseph, 144–6, 203
Ainsworth, David, 62, 65
Akenside, Mark, 94, 100, 187
Alkon, Paul K., 8
Allestree, Richard, 28
allusion, 7, 12, 184–94, 199, 205, 222
Anderson, Benedict, 167–8
anthologising, 11, 124, 143–4, 148–9, 152, 207, 208, 211, 212
Arnold, Matthew, 207
Auerbach, Erich, 33, 82–3
Augustine, Saint, 22, 57, 58, 59, 75

Baker, Jeffrey, 164, 171, 172, 178
Bakhtin, Mikhail, 4
Barrell, John, 41, 103, 155
  and Harriet Guest, 155
Bate, Jonathan, 117
Beck, Lewis White, 3
Beer, John, 164, 166
Benet, Diana Treviño, 38
Bentley, Richard, 54
Bible *see* Scripture
blank verse, 4, 99, 123, 165, 194
Bloom, Harold, 187, 191
Boesky, Amy, 21, 53
Boethius, 10, 20, 22–9, 31, 33, 42, 53, 58, 68, 148
Book of Nature, 93–4, 97, 134
Bostetter, Edward E., 176
Boswell, James, 149
Boyle, Robert, 96, 97–8, 112

Bramhall, John, 26–7, 28, 29, 32, 34
Brower, Reuben A., 134
Bushnell, Rebecca, 6
Byron, George Gordon, 73, 175

Carrithers, Gale H. and James D. Hardy, 76
Cassandra, 50, 181–4; *see also* prophecy
Chaplin, Gregory, 63
chronos, 12, 162–7, 175, 177–8, 193, 195, 202, 209, 213, 219
clock-time, 3, 164, 167, 168, 178, 183–4
Cohen, Ralph, 92, 93, 106, 108, 115n, 121, 122, 124, 134, 150
Coiro, Ann Boynes, 19
Colebrook, Claire, 38
Coleridge, Samuel Taylor, 72, 169, 172, 183, 184, 186, 204, 209–11
Colie, Rosalie, 43
commonplacing, 10, 51, 57–9, 63, 70, 71, 75, 80, 144, 207, 211, 216
Connell, Philip, 95, 96
Cook, Albert, 109
Cornes, Saskia, 40
Cowley, Abraham, 25–6, 27, 60, 68–9
Cowper, William, 96, 168, 186
Crawford, Rachel, 100
Cudworth, Ralph, 26, 28

Index   241

Danielson, Dennis Richard, 24
Davie, Donald, 74
Davis, James P., 164, 212
Defoe, Daniel, 8, 56, 97, 98, 112
delphic, 49–52, 55, 64, 181, 182;
    see also prophecy
De Man, Paul, 193,
Denham, John, 5, 17, 18, 19, 33, 41
De Quincey, Thomas, 185
Desroches, Dennis, 155
Donnelly, Phillip J., 75–6, 79
Drayton, Michael, 42
Driscoll, James P., 20
Dryden, John
    Georgics, 56, 99, 100, 101, 102, 105, 109
    The State of Innocence, 29–30
Duck, Stephen, 103
Dyer, John, 42

Eliot, T. S., 7, 70
epic, 5, 6, 9, 19, 25, 32–3, 34, 69, 72, 74, 77, 99, 165, 168, 212, 224; see also simile
eternity, 3, 20, 22–7, 31, 43, 44, 50, 58, 78–9, 80, 162, 164, 192, 212, 216, 224; see also nunc stans

Fairer, David, 100–1, 105–6, 119, 213
Favret, Mary A., 168
Ferris, David, 208
Ferry, Anne, 55, 79
Ferry, David, 177
Fish, Stanley, 10, 40, 43, 74–6
Foster, John Wilson, 40
Frank, Joseph, 7–8, 73, 141;
    see also reflexive reference;
    spatial form
free will, 3, 4, 10, 19–42, 50, 51, 77, 83, 222
French Revolution, 167, 208, 216–19
Fulford, Tim, 42

Genovese, Michael, 103
genre, 4, 5, 8–9, 17, 19, 20, 24, 33, 42, 56, 89, 90, 99–100, 212, 224; see also epic; georgic; long poem; lyric; non-narrative poem; novel; pastoral; philosophical long poem; prospect poem; romance
georgic, 5, 8–9, 11, 13, 19, 56, 89–90, 93, 99–106, 111, 112, 117, 118, 121, 135, 145, 147, 153, 161, 165, 203, 213, 223, 224; see also Dryden, John; Virgil
Gidal, Eric, 91
Gill, Stephen, 196, 199, 206, 207
Goodman, Kevis, 93–4, 121, 186
Gottlieb, Evan, 175
Grant, Roger Mathew, 94
Gray, Thomas, 42
Greene, Robert, 25, 26
Gregerson, Linda, 74–5, 80
Griffin, Dustin, 89, 106
Groom, Nick, 103
Grossman, Marshall, 30, 39, 82

Hartman, Geoffrey, 212
Haskin, Dayton, 60
Havens, R. D., 149
Haydn, Joseph, 190–1
Hazlitt, William, 72–3, 124, 183, 204–5,
Hegel, G. W. F., 6
Herbert, George, 59–60, 64, 65
Herman, Peter C., 29
Herz, Judith Scherer, 21, 48
Hewson, Mark, 170, 172
Hobbes, Thomas, 26–8, 44, 163
homogeneous time, 167–8
Horrocks, Ingrid, 91, 138–9
Horsley, John Calcott, 128–31
Hume, David, 98
Hunt, John Dixon, 115n
Hunt, Leigh, 1

Hunt, Lynn, 217
Hutchings, W. B., 92
Hutchinson, Lucy, 29, 78

illustration, 116, 122, 123, 126–31
Irlam, Shaun, 134

Jackson, Wallace, 144
Jarvis, Robin, 184
Jeffrey, Francis, 205, 206
Johnson, Jr, Karl R., 208
Johnson, Samuel, 68, 69, 141, 142, 143, 146, 148, 149
Johnstone, W. Michael, 206
Jung, Sandro, 90, 108, 118, 120, 124, 140n, 148

kairos, 12, 162–7, 170, 177, 178, 188, 193, 195, 196, 202, 209, 219
Keats, John, 1–2, 3, 7, 49–50, 51, 71, 76, 144, 181
Keenleyside, Heather, 144
Kelley, Theresa M., 216
Kenshur, Oscar, 148, 150, 157–8n
Kent, William, 126–7, 128
Kermode, Frank, 74, 164
Kerrigan, William, 50, 52, 65
Kinsley, Zoë, 146
Kramnick, Jonathan, 134
Krapp, John, 177

Lamb, Charles, 71–2, 73, 77, 168, 169, 183, 209–10
Lamb, Mary, 72
landscape, 4, 8, 10, 12, 13, 18, 28, 31, 33, 41–2, 60, 92, 107, 109, 146–7, 166, 169, 196, 204, 205–6, 208, 209, 211; see also prospect poem
Langer, Ayelet C., 21–2, 38
Larkin, Peter, 165, 174, 195
Leader, Zachary, 195
Leonard, John, 54, 70
Lessing, Gotthold Ephraim, 8

Lethbridge, Stefanie, 143–4, 148, 154–5
Lieb, Michael, 65
Lindenberger, Herbert, 213
Literature and Contingency, 5
Liu, Alan, 216
long poem, definition of, 1–9, 13, 68–9, 223–4
Lucretius, 5
lyric, 5, 6, 12, 71, 77, 107, 165, 214, 223
Lyttelton, George, 122, 135

Macauley, Thomas Babington, 206
McMahon, Robert, 75
Mallet, David, 100, 109–10, 185
Marcus, Leah S., 41–2
Marvell, Andrew, 18, 33, 74
Merivale, John Herman, 205, 206
Millar, Andrew, 126, 131
Miller, Christopher R., 115n, 163, 170, 172
Milnes, Tim, 206–7
Milton, John, 4, 9, 10, 11, 12, 89, 94, 99, 135, 164, 168, 181, 181–6, 190–1, 204
  De Doctrina Christiana, 27, 51, 57, 60–1, 63
  'Lycidas', 71, 183
  Paradise Lost, 1, 4, 6, 9, 10, 11, 13, 17–59, 68–83, 90, 91, 92, 95, 100–1, 103, 104, 105, 111, 118, 119, 132, 143, 144, 161, 163, 166, 177, 188, 190, 192, 193–4, 202, 217
  Paradise Regain'd, 10, 27, 34–5, 42, 50, 51, 52, 63–5, 77–9, 80, 92, 166
  Samson Agonistes, 24, 161
  Tetrachordon, 52, 57, 61, 62
mist, 49, 51, 134, 137, 187, 190, 193, 194
Mitchell, Sebastian, 126
More, John, 108, 142–3, 150, 153, 155

Morgan, Monique R., 165, 177, 178, 213–14
Morson, Gary Saul, 21, 22, 120
Myers, William, 24, 31

natural philosophy, 13, 89, 95, 97, 98, 155
Nellist, Brian, 208
Netzley, Ryan, 77–8
Newlyn, Lucy, 71, 182,
New Milton Criticism, 21, 75, 79
Newton, Isaac, 3, 94–6, 97, 121, 164
Newton, Thomas, 77
Nicolson, Marjorie Hope, 95
Noggle, James, 144
non-narrative poem, 5, 7, 8, 12, 13, 89, 116, 144, 165, 204, 223–4
novel, 5–7, 120, 223
nunc fluens, 22–3, 28, 31
nunc stans, 10, 20, 21–8, 32, 34, 35, 42, 43, 48, 50, 52, 56, 58, 68, 69, 73, 76, 77, 91, 163, 166, 203

Parker, Blanford, 106, 109
Parrish, Stephen M., 195
pastoral, 40, 101, 169, 212; *see also* shepherds
Pater, Walter, 207
Pellicer, Juan Christian, 100
Peterfreund, Stuart, 212
Philips, John, 99, 101
Phillips, Edward, 25
philosophical long poem, 5, 13, 100, 165, 223
physico-theology, 3, 11, 95
planetary time, 95, 167, 169, 175–6, 177
Poe, Edgar Allan, 223
Pope, Alexander, 41, 94, 141, 186
Potkay, Adam, 186
Poulet, Georges, 162

Priestman, Martin, 3
prophecy, 21, 42, 49–51, 71, 79, 181, 183–4; *see also* delphic; Cassandra
prospect poem, 4, 5, 8, 9, 10, 12, 13, 17–21, 24–5, 32–44, 48, 56, 62, 63, 69, 90, 91–2, 93, 103, 109, 136, 137–9, 146, 163–6, 168–9, 171–5, 203, 209, 223–4

Quint, David, 19, 79

reflexive reference, 7, 8, 81; *see also* Frank, Joseph
Regueiro, Helen, 163–4
Reid, David, 89, 115n
revision, 9, 11, 12, 59, 116, 122–8, 131–2, 135, 138, 184, 194–9, 214–5, 222
Ricks, Christopher, 74, 76
Rigby, Kate, 169
Roberts, Adam, 5, 223
Rogers, Pat, 122
romance, 5, 9, 97–8, 223

Sachs, Jonathan and Andrew Piper, 163
Sambrook, James, 122
Schuler, Stephen J., 24, 27, 28
Scott, John, 118, 153–4
Scripture, 10, 19, 33, 50, 51–2, 57–65, 77, 83
Setzer, Sharon M., 185
Shears, Jonathon, 73, 213
Shelley, Percy Bysshe, 72, 73
shepherds, 117, 119, 169, 172, 187–8, 190, 194
Shiels, Robert, 142, 143, 147, 148, 149, 155
Shoaf, R. A., 76, 77
Silver, Sean, 98
simile, 10, 51–7, 61, 64, 72, 100, 103, 119, 189
Sitter, John, 3, 94, 106, 115n, 149

Sjödin, Alfred, 100
Smith, Charlotte, 175
Smith, Courtney Weiss, 95, 96, 97
Southey, Robert, 206
Spacks, Patricia Meyer, 106, 115n, 149
spatial form, 2, 7–8, 10, 12, 52, 60, 68, 69, 71, 72, 73, 77, 144, 145, 156, 203, 204, 208, 210, 211; see also Frank, Joseph
Starke, Sue, 25
stars, 1, 18, 51, 53–6, 59, 60, 64, 171, 176–7, 210
Stein, Edwin, 186
Stenke, Katarina, 5, 118, 139n, 144
Stephen, Leslie, 175, 206
Stevenson, Randall, 5–6
Stockdale, Percival, 141–2, 153
storms, 56, 101, 104–5, 116–20; see also wind
Strachan, John, 185
Sugimura, N. K., 37
Sullivan, Hannah, 131
Swift, Jonathan, 144

Tayler, Edward W., 24, 33
Taylor, Jeffere100y H. and Leslie A., 24, 34
Taylor, Luke, 50, 51, 52, 63
Tennyson, Alfred, 223
Terry, Richard, 106, 115n, 150, 154
Thomas, Walter Keith and Warren U. Ober, 95
Thomson, James, 4, 11, 12, 56, 89–156, 161, 164, 167, 170, 185–6, 192
  Britannia, 93
  'Hymn', 90–1, 156
  Liberty, 41, 91, 93
  'Poem Sacred to the Memory of Sir Isaac Newton', 95, 96
  The Castle of Indolence, 1, 135, 161, 168, 169, 194
  The Seasons, 4, 9, 11, 161, 166, 171, 172, 184, 187–91, 193–4, 205, 208
Time and Literature, 5
Townsend, C. H., 186
Tristram Shandy (Laurence Sterne), 8

Van De Walle, Kwinten, 90, 139n.
Van Renen, Denys, 119
Virgil, 5, 56, 60, 90, 99, 100–5, 109, 144–5, 161, 186, 193; see also epic; georgic; pastoral

Waller, Edmund, 19, 33
Warminski, Andrzej, 193
Watson, J. R., 79
weather see mist, storms, wind
Welch, Anthony, 21, 80
Westall, Richard, 129
Whaler, James, 54, 65n, 72
wind, 53–6, 97, 102, 117, 146, 173, 176, 177; see also storms
Wittreich, Joseph, 65, 75
Wolfson, Susan J., 165, 196, 200n
Wordsworth, Dorothy, 172, 174, 177, 186
Wordsworth, William, 4, 12, 71, 161–219
  'Essays on Epitaphs', 188
  The Excursion, 12, 203–9, 211
  'Home at Grasmere', 163
  Letters, 17, 185
  Lyrical Ballads, 124, 165, 167, 185
  'Milton! thou should'st be living at this hour', 183
  Poems (1820), 198
  'Preface' (1815) to *Poems*, 193–4
  The Prelude, 4, 9, 12, 95, 133, 161–219

The Recluse, 184, 188, 203, 205
reviews of, 12, 205–7, 211–13
spots of time, 12, 162–79, 187, 190, 191, 192, 195–6, 197, 199, 202, 208–9, 212–16, 217, 224

'Stanzas written in my Pocket-copy of Thomson's Castle of Indolence', 161

Young, Edward, 94, 96, 98–9, 100
Youngren, William, 145, 157n.

EU representative:
Easy Access System Europe
Mustamäe tee 50, 10621 Tallinn, Estonia
Gpsr.requests@easproject.com

www.ingramcontent.com/pod-product-compliance
Lightning Source LLC
Chambersburg PA
CBHW070340240426
43671CB00013BA/2384